D1291629

D. W. WINNICOTT:
A BIOGRAPHICAL PORTRAIT

Photograph of Dr Donald Woods Winnicott, circa 1925.
This photograph is published here for the first time
by the kind permission of Mr John Ede and Dr Joseph Buist Loudon.

D. W. WINNICOTT:
A BIOGRAPHICAL PORTRAIT

Brett Kahr

INTERNATIONAL UNIVERSITIES PRESS, INC.

Madison   Connecticut

First published in 1996 by
H. Karnac (Books) Ltd.
58 Gloucester Road
London SW7 4QY

Library of Congress Cataloging-in-Publication Data

Kahr, Brett.
    D.W. Winnicott: a biographical portrait / Brett Kahr.
        p. cm.
    Includes bibliographical references (p.   ) and index.
    ISBN 0-8236-6684-0
    1. Winnicott, D.W. (Donald Woods), 1896-1971.
    2. Psychoanalysts—Great Britain—Biography.
    3. Psychoanalysis—History. I. Title.
    BF109.W55K34 1996
    150.19'5'092—dc20
    [B]   96-24407
                                         CIP

Dedicated to
my grandfather
Charles Edward Kahr

The healthy child who is negotiating all these hazards must be thought of as living in a relatively stable environment, with the mother happy in her marriage, and with the father ready to play his part with the children, to get to know his son and to give and take in the subtle way that comes fairly naturally to the father, who as a boy himself had a happy experience with his own father.

Winnicott, *Human Nature* (1988, p. 55)

CONTENTS

ACKNOWLEDGEMENTS

A very large number of generous colleagues have contributed significantly to the preparation of this book. In particular, I want to extend my thanks to the following individuals for sharing their reminiscences with me of the late Dr Donald Winnicott: Mr Leo Abse, Professor E. James Anthony, the late Mrs Enid Balint, Dr Reva Berstock, Mrs Francesca Bion, Mrs Mary Boston, the late Dr John Bowlby, C.B.E., Mrs Ursula Bowlby, Professor Anthony Bradshaw, F.R.S., Mrs Elizabeth Bradshaw, Mr Donald Campbell, Dr Audrey Cantlie, Mrs Joyce Coles, Dr Nina Coltart, Mrs Judy Cooper, Mrs Beta Copley, Dr Murray Cox, Professor John Davis, Mrs Dilys Daws, Mrs Barbara Dockar-Drysdale, Mr Stephen Dockar-Drysdale, Dr Michael Eigen, Ms Irmi Elkan, Dr Susanna Isaacs Elmhirst, Mr Kenneth Fenn, Mrs Phyllis Fenn, the late Dr Michael Fordham, Mrs Sadie Gillespie, Dr William Gillespie, Professor Peter Giovacchini, Dr Lawrence Goldie, Mrs Silvia Oclander Goldie, Dr Victoria Hamilton, the late Dr Thomas Hayley, Mr David Holbrook, Mrs Juliet Hopkins, Mr Hans Hoxter, Mrs Shirley Hoxter, Dr Athol Hughes, the late Dr Martin James, Dr Jennifer

Johns, Mr Mervyn Jones, Mr Harry Karnac, Mrs Ruth Karnac, Ms Rosalie Kerbekian, Ms Pearl King, Dr Robert Langs, Mrs Audrey Lees, Professor Julian Leff, Dr Arnold Linken, the late Dr Margaret I. Little, Dr Peter Lomas, Dr Josephine Lomax-Simpson, Dr Joseph Buist Loudon, Mrs Frederica Low-Beer, Dr Dora Lush, Mrs Isabel Menzies Lyth, Dr Harold Maxwell, Mrs Freny Mehta, Mr Simon Meyerson, Mrs Marion Milner, Mrs Eileen Orford, Mr Frank Orford, Mrs Edna O'Shaughnessy, Dr John Padel, Dr Jonathan Pedder, Mrs Irma Brenman Pick, Dr Malcolm Pines, Dr Eric Rayner, Dr Katharine Rees, Professor Paul Roazen, Dr Charles Rycroft, Dr Robin Skynner, Mrs Gloria Solomon, Professor Thomas Stapleton, Dr Elisabeth Swan, Dr Harold Swan, the late Mrs Frances Tustin, Dr Alan Tyson, C.B.E., Dr Ved Varma, Dr Estela Welldon, Dr John White, Dr Agnes Wilkinson, Mrs Jilian Wilson, Mrs Isca Wittenberg, Mrs Jennifer Woolland, and Mr Peter Woolland.

Professor James William Anderson, Mr Richard Buckle, C.B.E., Mr John Ede, Dr Matthew Gale, Professor Phyllis Grosskurth, Dr Lesley Hall, Professor André Haynal, Mr Jeremy Hazell, Mr Geoffrey Houghton, Mr Joel Kanter, Mr Sonu Shamdasani, Ms Joan Slater, and Ms Frances Wilks all made valuable contributions to the research project. Mrs Joyce Coles, Ms Irmi Elkan, Dr Susanna Isaacs Elmhirst, Professor Sander Gilman, Professor Jean Goodwin, Dr Athol Hughes, Dr Jennifer Johns, Mr Harry Karnac, Ms Pearl King, Dr George Makari, Ms Susie Orbach, Dr Charles Rycroft, Dr Joseph Schwartz, Ms Valerie Sinason, Mr David Livingstone Smith, and Dr Judith Trowell have all read the manuscript in its entirety or have read certain sections, and I have derived much benefit from their illuminating comments.

Dr Jennifer Johns of The Winnicott Trust studied the manuscript in particularly great detail, and I have managed to incorporate many of her very helpful suggestions, for which I thank her. Dr George Makari graciously took time from his own research on the history of transference in psychoanalysis to offer encouragement and to write the Introduction. And Dr Susanna Isaacs Elmhirst merits special mention for providing me with a Foreword to this text, for her meticulous comments on an earlier version of the typescript, and for bringing Winnicott and the

Paddington Green Children's Hospital back to life in a most extraordinarily vivid manner.

I also want to thank the many librarians and archivists who have assisted me in the research for this text, notably Mr Paul Bunten, Curator of The Oskar Diethelm Library of the History of Psychiatry at the Cornell Medical Center in New York City. As custodian of the Donald W. Winnicott Papers, Mr Bunten has provided invaluable academic support during my visits to Manhattan. Quotations from the Donald W. Winnicott Papers at the New York Academy of Medicine appear by courtesy of The Oskar Diethelm Library of the History of Psychiatry. I also want to express my appreciation to the library staff at Regent's College, at the Tavistock Clinic, at The Wellcome Institute for the History of Medicine in London, at the Malloch Reading Room of the New York Academy of Medicine in New York City, and at the Rare Book and Manuscript Library in the Butler Library at Columbia University, also in New York City.

I owe a great debt of gratitude to my students and colleagues at Regent's College, and at the Tavistock Clinic, the Tavistock Clinic Foundation Young Abusers Project, and at the Tavistock Mulberry Bush Day Unit, who have permitted me to indulge my interest in Winnicott. Mrs Gillian Payne, President of Regent's College, Professor Emmy van Deurzen-Smith, Academic Dean of the School of Psychotherapy and Counselling at Regent's College, and Mr David Livingstone Smith, the Associate Dean, have proved particularly supportive of my research.

The administrative staff at Regent's College deserve my very sincerest thanks for their cheerful and responsible cooperation with so many aspects of this book, and for their ongoing interest in this project. Mr Ian Jones-Healey, our Academic Registrar, and Ms Claire Penhallow, the Administrative Officer, offered me a great deal of necessary guidance on the vicissitudes of the College computer system, as did Mrs Teresa Smith, the Administrative Assistant, and Ms Jacqueline de Silva, our Secretary.

Additionally, I want to express my gratitude to The Winnicott Trust and to the Winnicott Publications Committee for their dedicated scholarship, and for their careful editing of Winnicott's writings. It must be mentioned that the majority of Winnicott's books have appeared posthumously, as a direct result of the

sustained efforts of The Winnicott Trust. And I do want to express
my appreciation for the yeoman activities of The Squiggle Foundation and The Winnicott Clinic of Psychotherapy, and for their
successful efforts to foster interest in Winnicott's work.

Mrs Joyce Coles, the loyal secretary who served Winnicott
from 1948 until 1971, has proved an inestimably valuable
source of information during the writing of this book. I learned
more about Winnicott in one morning's discussion with Mrs
Coles than I did from a multitude of other sources combined.
She has graciously granted me many interviews over the last few
years. Sadly, because of the sheer extent of the information that
I have gleaned from Mrs Coles, most of her reminiscences will
have to appear in a subsequent work. I do want to thank her for
providing a special glimpse into Winnicott's daily world and for
her generosity in letting me use Winnicott's drawing of the
"santa-mums", from 1966, for the front cover of this book.

I want to convey my special thanks to some very cherished
colleagues for their continuing encouragement of this project,
particularly Mr Leo Abse, Mrs Margaret Baron, Professor
Rudolph Binion, Professor Robert Bore, Mrs Judy Cooper, Mr
Lloyd deMause, Ms Zack Eleftheriadou, Mrs Lucy Freeman,
Professor Jean Goodwin, Dr Robert Langs, Ms Alessandra
Lemma, Dr Margaret Lloyd, Ms Jeannie Milligan, Ms Susie
Orbach, Mrs Rosalind Pearmain, Dr Joseph Schwartz, Mr Sonu
Shamdasani, Ms Valerie Sinason, Mr David Livingstone Smith,
Mrs Judith Usiskin, Dr Eileen Vizard, and Dr Estela Welldon.
The late Professor William Niederland and the late Professor
Flora Rheta Schreiber offered very welcome encouragement of
my writing and research at an early stage in my career, for
which I shall always remain very grateful.

No author could ask for a more intelligent, convivial, and
gentlemanly publisher than Mr Cesare Sacerdoti of Karnac
Books. Mr Sacerdoti has facilitated many aspects of this work,
and he has continued to provide unfailing moral support and
judicious guidance throughout the long process of transforming
a set of ideas and observations into a workable manuscript. He
possesses an unusually fine knowledge of Winnicott and of
psychoanalytic theory, and he has improved the book vastly,
in many ways. His assistant, Mr Graham Sleight, also deserves
my kudos for his perspicacity and good cheer, and for his

fine attention to detail during the preparation of the final text. Mr Eric King and Mrs Klara King undertook the copyediting of the manuscript with unusual swiftness and magnificent professionalism. And Mr Malcolm Smith not only designed the beautiful cover of this book, but he has assisted my research over the years, as have all the bibliographically skilled staff at H. Karnac (Books) Limited.

Above all, I thank my family for their love and for providing such continuity.

Brett Kahr
Regent's Park, London
15 February 1996

FOREWORD

Dr Susanna Isaacs Elmhirst, F.R.C.P., F.R.C. Psych.

I t is now over forty years since my path first crossed, and became in some ways intertwined with, Donald Winnicott's. I had worked my way up to consultant status in paediatrics, a journey during which I had become increasingly intrigued by the high proportion of child patients whose sufferings were not primarily of physical origin; in other words, their problems were psychosomatic in origin "at best", and often apparently purely psychogenic. The climate of paediatric opinion was strongly opposed to the view that the unconscious mind existed at all, let alone that its manifestations in children might include disturbances of bodily functions and structures. As for psychogenic pain, children were all too often treated as though they

---

Training Analyst at The Institute of Psycho-Analysis, London, and Consultant Psychiatrist at The Adoption Unit of the Thomas Coram Foundation, London. Former Vice-President of The British Psycho-Analytical Society, Former Director of the Children's Department at The London Clinic of Psycho-Analysis, and Former Consultant Psychiatrist and Physician-in-Charge of the Department of Child Psychiatry at the Paddington Green Children's Hospital and St. Mary's Hospital, London.

experienced no pain—not even physical. Adults whom the psychodynamically inclined might surmise as suffering from psychogenic pain or behavioural disorders beyond their conscious control were frequently seen as lazy, or even malingerers who could and should pull up their socks, or pull themselves together, and would be firmly warned that non-compliance with medical instructions would lead to referral to a psychiatrist.

In 1953, when I went to Winnicott for the first of the two admissions interviews required by the selection procedures of The Institute of Psycho-Analysis, I had not heard of him, or read any of his writings, nor, indeed, at that time, had I read very widely in Freud, Melanie Klein, or Anna Freud. However, an important motive for my wish to do the psychoanalytic training was the hope of enlarging my understanding of human beings of all ages, including myself. Only later did I discover that both Winnicott and Milton Senn (of Yale University) had also undertaken this arduous endeavour because, in Senn's words, he "did not want to be a cook-book paediatrician."

Whatever Winnicott's conscious and unconscious feelings about my experience, my ignorance, and my pregnancy, I was accepted for analytic training in the group of my choice, which was then called the "A Group". This group comprised the Kleinians and those who later hived off as the Middle (now the Independent) Group, as separate from, and often opposed to, the B Group of Anna Freud's followers, now renamed the Contemporary Freudians.

I think that Melanie Klein's work opened up more areas of understanding and avenues of enquiry than that of any other analyst since Freud. Therefore I am "a Kleinian", and do not "belong" to any group. However, I am an "abolitionist", in the sense that I am one of the not inconsiderable number of psychoanalysts who think that the "Groups" have outlived their time and are more divisive than cohesive.

In the course of changing career specialities, it was Dr Zena Moncrieff, a paediatrician friend of Winnicott's locum Dr Barbara Woodhead, who first appointed me to a niche in her out-patient clinic, as a Clinical Assistant in St. Charles Hospital, London. Barbara Woodhead was an analyst of adults and children who was Winnicott's locum at Paddington Green whenever illness prevented him from working at all or for the full number of his allotted sessions. St. Charles Hospital was part of the "St. Mary's Group"; so too was 17, Paddington Green, the lovely old house which D.W.W. was responsible for finding and persuading the powers-that-were to purchase as the headquarters of the work of the first-ever Department of Child Psychiatry of St. Mary's Hospital, London.

In due course I applied for, and was appointed to, a part-time Senior Registrar post in "The Green", and I began my close involvement with Winnicott and his work in the National Health Service with children and parents who did not "pay to teach" him in the financial sense. During the years I was learning from him, the parents, the departmental staff, and the varied people in the lives of his child patients, Donald was often ill and was never well enough to work his full complement of N.H.S. sessions. Yet it was in this area of his work that I came to realize that he was a genius. Any genius has to be a genius at something; exquisite perceptiveness does not alone constitute genius even if it is combined, as in Winnicott, with a capacity to approach anew anything in his field of interest, however apparently ordinary or mundane the activity. One of my favourites of his many, usually beautifully written papers is an early gem, "The Observation of Infants in a Set Situation" (1941a). The observations described in it were made in a big room in the large out-patient central area of Paddington Green Children's Hospital. It was there that he began to hold the non-appointment sessions he called "the snack bar" and also started having people sit in on consultations. When he was there, within hearing distance of the children's wards, it was the task of the Senior Registrar to remind, and re-remind, the nursing staff that babies must not be left to cry for more than the merest moment when Dr Winnicott was "doing his out-patients".

In my experience, Winnicott's acute sensitivity was in his N.H.S. work, mainly focused on babies, young children, and their mothers; not on their fathers or on adolescents. This intensely sensitive interest, and his capacity non-verbally to convince the object of this interest, is illustrated by the true story of a Scandinavian colleague who told his non–English-speaking children that Dr Winnicott would soon be visiting them again. There was considerable enthusiasm even from the two youngest, who cannot have been more than two and four years old when

Donald had stayed with the family previously. All the children agreed that the non-Scandinavian D.W.W. had been so interested and interesting; he had "understood so much", that they could not readily believe that there had been no common spoken language. This vignette supports the conclusion I reached over several years of observing D.W.W. using the squiggle technique in his Monday clinics at 17, Paddington Green (which is where he regularly came, if physically able to do so). I did not think that Winnicott needed the squiggle technique to get in touch even with latency-age children. Furthermore, I decided against using or recommending it as I came to realize its seductive encouragement of a belief in the equivalence of need and dependence in patient and professional, child and adult; a belief that undermined the vital importance of the interdependence that Winnicott once summarized as "there is no such thing as a baby". One consequence of the depth of Winnicott's ambivalent attitude to his own and other people's discoveries, and the development of them, was that it was more than ordinarily difficult to take over a patient from him, even one specifically referred for treatment after a single consultation. It took me years to discover that this experience was not always a totally personal failure, rooted in my reaction to the inevitability of there having been only one D.W.W.

In my opinion Winnicott's genius was also shown in his ability to communicate with many of the adults practically concerned with the physical and emotional needs of children from birth onwards. Important examples of this are his radio talks, published in two volumes as *The Child and the Family* (1957a) and *The Child and the Outside World* (1957b). Of at least equal importance as a manifestation of genius was his work with children whose families needed more than the usual amount of help from the world outside the home. Donald's interest in this varied group was first focused by his involvement with the disturbances caused to evacuated children by being separated from their families in the hope of protecting them physically from what war had become.

It was in the course of this "war work" that he met Clare Britton; between them they developed unique experience and skill in devising and supporting environmental changes which nourished the emotional and physical growth of children. Out of this lively mutual co-operation, involving various non-medical, and often non-parent, adults, gradually developed Winnicott's "Monday afternoons" at the Green. To begin with, the group of alert but silent observers sitting in the room where Winnicott was doing a diagnostic consultation on, or a "follow-up" of, a troubled and troubling child, consisted of members of the department staff and of the varied personnel professionally involved: mainly teachers, nurses, and social workers. Over the years, the number of would-be observers had to be limited and formalized because people came to the Winnicott Mondays from literally all over the world, although almost never from the main body of its parent hospital. When later I succeeded Winnicott as Physician-in-Charge of Child Psychiatry in St. Mary's Hospital, the particular difficulties of taking over from him were vividly illustrated by there being only five rooms for the equivalent of eight full-time staff, also by the fact that when it was agreed that medical students would at least have a taste of child psychiatry during their training, I was allowed to "have" them on Wednesdays, i.e. on what I discovered in due course were Rugger Days, in that predominantly masculine stronghold of sport. Unfortunately it is not yet firmly established whether or not D.W.W.'s clinical notes (illegible even to him after retirement) and wonderfully clear and helpful typewritten letters to social workers, teachers, and the Inner London Education Authority, etc., have been preserved for the necessary follow-up of child patients as well as for longer-term research and teaching.

Winnicott's awareness of the need for cooperative work in support of children in difficulties led him to ensure, by dint of much hard work, that child analysis not only had a purpose-built "home" in The London Clinic of Psycho-Analysis, but that support for the parents or others responsible for the day-to-day care of those children needing five sessions a week should be provided by Paddington Green if the diagnostic assessment had been made there and sometimes even in cases referred for analysis by other clinics or individuals. Statistically valid measurement of the short- and long-term clinical outcome of such stupendous and original efforts is, even now, in these days of computerised records, word-processors, etc., impossible beyond a limited extent, but from the 1930s to the 1970s it was out of the question because of staff shortages and the absence of the not-as-yet invented equipment.

I had almost no direct involvement with Winnicott's post-N.H.S. work with children and parents. His writings about this aspect of his work do, for me, confirm my view that one of D.W.W.'s limitations as a diagnostician, psychotherapist, and communicator was his failure to afford fathers their full developmental importance. This interweaves with his relative failure to communicate with or about adolescents, and adolescence. In his clinic work, these omissions were to some extent compensated for by the many and varied professional colleagues working with him. One outcome was that D.W.W. could be very disappointed in the long-term outcome of his clinical interactions with children and families not supported by a wider "team" of co-operating colleagues from different fields. A poignant, if partial, recognition of this is given by D.W.W. in his follow-up of the boy whose treatment within the family he described in "String" (1960a). In the "Added Note" in *Playing and Reality* (1971a, p. 20), D.W.W. wrote: "I have come to see that the boy *could not be cured of his illness*" (my italics). In this written contribution, D.W.W. did not acknowledge, as he undoubtedly could have in different moods about similar situations, that the outcome might have been very different if there had been adequate local "management" or even that someone else might have involved father, son, and mother more imaginatively and constructively than he himself had been able to do on this occasion.

Donald would sometimes make provocatively over-inclusive verbal statements, such as "no one could become an artist who had not had a transitional object". My response to this particular claim was "how do you know whether Michelangelo or Rembrandt had transitional objects?" On this occasion he laughed appreciatively, indicating that I had struck home in a more vitalizing than persecuting way, as was my intention. I did not then know of Donald's "Lily", or his sisters' "Rosie", as recounted in the first chapter of Brett Kahr's absorbing book. I think Kahr "strikes home" a great deal in this book, and it is my hope that this Foreword will similarly encourage readers to approach it, and their thoughts about Winnicott in general, with a healthily sceptical appetite.

Although I do not myself agree with Kahr and many others that Winnicott was a psychoanalyst of genius, I do firmly believe that he was a psychoanalyst who was a genius in certain areas of work relating to children's mental health and welfare and have tried to give a glimpse of my grounds for this view. Kahr writes in a clear, flowing, and economical way, revealing an honest, genuinely scientific attitude of enquiry. It seems clear to me that many readers will find his book to be a very interesting introduction to the life and work of a very interesting person and that many will, as I do, look forward to his next, longer, book on D.W.W., which is already under way. Whatever our differences about Donald Winnicott, I recommend this book as a stimulus to discussion and further research on his life and work.

INTRODUCTION

Dr George Makari, M.D.

Is it with psychoanalysts, as Friedrich Nietzsche once remarked of philosophers, that their theories are necessarily
concealed autobiography? Sigmund Freud himself worried
that incompletely analysed psychoanalysts might project out-
ward "some of the peculiarities of their own personality . . . into
the field of science, as a theory having universal validity" (Freud,
1912, p. 117). And if this is at least in some part necessarily
so, where do the lines between theory and theorist get drawn? In
the case of an original and creative psychoanalytic thinker, for
instance, how and where do inner subjectivity and outer experience meet, mingle, and in the end create not just a therapy, but
also a new theory? It is fitting that Donald Woods Winnicott, the
man who beautifully described this in-between creative space,
would himself present tantalizing questions about the relation-

Assistant Professor of Psychiatry and Acting Director, History of Psychiatry Section, Department of Psychiatry, Cornell University Medical
College, New York, NY, and at the Columbia University Center for Psychoanalytic Training and Research, New York, NY.

ship between the psychoanalyst's theories, his historical milieu, and his own biography.

Winnicott's theories announce their own originality; they seem to demand that the reader look for the origins of these thoughts not in a tradition but, rather, inside a creator—D. W. Winnicott. A friend once wryly commented that there are two kinds of "original geniuses": those who cite their sources and those who do not. Winnicott was—to the chagrin of some of his colleagues, like Balint—of the latter breed. Seeking "live" language in psychoanalytic theory, feeling the need to mull over and rework other's theories and make them his own, Winnicott rejected the repetition of others' terminology, hoping instead to create his own way of naming. To his detractors, Winnicott's ideas were wilfully obscure and idiosyncratic, while to his admirers they were fresh, undogmatic, and brilliantly original.

For the followers of the man who penned *Totem and Taboo* (Freud, 1912–13), claims of such originality have always been scented with danger and inhibition. But in the bitter and strident atmosphere within psychoanalytic discourse in America and Britain during and after the Second World War, the pressures for conformity and communal allegiance made for unusually heavy burdens. Yet, despite the great pull of two towering leaders, Melanie Klein and Anna Freud, Winnicott ended up holding steadfast on a course that was his own. Though first identified as a Kleinian, Winnicott created and then maintained his independence, while at the same time remaining in the thick of it at The British Psycho-Analytical Society. By remaining within psychoanalysis while preserving a place for his own theoretical creativity, Winnicott can be seen as an exemplary antithesis to the unfortunate tendency in the history of the field to encourage dogmatism or exile.

Given this independence of character and originality of thought, it is no wonder that we would be interested in Winnicott, the man. Genius, quixotic hero, English eccentric, clinician extraordinaire, impish wiseman: these are some of the idealized Winnicotts that we have so far possessed. But, amazingly, this extraordinary man had previously received little in-depth attention from biographers. Brett Kahr's elegant biographical portrait stands as the first book-length attempt to grapple with the complexities of Winnicott's life. Kahr has stuck close to sound ground, and the result is that Winnicott's life resonates for us clearly and directly, without the haze of injudicious psychohistorical inference. The overall effect is liberating. Kahr allows the reader who is familiar with Winnicott's theories to imagine and play with the crucial intersection between the Donald Woods Winnicott of Plymouth and the D. W. Winnicott of the transitional object.

Kahr's book provides another service for students of Winnicott and for practitioners of psychoanalysis. Winnicott was himself a not unimportant figure in the development of countertransference theory. Hence he played his own part in the demystification of the role of the "objective" analyst. To my mind, part of this evolutionary process for the field involves not only increased internal examination by the psychoanalyst in the clinical situation, but also a modification of our psychoanalytic identities by the adoption of less idealized, more nuanced visions of our predecessors. Without animus or blinding admiration, Kahr guides us towards seeing a Winnicott of flesh and history, a Winnicott of extraordinary resolve as well as complicated weaknesses and tribulations. This biographical Winnicott now stands alongside the authorial Winnicott, giving us a new point of reference. By drawing a picture of Donald Winnicott's origins, Brett Kahr allows us to appreciate more deeply the bounds and dimensions of the originality of this extraordinary psychoanalyst.

PREFACE

With the obvious exception of Sigmund Freud, perhaps no other figure in the history of psychoanalysis has contributed as much to our understanding of the origins and treatment of mental distress as Donald Winnicott has done. Winnicott (1919) first encountered psychoanalytic ideas as a young medical student at St. Bartholomew's Hospital in London, while seeking to understand his often baffling dreams. After reading Freud's (1900) magnum opus, *The Interpretation of Dreams*, Winnicott decided that he would devote his life to the study of the human mind—in particular, that he would bring psychoanalytic ideas and concepts to the attention of the wider British public. Throughout the following five decades, Winnicott dedicated himself single-mindedly to the study and treatment of human psychopathology, and he did so with such verve and determination that he often became ill from overwork. By the time he died in 1971, he had already completed nine volumes of his written work (Winnicott, 1931a, 1945a, 1949a, 1957a, 1957b, 1958a, 1964a, 1965a, 1965b); after his death, a number of devoted editors, initially spearheaded by his widow Clare Winnicott, ensured the publication of no fewer than twelve further books on a variety of clinical and developmental topics (Winnicott, 1971a, 1971b, 1978, 1984, 1986a, 1986b, 1987a, 1987b, 1988, 1989, 1993, 1996).

Although he first practised solely as a paediatrician, Winnicott eventually underwent a complete training in psycho-analysis, and he spent the whole of his professional career working not only with infants and toddlers, but with adolescents and adults as well. His incomparably extensive clinical experiences, both as a hospital doctor and as a private practitioner, permitted him a privileged insight into the functioning of all types and degrees of psychopathology, from the most mild neurotic manifestations to the most severe psychotic states. With his unusual genius and his dogged perseverance, Winnicott strove to understand all aspects of the human mind, and he did so with great aplomb, writing memorable books and articles on every conceivable topic within the mental health field, ranging from adoption, birth trauma, breakdown, and breast-feeding to electroconvulsive shock treatment, enuresis, envy, juvenile rheumatism, and many more besides, not to mention his detailed technical contributions to the practice of psychoanalysis, psychotherapy, and child psychiatry.

Winnicott will perhaps be best remembered for teaching us that madness begins in the nursery, and that madness can be prevented by providing our infants with consistent, loving care, free from impingements and abuses. Moreover, in an era when most parents chastised their offspring in keeping with Blanche Bellamy's popular injunction that "children must be seen, not heard", Winnicott tried to talk to mothers and fathers from every walk of life, in order to help them to understand that their babies and toddlers could be interesting people in their own right, not mere bundles of nuisance languishing in their cots.

With the exception of his first book on clinical paediatrics (Winnicott, 1931a) and his two early volumes of radio broadcasts (Winnicott, 1945a, 1949a), all of Winnicott's other writings remain in print today, and they can easily be found in most professional bookshops and libraries. In addition, quite a number of expository volumes in the English language in recent years have provided useful summaries of Donald Winnicott's extensive body of writings (e.g. Davis & Wallbridge, 1981; Clancier & Kalmanovitch, 1984; Phillips, 1988; Hughes, 1989;

Grolnick, 1990; Rudnytsky, 1991; Goldman, 1993; Jacobs, 1995; Newman, 1995). My own guide to Winnicott's oeuvre, entitled *Donald Winnicott: The Life and Work of a Pioneer Psycho-Analyst* (Kahr, in preparation a), will appear shortly from Karnac Books, followed by a volume of essays compiled to celebrate Winnicott's one-hundredth birthday (Kahr, in preparation b). In view of this profusion of Winnicottiana, yet another volume on the great man might seem wholly unnecessary.

However, this current text, *D. W. Winnicott: A Biographical Portrait*, attempts neither a review of Winnicott's work nor a critical account of his ideas and their influence. Rather, I have written a short biography, which sketches out for the first time the details of Donald Winnicott's private life. Within the intimate science of psychoanalysis, the theoretical ideas of our foremothers and forefathers cannot easily be separated from their own personal histories, and this certainly holds true in Winnicott's case. I trust that by understanding more about the background of Winnicott's concepts, students of psychoanalytic ideas will derive a greater comprehension of the vicissitudes of Winnicott's life and work. I remain only too aware that this book serves as a mere *sketch*, and it does not in any way constitute a comprehensive biography. I have, in fact, begun the groundwork for a more extensive project, and the current text represents a preliminary portion of my ongoing archival and biographical research on Winnicott. In the meanwhile, I very much hope that this brief guide to the phases of Winnicott's life will stimulate further interest in his clinical and technical contributions, which remain immensely useful for all contemporary mental health practitioners.

D. W. WINNICOTT:
A BIOGRAPHICAL PORTRAIT

The most important element in our country at any one moment is the ordinary home in which ordinary parents are doing an ordinary good job, starting off infants and children with that basis for mental health which enables them eventually to become part of the community.

Winnicott, *The Spontaneous Gesture* (1950d, p. 21)

D. W. WINNICOTT.
A BIOGRAPHICAL PORTRAIT

CHAPTER ONE

Infancy and childhood

Donald Woods Winnicott, the youngest child of John Frederick Winnicott and Elizabeth Martha Woods Winnicott, entered the world on the night of Tuesday, 7 April, 1896, in the twilight years of Queen Victoria's reign. At the time of Winnicott's birth, Robert Salisbury, the Third Marquess of Salisbury (1830–1903), had only recently begun his third term as the Conservative Prime Minister of Great Britain, having assumed office once again in June of 1895. The English enjoyed an unusual period of peace, as the country had not yet plunged into the Anglo–Boer conflict, which would claim so many lives. It was a time of relative repose and of trust, when most people had no locks on their doors. The ladies wore corsets, the gentlemen smoked cigars after their evening meal, and most of the landed and monied citizens of Great Britain took pride in the increasing size and the growing international stature of the Empire.

The parents of the healthy new addition to the Winnicott home dubbed their son "Donald"—a prophetic name that derives from the old Celtic word meaning "mighty". The Winnicott family lived in the restful English coastal city of Plymouth, Devon, far from the hustle and bustle of London. They had lived in the West

Country for many generations. In all likelihood, the family surname derives from the Old English "Winn", possibly meaning "friend", and from "Cott", meaning "home". One can even locate a town called "Winnicott" on the map of Devon.

Donald Winnicott's paternal grandfather, Richard R. Winnicott, who styled himself as a "furnishing and general ironmonger, plumber and gas fitter" (quoted in Robinson, 1991, p. 59), had founded the firm of Winnicott Brothers, Merchants and Shippers, in George Street, in Plymouth, as far back as 1846, some fifty years before Donald's birth.

Winnicott's father, Frederick, born in Plymouth on 8 September 1855, the younger son of Richard R. Winnicott, grew up to become a tall, slender man with considerable talent and energy. He attended the George Street School in Plymouth; and after he left school, he entered into business partnership with his brother, Richard Weeks Winnicott. The Winnicott brothers established themselves first in their father's red-brick and limestone offices on Frankfort Street in Plymouth, an imposing building designed by the local architect Henry Snell, which extended more than one hundred feet in length (Robinson, 1991); eventually, they expanded the firm to other locations too, including branches on George Lane and on Frankfort Lane, and, in 1941, on Ebrington Street as well. Frederick Winnicott had a tremendous flair for business deals, and he no doubt received much wise instruction from his own father, Richard Winnicott, Senior. Frederick would eventually become Managing Director of Winnicott Brothers. The two sons—Frederick, and his elder brother, Richard Weeks Winnicott—expanded their father's stock, and they specialized in wholesale merchandise, selling items of every variety, including table cutlery, tin goods and iron goods, galvanized baths, electro-plated wares, and Japanese-style travelling trunks. They also maintained a Fancy Department in their shops, offering an "endless variety of Japanese and other useful and fancy articles of general sale" (quoted in Robinson, 1991, p. 59). They manufactured women's corsets (Phillips, 1988); they produced sweets and assorted confectionery (Fuller, 1987), including the well-known local treat, Winnicott Sweets; and they also served as outfitters for the sailors in the Royal Navy, as their shop proved rather convenient for the multitude of seamen who embarked at Plymouth. According to Richard Winnicott's grandson, Mr Peter Woolland (personal communication, 22 September 1994), the two brothers got on "extremely well", and after a long day at work they would often play billiards together.

In addition to his work for the family enterprise, Frederick Winnicott devoted much energy to religious activities and to other business affairs and, subsequently, to local politics as well. In his early twenties, Frederick had taught Sunday School at the King Street Wesleyan Church; in 1876, he became the Honorary Secretary to the class in Biblical Instruction. During 1879 and 1880, he helped to build the Wesleyan Church on Mutley Plain, raising funds from neighbours and contributing money of his own. He also served as a Steward of this church until his death. He held the post of Treasurer for his church, he sang in the choir, and he also worked as Circuit Steward and Honorary Treasurer for the local Theological Colleges, and he became a member of the Wesleyan Synod.

In later years, Frederick Winnicott turned his attention to more civic pursuits. He worked as Honorary Secretary to the Mechanics' Institute, and from 1899 until 1900, shortly after the birth of his son Donald, he became Chairman of the Plymouth Mercantile Association. Additionally, he served as the Chairman of the Plymouth Chamber of Commerce in 1908, as a Trustee of the Plymouth and South Devon Savings Bank, and as a Justice of the Peace. Frederick Winnicott's formal political career seems to have begun when he became elected as a member of the Plymouth Town Council; thereafter, he rose to the position of Alderman, and he eventually became the Lord Mayor of Plymouth, serving two terms of office, from 1906 until 1907, representing Plymouth Town, and again from 1921 until 1922, as Mayor of Greater Plymouth.

Not surprisingly, in honour of his varied services to public welfare, he received a Knighthood in 1924, from King George V, in the Ballroom at Buckingham Palace. He earned a political Knighthood, having received a nomination through the office of the Prime Minister at 10, Downing Street. Frederick Winnicott entered the order of the Knights Bachelor, not one of the Royal Orders, but a rather old and impressive title nonetheless, created originally in the seventeenth century by King James I (David Pogson, personal communication, 28 September 1994). In his newly beknighted life, Sir Frederick seems to have spent quite a lot of his time laying the foundation stones for various buildings in Plymouth, including the Plymouth Free Library (now known as the Plymouth Central Library) and the crematorium (Kenneth Fenn, personal communication, 18 September 1994). The City of Plymouth awarded him the status of Freeman in 1934.

Frederick Winnicott did aspire to become a Member of Parliament, but he had experienced learning difficulties as a youth, and this deprived him of both the education and the confidence to move beyond the sphere of local politics. He did, however, make the acquaintance of Nancy, Viscountess Astor; and after her husband became ennobled as Lord Astor, Frederick Winnicott suggested that Lady Astor stand for Parliament. Of course, Lady Astor did so, and she triumphed as the first woman to serve as a Member of Parliament in Great Britain, representing the Sutton Division of Plymouth. Frederick Winnicott even helped her to obtain this office in the House of Commons (interview with Clare Winnicott: Neve, 1983). Years later, Donald Winnicott would describe his father as "extremely preoccupied in my younger years with town as well as business matters" (quoted in Clare Winnicott, 1978, p. 23). Frederick Winnicott's brother, Richard, also participated in numerous municipal activities, such as serving as Chairman of the water company in Plymouth. Because of these many undertakings, Richard Winnicott's grandson referred to the two Winnicott brothers as "very public-spirited" (Peter Woolland, personal communication, 22 September 1994).

The Winnicott family lived in a spacious home, known as Rockville, located on Seymour Road, in the Mannamead section of Plymouth. Rockville consisted of a large house, spacious gardens on no fewer than four levels, a croquet lawn, an orchard, a pond, and a vegetable garden, all surrounded by large, lofty trees (Clare Winnicott, 1978). Rockville still stands today, and it remains a rather beautiful and very impressive private residence, with a host of bedrooms. Frederick's wife, Elizabeth, took great pride in her home, and she maintained a visitors' book at Rockville, as did many ladies of the period.

Elizabeth Winnicott, the daughter of the chemist and druggist, Mr William Woods of Plymouth, supervised the household and cared for Donald and her two elder daughters, Violet, born in 1889, and Kathleen, born in 1891. In addition to the nuclear family, the Winnicott household also included an aunt, Delia (interview with Clare Winnicott: Neve, 1983), a nanny called Allie for the young Donald, and a governess for Violet and Kathleen (Clare Winnicott, 1978), not to mention a cook and several parlour-maids (Johns, 1991). Another aunt lived with the family from time to time (interview with Clare Winnicott: Neve, 1983). The Winnicott clan also kept a favoured pet cat. Donald Winnicott maintained a great feeling of affection for his nanny in particular, throughout his life (Clancier & Kalmano-vitch, 1984).

Father Winnicott dedicated so much time to the city that he seems to have spent very few hours at home, leaving his son surrounded by this veritable bevy of women: mother, sisters, aunts, nanny, governess, cook, maids, as well as the many female relations who lived across the road in the home of Donald's uncle, Richard. Every Sunday, young Donald Winnicott would have the treat of walking home from the local Nonconformist church with his father, a short stroll of some ten minutes' duration (interview with Clare Winnicott: Neve, 1983). Apart from these brief interludes with his father, Donald passed virtually all of his time in the presence of women, often enjoying their attentions quite considerably and developing an exquisite understanding of their private lives and their personal preoccupations. He felt so comfortable with women that he spent countless hours in the family kitchen, the most traditionally female room in the house. Apparently, Elizabeth Winnicott used to complain that young Donald frittered away too much time there with the cook (Clare Winnicott, 1978). Donald must have enjoyed being doted on by the women who surrounded him during his childhood. He referred to them collectively as his "multiple mothers" (quoted in Clare Winnicott, 1978, p. 23). The servants, in particular, played a vital role in Donald Winnicott's development. In later years, he would advise some of his patients to spend more time "below stairs", with the domestic staff, as part of their treatment. Presumably, he knew that the hired help often had more time and compassion for the children than did the biological parents (Jilian Wilson, personal communication, 25 February 1993). Dr

Charles Rycroft, a former Member of The British Psycho-Analytical Society, who knew Winnicott well, noted that although the Winnicott family had a good deal of money, they certainly did not qualify as "top-drawer" landed gentry, and thus they did not employ any male servants such as a butler, footmen, or even coachmen, as a wealthier family would have done (personal communication, 29 November 1993). One wonders what might have happened if Winnicott had had more access to male figures—whether their presence would perhaps have muted what would become an unusual immersion into the lives of mothers and children.

This unique constellation of a little boy fully enveloped by mothers and virtually deprived of a father seems to have left an indelible impression on Winnicott's psychological development, resulting in a powerful female identification. First of all, because young Donald received so much affection from so many women with whom he interacted in a reliable manner, he felt protected, safe, and secure, and this emotional stability provided him with a solid foundation for a sturdy, productive, and creative adult life. Secondly, the preponderance of women in Winnicott's childhood stimulated an extreme fascination with the inner world of the female—an interest that eventually became his life's work; as a professional, he devoted more than forty years of research to the exploration of the essence of motherhood and to the examination of the child's relationship with the mother. Even Winnicott's father earned his livelihood, in part, as a corsetier, selling intimate clothing to untold numbers of women (cf. Cooper, 1989). In fact, at every turn the young Donald Winnicott found himself confronting the nature of femaleness.

Although Winnicott eventually developed a relatively firm sense of masculinity, fuelled by many years in typically male institutions such as public school, university, and the Royal Navy, he always spoke in a high-pitched and vaguely squeaky voice. Apparently, he detested the sound of his own voice—a legacy of a childhood filled with too many females (Barbara Dockar-Drysdale, personal communication, 1 October 1994). In his book on *Clinical Notes on Disorders of Childhood*, Winnicott (1931a, p. 119) remarked that, "Sometimes a boy at puberty cannot make use of the new power of manly speech, but either must speak falsetto, or else unconsciously imitate the voice of a girl or woman he has known." In fact, when he began to deliver radio broadcasts in the 1940s, many listeners thought him to be a woman, and he received quite a few letters at the British Broadcasting Corporation addressed to "Mrs Winnicott" (Martin James, personal communication, 24 November 1991; cf. Casement, 1991). Also for many years, whenever he telephoned Harry Karnac, the original proprietor of H. Karnac (Books), Winnicott would say hello in such a high voice that Karnac would reply (personal communication, 3 August 1994), in all seriousness: "How can I help you, Madam?"

Classical psychoanalytic theory has always focused on the child's position in relation to both parents. The oedipal drama of Freudian theory requires *three* participants: mother, father, and child. Winnicott, in contrast, rarely ever wrote about the father; most of his work concentrated only on the mother and the baby. In view of his early experiences, this relative neglect of the father should not surprise us. No doubt his emphasis on the mother— a vital contribution to psychoanalytic research—also derived from Winnicott's close bonds with his female caretakers. Interestingly enough, even contemporary students of psychology often express sincere surprise when they discover that D. W. Winnicott is actually a man—he writes about mothers and babies with such intimate familiarity that people imagine him to have personally breast-fed scores of young infants.

On the whole, Winnicott seems to have enjoyed a fairly solid and predictable childhood. He suffered no bereavements or physical losses, he had no younger siblings to displace him, and he experienced tremendous continuity and consistency. In a profile of Winnicott published shortly after his sixty-fifth birthday, a journalist wrote: "He had a happy childhood; and he regards himself particularly fortunate because his childhood home is still as it was when he was 18 months old, so that he has always been able to go back and recapture the feelings of his past history" (Anonymous, 1961, p. 138). The young Donald Winnicott could play exhaustively with his siblings and with his cousins, and he cherished the regular experience of having his needs anticipated. Many years later, he recalled: "I remember when I was four years old I woke up on Christmas morning and found I possessed a blue cart made in Switzerland, like those that the people there use for bringing home wood. How did my parents know that this was exactly what I wanted?" (Winnicott, 1962c, p. 70). Furthermore, his close relationship to his nanny, Allie, lasted for more than fifty years. Winnicott (1957j) maintained a lively interest in the nanny's well-being until her death, and he must have derived great sustenance from this relationship.

Young Winnicott had a transitional object—a special possession of childhood: a doll called "Lily", which had belonged previously to Kathleen, the younger of his two sisters. Violet and Kathleen also owned another doll, named "Rosie", and at the age of three years Donald smashed Rosie's nose with a croquet mallet, possibly in a symbolically rivalrous attack on one or both of his sisters. Frederick Winnicott used a number of lighted matches to warm up the doll's wax nose, and he succeeded in remoulding the face. This episode seems to have left a profound impression on Donald, providing him with an experience of being *aggressive* without ultimately being *destructive*—a piece of knowledge that would fortify him in his subsequent psycho-analytic practice. And Winnicott (1970c) would eventually come to believe in the vital role of expressing hostility without annihilating the object of one's rage and anger. Fundamentally, Frederick Winnicott unwittingly demonstrated to his young son that violent behaviour could be contained and survived, and that the shattered remnants of hostile assaults could even be repaired. It should perhaps not surprise us that Winnicott would eventually become very adept in working with violent and delinquent patients (e.g. Winnicott, 1943a, 1956c, 1963f).

Eventually, Winnicott's second wife, Clare Winnicott (1978, p. 25), would comment that her husband's childhood "sounds too good to be true. But the truth is that it *was* good, and try as I will I cannot present it in any other light." Winnicott (1957c, p. 143) expressed a "fully informed and fully felt acknowledgement" for his mother and for her bountifulness. Undoubtedly, Elizabeth Winnicott provided a sound anchoring for her offspring. At one time, when the water tank in the Winnicott household burst and caused terrific floods, the family treated this as an adventure, rather than as a catastrophe as most families would have done (Clare Winnicott, 1978). This anecdote certainly illustrates something about the emotional resilience and the durability of life within the Winnicott family.

In addition to the solidity that Winnicott absorbed from his reliable and steadfast caretakers, he also acquired the permission to be free-spirited and unshackled by dogma. One day, while walking home from church with his father, the youthful Donald Winnicott asked some questions about religion. Frederick Winnicott responded, "Listen, my boy. You read the Bible—what you find there. And you decide for yourself what you want, you know. It's free. You don't have to believe what I think. Make up your own mind about it. Just read the Bible" (interview with Clare Winnicott: Neve, 1983). Not surprisingly, as the decades went by, Winnicott would become the leading figure in the *Independent* tradition within British psychoanalysis, unfettered by the strictures of the more orthodox theoretical positions (cf. Rayner, 1991).

Donald Winnicott may have enjoyed considerable security and peace of mind during his formative years, but something unsettled him and drove him in search of a career devoted to the study of severe mental illness. As the only son in the family, he should have entered into his father's business ventures, but instead he defied convention and became a doctor, and then a psychoanalyst. The presence of Winnicott's "multiple mothers" may, in fact, explain to a large extent why he wrote so much about the psychology of the mother–child bond, but the presence of so many maternal figures hardly illuminates why Winnicott chose to become a clinical *psychoanalyst*. In view of Winnicott's great ease among women, he might just as readily have become a couturier or a gynaecologist. Winnicott never discussed in any of his published writings his deep motivations for pursuing an analytic training; but during his sixty-seventh year, he wrote a moving poem about his mother, Elizabeth, which provides a strong clue to the source of his profound interest in healing emotional distress. Winnicott sent the poem to his brother-in-law, James Britton, with the following note attached: "Do you mind seeing this that hurt coming out of me." Winnicott's poem, "The Tree", consists of these tender phrases:

Mother below is weeping
            weeping
            weeping
Thus I knew her

Once, stretched out on her lap
        as now on dead tree
I learned to make her smile
        to stem her tears
        to undo her guilt
        to cure her inward death
To enliven her was my living.

[quoted in Phillips, 1988, p. 29]

The poem suggests that Elizabeth Winnicott may have suffered from depression (cf. Winnicott, 1948c) and that as a boy Donald had assumed the role of cheering her up. One of Winnicott's associates, Dr Margaret I. Little, later confirmed (interview, 1 November 1981, in Anderson, 1982a) that Elizabeth Winnicott did indeed contend with bouts of depression. Winnicott also implied that his busy father unconsciously delegated him to look after his forlorn mother. In his unpublished autobiography, he noted that Frederick Winnicott "left me too much to all my mothers. Things never quite righted themselves" (quoted in Clare Winnicott, 1978, p. 24). Thus it seems that Winnicott regarded the presence of his multiple mothers not only as a great asset, but as a psychological liability as well.

The Swiss psychotherapist Alice Miller (1979) has written a very insightful essay on the childhood experiences of psychoanalysts, postulating that many of these clinicians entered the profession after having served an apprenticeship in infancy as miniature psychotherapists, listening to the miseries and woes of their depressed parents and comforting them during periods of anguish. Who else but the children of very unhappy mothers or fathers would wish to devote their careers to the study of emotional casualties? As a child, Winnicott had enough strength to survive his mother's episodic depressions, and he had received enough nurturance to experience true joy and creativity as well. But the experience of ministering to the needs of a sad mother might have stimulated rescue phantasies in young Donald, prompting him to devote his life to the care of other sad individuals. In later years he wrote that "Analysis is my chosen job, the way I feel I will best deal with my own guilt, the way I can express myself in a constructive way" (Winnicott, 1949b, p. 70). In his essay on "Reparation in Respect of Mother's Organized Defence Against Depression", Donald Winnicott (1948c, p. 93) suggested that often children will attune themselves to the mental state of the mother: "Their task is first to deal with mother's mood." Undoubtedly, Winnicott spoke from some deep personal experience in this regard, and he may well have felt intensely guilty in later life that he did not succeed in curing his mother or in saving her from an untimely death from catarrhal pulmonary congestion and cardiac fatty infiltration in 1925.

We must proceed with caution in our attempt to understand the influence of Donald Winnicott's early childhood experiences on his later life and work; however, it does seem very suggestive that Winnicott's awareness of nurturant women, especially those with depressive tendencies, fostered his interest in the trials of the nursing mother and thus facilitated his understanding quite considerably. Winnicott's great sensitivity to mothers and their babies will become increasingly apparent in the coming pages.

Donald enjoyed a rich childhood, full of play and companionship. Not only did he write poetry and participate in amateur dramatics, but he revelled in singing and practising the piano, and he also engaged with relish in various sporting activities, especially swimming and running (Clare Winnicott, 1978). Actually, Winnicott ran with such skill and speed that he planned to join the British Olympic Team, to represent his country in the international games; sadly, a hip injury prevented Winnicott from participating (Khan, 1988). Had Winnicott earned a place on the British team, he would have begun the arduous training for The Sixth Olympic Games, scheduled for 1916 in Berlin. Needless to say, this pageant never materialized, because of the onslaught of the First World War. By the time of The Seventh Olympic Games in 1920 in Antwerp, Winnicott had already begun his medical career (cf. Weyand, 1952).

Winnicott very much enjoyed bathing in the water in Plymouth Sound, near his home; and years later, he would still recall the beauty of the sunlight shimmering on the waves (Dockar-Drysdale, personal communication, 13 July 1991). He also derived great pleasure from small animals, and as a boy he kept mice, ever observant of the interactions between the mother mouse and her babies (Winnicott, 1969e). On one occasion, he erected a concentration camp for woodlice, trapping the poor creatures inside. He continued to experience pangs of guilt about this for many years to come (Barbara Dockar-Drysdale, personal communication, 13 July 1991).

Winnicott attended a local preparatory school in Plymouth, and he continued to live at home. By all accounts, he performed outstandingly well in his academic subjects, apart from a brief period during his ninth year when he messed up his school notebooks and received very poor scores on his examinations (Khan, 1975). We know nothing of the specific details of this phase of Winnicott's latency years. It would be tempting to speculate that his mother may have experienced yet another episode of depression at this time, thus affecting her son's mood and hence his subsequent performance at school.

On the whole, the young Donald Winnicott enjoyed a very good childhood. Certainly, his parents provided him with enough love and protection to prevent him from experiencing any major mental illness in later life. However, the lingering shadow of Elizabeth Winnicott's depressions and the unusual psychosexual constellation of Winnicott's multiple mothers prompted him to develop extensive rescue phantasies towards women in distress. In 1923 he would re-enact a childhood scenario by marrying a very ill young woman who brought him many years of misery and turmoil. In spite of all these tribulations, Winnicott's family offered him the foundation that he needed to pursue a full and creative life, touched by genius and great works.

CHAPTER TWO

Boarding-school

One afternoon, at a family meal, the twelve-year-old Donald shocked his father by using the word "drat". Frederick Winnicott, born in 1855 during the apogee of public prudery, found this epithet rather shocking. Donald reminisced, "My father looked pained as only he could look, blamed my mother for not seeing to it that I had decent friends, and from that moment he prepared himself to send me away to boarding-school, which he did when I was 13" (quoted in Clare Winnicott, 1978, p. 23). In September 1910, some months *after* he had, in fact, turned fourteen years of age, Donald left his preparatory school in Plymouth and travelled north to the exclusive Leys School for boys, in Cambridge. Significantly, Winnicott remembered having gone to boarding-school at the age of *thirteen*, thus committing a parapraxis—perhaps the trauma of leaving home at that time made him feel rather younger and more vulnerable. No doubt his expulsion from the family home contributed to Winnicott's ultimate professional interest in the ruptures and impingements that can shatter the continuity of a child's environment.

The Leys School, on Trumpington Street in Cambridge, first opened its doors to pupils on 16 February 1875, as a specialist Wesleyan First Grade School. Its name derives from the surrounding Cowfenleys meadowland fields. Dr William Fiddian Moulton, a scholar descended from a long line of Methodist ministers and preachers, served as the first Headmaster of the school. Frederick Winnicott would have held The Leys School in very high regard, because of its staunch and long-standing tradition of English Methodism and its status as a very respectable school for the middle classes. Early pupils included Joseph Arthur Rank, later the first Baron Rank, the well-known film producer; Henry Hallett Dale, a physician who would eventually win both a knighthood and the Nobel Prize; and Samuel Gurney-Dixon, who would eventually become the Pro-Chancellor of Southampton University (Stirland, 1963).

Dr Moulton had created an environment in which scholarship, religion, and athletics could be pursued simultaneously. At the time of Donald Winnicott's stay there, the boys would have been awakened early in their dormitory rooms by the clanging of a bell. Breakfast and morning chapel would be followed by an hour of academic lessons. After a period of gymnastic activities, they would then proceed to luncheon. After the midday meal, the students would have a further hour of academic work, with additional playtime afterwards. Between 4.30 p.m. and 6.30 p.m., the boys attended two further periods of lessons, and then, following dinner in the Hall, there would be evening preparation from 7.05 p.m. until 7.35 p.m., and evening prayers. On Wednesdays and Saturdays the boys enjoyed special half-days (Baker, 1975).

Donald Winnicott began his boarding-school career as a Fifth Form student, in tandem with twenty-one other boys. Contemporaries who had matriculated in the previous year included the colourful George Eric Whelpton, a young gentleman who attended The Leys from 1909 until 1913 and who seems to have inspired Dorothy L. Sayers to create the popular, fictional detective, Lord Peter Wimsey (Stirland, 1975; Geoffrey C. Houghton, personal communication, 27 September 1994). Virtually all of the boys had come from proud, successful, gentrified families, and many had followed their fathers or elder brothers or cousins to The Leys School, thus perpetuating a family tradition.

In all likelihood, the young Winnicott arrived at the school on Friday, 16 September, 1910. He would have taken the train from Plymouth to the railway station at Cambridge, where the school servants would have greeted him and then conveyed his luggage to his dormitory, a bleak room shared by many boys, with little more than narrow beds lined up in a row, affording no privacy at all. We do not know whether Winnicott arrived in time for lunch at 1.30 p.m., but he certainly would have eaten the "meat tea" dinner at 7.00 p.m., followed by prayers in the school chapel at 8.15 p.m. (Baker, 1975).

Winnicott lodged in North House "B", one of the rather large and spartan residential halls. Of the new arrivals, William Norman Cleland, Wilfrid Arnold Grace, William Arthur Hinchcliffe, Herbert Lumsden, Andrew Montgomery Rees, William Henry Robinson, and Clifford Huddart Walker also lived in North House "B". Eric Whelpton had also resided in "B" House (Stirland, 1963). Winnicott would have enjoyed the protection of his young Housemaster, one James Edgar Mellor, better known as Jesse Mellor, a devoted alumnus of the school—he had been a student there from 1898 until 1903. After training as a classicist at Jesus College at the University of Cambridge, Mellor returned to The Leys in 1906 as a Master, remaining on the faculty until 1947 and immersing himself enthusiastically in all aspects of school life. He held many additional positions at the school, including those of Honorary Secretary and Treasurer of the Old Leysian Union, and he later served as President of the Old Leysian Union, the school's alumni society. Eventually, Mellor became a Governor of the school. Jesse Mellor also took most of the school's photographs during the first half of the twentieth century (Geoffrey C. Houghton, personal communication, 27 September 1994). His younger brother, William Algernon Mellor, also attended as a pupil from 1903 until 1905, and the latter's son, Hugh Wright Mellor, would eventually matriculate to The Leys as well.

Jesse Mellor enjoyed tremendous popularity with the boys; as a young man himself and as an Old Leysian, Mellor would have had a much greater understanding of school life than the more antiquated masters would have done. Mellor also became very involved in school sports, serving as Captain of "Mr Mellor's XV" rugby football team, thus affording him many additional interactions with his young charges. In view of the fact that Winnicott would eventually transfer from The Leys School to Jesus College, at the University of Cambridge, exactly as Mellor had done, one cannot help but speculate whether Winnicott would have turned to Mellor for guidance in selecting a Cambridge college. Like Winnicott, Mellor had two sisters, and after his retirement, the bachelor school-teacher moved in with his two sisters, where he lived a quiet and retiring life (Geoffrey C. Houghton, personal communication, 27 September 1994). He died on 5 October 1963 (Howard & Houghton, 1991).

Among the other masters were The Reverend William Theodore Aquilla Barber, the venerable Headmaster of the school from 1898 until 1919, Joseph Clark Isard, the Bursar, and an Old Leysian in his own right, and, above all, the legendary William H. Balgarnie (Howard & Houghton, 1991). Mr Balgarnie worked at The Leys from 1900 until 1930 and again from 1940 until 1946. A superb teacher, Balgarnie served as the real-life model for the immortal literary character "Mr Chips", the protagonist of the classic novel by James Hilton, himself a pupil at The Leys School from 1915 until 1918 (Geoffrey C. Houghton, personal communication, 27 September 1994). Though he made no public references to Balgarnie, Winnicott did indeed bear a certain similarity to his former Master. He, too, would be remembered by generations of students as a truly inspiring teacher, and so it may be that Donald Winnicott identified with certain charismatic aspects of Balgarnie's pedagogical approach.

As the autumn term of 1910 unfolded, Winnicott began to immerse himself in school life as one of the new boys. The editorial of 30 September 1910, in the school's magazine, *The Leys Fortnightly*, notes:

> Another School year has begun, and with it all those signs of change are manifest which make the beginning of a new year a quiet and somewhat trying experience. In all departments of School life others fill the places of those whose absence we deplore; those who so recently have been the leaders and strong ones among us. We wish them all every success in their new positions. We also welcome very heartily those who have come to fill up our depleted ranks. [p. 2]

One can certainly imagine the newly pubescent Winnicott reading this inaugural editorial of the new school year, away from his
family home for the first extended period in his life. Whatever
loneliness Winnicott may have felt, having left the bright red soil
of Plymouth, he would have had numerous opportunities to
immerse himself into the solid studies and the vast array of
extracurricular activities at The Leys School; and if he did feel
homesick, he might have visited the school's matron, Nurse
Pople, who had herself only recently joined the staff in the
autumn of 1910.

The school clubs included *The Leys Fortnightly* Committee,
The Literary and Debating Society Committee, The Natural History Society Committee, The Bicycle Club Committee, and, of
course, the Games Committee. On Monday, 3 October, 1910,
The Literary and Debating Society convened in the Prefects'
Room to hear the reading of Entrance Papers into the Society by
eight boys, including that of Winnicott's classmate, Syed Mafid
Alam, who spoke on his "Journey from India to England". *The
Leys Fortnightly* (14 October 1910, p. 26) commented: "This
paper was also distinguished by the manner in which the candidate overcame his linguistic difficulties. Alam was unanimously
elected." We do not know whether Winnicott attended this meeting, but in view of the fact that boys had access to neither radio
nor television in those days, as modern students do, an evening
at The Literary and Debating Society would have constituted
rather an entertainment, and it seems likely that Winnicott
might have participated in some way. If so, he would have heard
another paper that night presented by John Hodson Alcock, a
boy from the North House "A", next door to Winnicott's "B"
House. Alcock spoke on "A Personal Visit to a Coal Mine". The
newspaper reported: "He gave a clear and interesting description
of the working of the mine, and was elected" (*The Leys Fortnightly*, 14 October 1910, p. 25). Alcock, a native of Mansfield, in
Nottinghamshire, would become one of Winnicott's two closest
friends at The Leys, in spite of the fact that he had arrived at the
school more than two years before Winnicott. Alcock eventually
matriculated to Peterhouse at the University of Cambridge. His
studies became interrupted by the First World War, and he
served as a Lieutenant in the Lincolnshire Regiment. He became

a prisoner of war in Germany and also in Holland (Winnicott, 1919). After the fighting ceased, Alcock returned to Cambridge to complete his university studies, graduating in 1920. He qualified as a solicitor, working for most of his life in the Bank Chambers on Market Street, in Mansfield, Nottinghamshire. Winnicott's other great friend, Harold Stanely Ede, a budding art historian from North House "A", will be discussed in greater detail in due course. Winnicott and Ede would maintain lifelong affectional ties.

It may be interesting to know something more about the papers presented to The Literary and Debating Society in 1910, to provide us not only with information about the talks that the impressionable adolescent Winnicott may have heard in the Prefects' Room, but to offer a glimpse into the concerns and preoccupations of an English schoolboy in the late Edwardian era. These included: "Has England Degenerated?", "A Short Glance at Astrology", "India Under Hindu Rule", "Is Life Worth Living?", and "The Justice or Injustice of the Execution of Chas. I. and Mary Queen of Scots". On 10 October 1910, Max Crutchley Ede, the elder brother of Winnicott's friend Harold Stanely Ede, delivered a highly praised impromptu talk on the "Revolution in Portugal".

Other events in Winnicott's first term would have consisted of a continuous round of sporting activities, such as a cycle run along the ancient Cambridgeshire road to Ely and another to King's Lynn, as well as football matches in which the school played against a variety of teams such as the Haileybury Wanderers, St. Paul's School, and Corpus Christi College of the University of Cambridge. Strikingly, on Saturday, 24 September 1910, only days after his arrival, Winnicott played for The Leys Minimi in a junior league football Association Match, competing against the Caldicott School from Hitchin, Hertfordshire. Winnicott assumed the position of forward, and The Leys Minimi defeated the Caldicott School by two goals to nil. Winnicott certainly did not shine in this match, and an anonymous commentator wrote that, "Howard kept goal well for Caldicott, but our centre and inside forwards did not bustle him enough, and lost many chances" (*The Leys Fortnightly*, 14 October 1910, p. 33). Furthermore, the school newspaper singled out three of Winnicott's team-mates, Henry Myles Carrick, Donald Holman, and his cousin, Richard Boyce Holman, for special praise. When The Leys Minimi played the Caldicott School again on 12 November 1910, Winnicott did not participate (*The Leys Fortnightly*, 25 November 1910). Undeterred, however, he would continue to play football throughout his time at school, eventually representing the First Football side. Winnicott did join in at least one more sporting event during his first term at school, on Tuesday, 13 December 1910, in a rugby match between North House "B" and the School Junior House. "B" House lost grievously with only eight points to School House's thirty-one points. On this occasion, however, Winnicott received special commendation along with his colleague, William Norman Cleland, for being "very good" (*The Leys Fortnightly*, 20 December 1910, p. 137).

One cannot readily ascertain the calibre of academic studies at The Leys School in 1910. The Library did acquire two volumes of poems by Robert Browning and a volume of poetry by John Keats, as well as a copy of George Eliot's novel *Silas Marner* (*The Leys Fortnightly*, 11 November 1910). Both Masters and visiting specialists alike would also contribute to the school's lecture series, which would convene on Saturday afternoons at 5.00 p.m. Speakers for the autumn term of 1910 included James Hurst Hayes, Esq., a member of the faculty, talking on "With a Motor in Algeria", Harry Brownsword, Esq., another Master, on "Dyes and Their Use", and Dr A. Hill, on "How We Come to Know" (*The Leys Fortnightly*, 28 October 1910). On 29 October, Professor German Sims Woodhead, Professor of Pathology at the University of Cambridge and a Fellow of the Royal College of Physicians, spoke to The Natural History and Science Society on "What Our Faces Tell", illustrated with slides. Professor Woodhead spoke about emotions in human beings and in other animals, concentrating on the links between emotions and the body. The description of the talk seems to indicate that Woodhead had studied Charles Darwin's topical work on this subject, and in later years Winnicott (1967c) would indicate the importance of Darwinian ideas in the shaping of his own intellectual development as a psychoanalyst. If Winnicott did indeed listen to Professor Woodhead, he would have heard the speaker's outrageous remark that mentally defective idiots do not display facial expressions owing to a weakened brain which cannot control the facial muscles (*The Leys Fortnightly*, 11 November

1910). Years later, Winnicott (1931a) would make important contributions to a more enlightened study of mental defect and mental handicap (Susanna Isaacs Elmhirst, personal communication, 4 September 1995).

In addition to academic activities and sporting events, religion featured prominently in the life of this Methodist school, as one might expect. All the pupils had to attend chapel twice daily for compulsory prayers, once in the morning, and once in the evening. Often, guest preachers would lead the prayers. Music and drama also featured quite strongly at The Leys, which boasted both a fine orchestra and a choir, and the students could often attend musical concerts. For light entertainment, the boys would contribute comical verse to *The Leys Fortnightly*, and on one occasion Winnicott's dear friend, John Alcock, treated The Literary and Debating Society to an amusing reading of a case of mesmerism on board a ship (*The Leys Fortnightly*, 9 December 1910).

As Christmas of 1910 approached, the boys wrote humorous poems for *The Leys Fortnightly*, all printed anonymously. One ditty, "A Song of the Holidays", begins:

Now is the time to be off for the holidays,
　　Joyful relief for our overtaxed brain!
Adipose Y's, thick X's, and solid A's
　　Cease for a while to give sorrow and pain!
　　　　Hey for the jolly days!
　　Strap your portmanteaus and off for the train.
　　　　　　[*The Leys Fortnightly*, 20 December 1910, p. 117]

And so, on Wednesday, 21 December, 1910, Winnicott would have completed his first term at school.

As the new calendar year commenced, on Wednesday, 18 January, 1911, Winnicott began to become better acclimatized to life at his boarding-school, and as the terms progressed, his name started to appear with increasing frequency in the school magazine. For example, he had already begun to acquire a reputation for fleet-footedness, and he ran well in various track events. On Friday, 31 March, 1911, Winnicott entered the Half-Mile Handicap race for boys under sixteen years of age, one of the competitions in a marathon three-day sporting extravaganza. The school newspaper reported that "Winnicott ran excellently" (*The Leys Fortnightly*, 3 April 1911, p. 226), but he lost to his contemporary, Wilfrid Arnold Grace. Not only did Winnicott play football and participate in track events, but he also joined the cricket team for a time, having earned the praise of a more senior student, Arthur Cyril Waddy (*5th Pitch*. Pitch Reports. *The Leys Fortnightly*, 2 June 1911, p. 267), who described Winnicott on the cricket pitch as "very plucky in attempting to stop hard drives".

During the winter and spring terms of 1911 Winnicott continued with his studies and with his participation in athletic events. He joined the choir, and he also became a member of the School Scouts. As he had no lessons during the afternoons, he used this time for running, swimming, cycling, and playing rugby (Clare Winnicott, 1978). He also consolidated his friendships with Alcock and Ede, both older boys who shared Winnicott's imaginative and artistic temperament.

Fortunately, we have a very vivid portrait of life at The Leys School during this period of time through the careful record of daily detail preserved for posterity in *The Leys Fortnightly*. For example, the family of three old boys, Alexander, Ernest, and John Forrester Paton, donated £250 to improve the organ in the school's Chapel, and the Modern Languages classroom acquired newly painted and varnished desks. The Library obtained the twelfth volume of *The Cambridge Modern History*, recently published; and on St. Valentine's Day, the Bicycle Club participated in a cycle run from Hitchin to St. Albans, in the neighbouring county of Hertfordshire, because the Headmaster had granted a special holiday in honour of several students who had won scholarships to Cambridge (*The Leys Fortnightly*, 17 February 1911). In the absence of female pupils, the boys celebrated St. Valentine's Day by sending secret love messages to one another, in keeping with the homoerotic tradition of the British public school of the early twentieth century.

As Winnicott's first year at school drew to a close, the boys enjoyed a special holiday from Tuesday, 20 June, 1911, until Monday, 26 June, 1911, to commemorate the Coronation of King George V (*The Leys Fortnightly*, 16 June 1911). Several weeks later, on Thursday, 6 July, a swelteringly hot day, the entire school celebrated its Annual Speech Day, with no fewer than one thousand invitations having been sent out to family members and to selected dignitaries. The Right Honourable Walter Runciman, M.P., President of the Board of Education, distributed the prizes in the Great Hall and then delivered a speech to the assembled gathering of adults dressed in their finery, with the boys sporting their school blazers.

The Headmaster, The Reverend Dr William Theodore Aquilla Barber, also spoke, as did the Head Prefect, Roy Evans Bullen, a bright and articulate man who would soon be killed in the First World War while serving as a Captain in the British army (Stirland, 1963). Winnicott's friends both shone during the awards ceremony: Harold Stanley Ede received the honour of delivering a special recitation in French, followed by loud applause; and John Hodson Alcock won a Form Prize and one for Success in the University Examinations, as well as a prize for General Drawing. Alcock also garnered a Lower Certificate in the Oxford and Cambridge School Examination Board. In view of Alcock's prominence in the Speech Day events, his mother and father, Mr and Mrs J. E. Alcock of Mansfield, in Nottinghamshire, travelled to Cambridge for the ceremony. Sadly, Winnicott received no prizes, and his parents did not attend the Speech Day. Perhaps Frederick Winnicott had preferred to commit his time to municipal activities in Plymouth.

After the formal speeches and prizes, some of the boys performed a swimming display, followed by a tea on the shaded lawn (*The Leys Fortnightly*, 15 July 1911). The grand day concluded with a Concert in the Great Hall, which featured a pianoforte solo performance of the Adagio section from Ludwig van Beethoven's "Moonlight Sonata", played by the graduating student Henry Wright Eyre. In only five years' time, in 1916, the young Eyre would die from war wounds during his tenure as a Captain in the army (Stirland, 1963). On Saturday, 29 July, 1911 (*The Leys Fortnightly*, 28 July 1911), Winnicott departed from The Leys School, having survived his first year as a boarder.

Winnicott returned to school on Wednesday, 20 September, 1911, fully able to enjoy his more senior status among the student body. Gradually, he seems to have become something of a ringleader among his peers, and every night in the dormitory he would read a story aloud to the other boys (Clare Winnicott, 1978). He also started to ride a motorcycle at this juncture

(Khan, 1975), and bicycling and motorcycling would continue to play a vital role in Winnicott's life.

At least one letter written by Winnicott survives from this period, and it deserves to be quoted fully for its charm and for its insight:

My dearest Mother,

On September 2nd all true Scouts think of their mothers, since that was the birthday of Baden Powell's mother when she was alive.

And so when you get this letter I shall be thinking of you in particular, and I only hope you will get it in the morning.

But to please me very much I must trouble you to do me a little favour. Before turning over the page I want you to go up into my bedroom and in the right-hand cupboard find a small parcel . . . Now, have you opened it? Well I hope you will like it. You can change it at Pophams if you don't. Only if you do so, you must ask to see No. 1 who knows about it.

I have had a ripping holiday, and I cannot thank you enough for all you have done and for your donation to the Scouts.

My home is a beautiful home and I only wish I could live up to it. However I will do my best and work hard and that's all I can do at present.

Give my love to the others: thank Dad for his game of billiards and V and K for being so nice and silly so as to make me laugh. But, it being Mother's day, most love goes to you,

from your loving boy

Donald.

[quoted in Clare Winnicott, 1978, pp. 24–25]

Winnicott's youthful letter to his mother reveals not only poignancy, but also a great sensitivity to the needs of the intermittently depressed Elizabeth Winnicott. It should hardly surprise us that a young boy who wrapped a present for his mother in such a thoughtful manner—providing her with detailed instructions on how she might find the gift, and with advice on how she might return it to Popham's shop—would then choose to specialize in a profession devoted to an understanding of the internal world of the mother.

At boarding-school, Winnicott began to develop a very serious interest in the natural sciences, and he particularly enjoyed reading Charles Darwin's classic treatise of 1859, *On the Origin of Species by Means of Natural Selection, or the Preservation of Favoured Races in the Struggle for Life*. Of Darwin's magnum opus, Winnicott (1945c, p. 180) reminisced, "I couldn't leave off reading it, and this got me into serious trouble because it seemed so much more interesting than prep., and I believe it was." Indeed, Winnicott enjoyed all of Darwin's writings, and he purchased second-hand copies from the bookstalls in the Cambridge market (interview with Clare Winnicott: Neve, 1983). In his quintessentially English phraseology, Winnicott (1967c, p. 574) explained: "Suddenly I knew that Darwin was my cup of tea." The young student did not know exactly why Darwin intrigued him so much, but in middle age a more insightful Winnicott (1945c, p. 181) reflected in a talk before the Eighth Form at St. Paul's School, in London: "The main thing was that it showed that living things could be examined scientifically, with the corollary that gaps in knowledge and understanding need not scare me. For me this new idea meant a great lessening of tension and consequently a release of energy for work and play." The similarities between Darwin and Winnicott seem quite apparent. Throughout his later endeavours as a paediatrician and as a psychoanalyst, Donald Winnicott would always observe children very carefully, just as Darwin had done with different species. And Winnicott, like Darwin, could tolerate *not knowing*—an essential attribute for a psychotherapist who might have to wait many long years before patients would reveal their innermost secrets. After all, Darwin had written extensively about the evolution of the human species, in spite of large gaps in the fossil records. Winnicott, too, would survive the uncertainty of not knowing all the details of a patient's life history; yet with his clinical acumen and his psychological sensitivity he could nevertheless rely on important clues to reconstruct the origins of a person's symptomatology with a certain facility.

By 1914, Winnicott had completed his studies at The Leys School, and at the passing-out ceremony, he won special commendation for his musical abilities, in particular. Although he could readily have become a professional musician, his infantile need to repair the depression of his mother drove him inexorably into the helping professions, and he decided that he would study at university in order to become a physician.

After Winnicott had graduated from school, he maintained occasional contact with The Leys over the years. He even attended at least one of the dinners for graduates of the school. On 15 March 1929, Winnicott would dine with his fellow Old Leysians at the Jubilee Annual Dinner in the Connaught Rooms, in London, where he sat next to his dear friend, Alcock. The menu for this meal included such delicacies as Hors d'Oeuvre Connaught and Turtle Consommé. Winnicott also signed the visitors' book at this dinner, still preserved in the archival collection at The Leys School. But the school remained most alive for him through his contact with Alcock and Ede. Years later, when visiting his fiancée, John Alcock would sometimes stay with Winnicott in London (Winnicott, 1919). And Ede eventually purchased a house in Hampstead, near Winnicott's residence of the 1930s and 1940s.

In general, The Leys School seems to have suited Donald well, because he certainly relished his studies and his many extracurricular activities. But we do not know how successfully he weathered the long periods of separation from his multiple mothers—he must have missed them a great deal, in view of the depth of his attachments. During the Second World War, Winnicott demonstrated great skill and sensitivity in his clinical work with evacuated children, kept apart from their parents. No doubt his own experiences at boarding-school permitted him better to empathize with his wartime child patients.

In many respects, The Leys School may have proved a blessing for Winnicott, because it offered him the opportunity to leave his family home. Violet and Kathleen appear to have assumed the role of caretaker for their mother, and, as such, they experienced great difficulties in separation. In contrast to their brother, neither sister succeeded in living independently, and they remained spinsters at Rockville, devoting themselves to singing, painting, and playing the piano, one of them going blind. Kathleen passed away first, in 1979, and Violet died in 1984, at the Nelson House Nursing Home, in the Stoke section of Plymouth. But Donald managed to escape from his home, and towards the end of his life he exclaimed to his second wife, "I was left too much to all my mothers. Thank goodness I was sent away at thirteen!" (interview with Clare Winnicott: Neve, 1983, quoted in Rudnytsky, 1991, p. 185).

CHAPTER THREE

Medicine and paediatrics

F rederick Winnicott attempted to persuade his son to enter the family business, but Donald had already begun to manifest that healthy sense of independence which would become so apparent in his later negotiations within the British psychoanalytic community. Donald Winnicott did not relish the prospect of training as a manufacturer. He had other ideas: he would become a medical doctor. One day, while convalescing in the sick room at The Leys School after having broken his clavicle on the sports field, Winnicott resolved: "I could see that for the rest of my life I should have to depend on doctors if I damaged myself or became ill, and the only way out of this position was to become a doctor myself" (quoted in Clare Winnicott, 1978, p. 25; cf. Winnicott, 1970b). This statement suggests that in spite of Winnicott's considerable ego strength and his notable psychological health, he also suffered from a marked fear of dependency—possibly a residue of the breaches in his earliest relationship with his mother. When Winnicott asked his headmaster at The Leys School whether medicine would suit him as a career, he replied, "Boy, not brilliant, but will get on" (quoted in Anonymous, 1961, p. 137). Fortunately, this discouragement did not deter Winnicott. He contended that, "I have never wanted to be anything else but a doctor" (Winnicott, 1970b, p. 114), and he set about this plan with resolute determination.

As we have already noted, the Winnicott family had a good deal of financial security, and Donald could have enjoyed a comfortable life as the manager of Winnicott Brothers, without pursuing a career as academically demanding as medicine; nevertheless, he chose to embark upon the arduous training, perhaps out of a deep need to heal his mother and to compete with his powerful father—an aspiring parliamentarian who had by then already completed his first term of office as Lord Mayor of Plymouth, and who enjoyed the company of many influential personalities. But Winnicott's wish to study medicine eventually triumphed. At sixteen years of age, he confessed to his long-time chum from The Leys School, Harold Stanley Ede, that, "All the stored-up feelings about doctors which I have bottled up for so many years seemed to burst and bubble up at once" (quoted in Clare Winnicott, 1978, p. 26). Apparently, young Ede interceded with Frederick Winnicott on Donald's behalf, and he helped to convince the father to relinquish any wishes that his son should enter the family business.

As a matter of interest, Winnicott's dear friend Stanley Ede, better known as "Jim" Ede, also went on to a splendid career in his own chosen field of art history. He became a collector of paintings and other art works, which formed the basis of the Kettle's Yard museum in Cambridge, a part of the University of Cambridge. Ede (1931) also wrote a solid dual portrait, entitled *Savage Messiah*, of the anguished artists Sophie Suzanne Brzeska and Henri Gaudier (cf. Ede, 1930). Brzeska spent a goodly amount of time in a mad-house, and one cannot help but speculate whether Ede's preoccupation with an unstable woman mirrored Winnicott's own interests in psychopathology. Extraordinarily, Ede's book appeared in 1931 under the imprint of the publishers William Heinemann Limited. Winnicott's first book, *Clinical Notes on Disorders of Childhood*, also appeared in 1931, produced by William Heinemann (Medical Books). In view of the fact that Winnicott wrote a commissioned book for William Heinemann's "Practitioner's Aid Series", one wonders whether he had, in fact, introduced Ede to his editor. In addition to his writing, Ede worked for a time at the National Gallery in Central London and then transferred to the National Gallery at Millbank in Southwest London, now the Tate Gallery, where he worked until 1936. He acquired a reputation for riding to luncheon parties in London on his bicycle (Richard Buckle, personal communication, 14 September 1994). Ede knew most of the English painters of the post-War period, and he became a patron of modern art. He also enjoyed a particularly warm relationship with the artist Ben Nicholson. Winnicott continued to socialize with Ede after both men had left The Leys School, and the friendship seems to have endured until Winnicott's death.

As Winnicott had attended school in Cambridge, just yards away from the picturesque colleges, it seemed only natural that he should have wished to continue his studies in that very locale; and in 1914 he matriculated to the University of Cambridge, residing at Jesus College, one of the most ancient and beautiful of the Cambridge colleges. His curriculum consisted of biology, zoology, physiology, and anatomy, the prerequisites for his subsequent clinical studies and hospital posts. Winnicott seems to have found the pre-medical course at the University of Cambridge exceedingly dry: "The physiology I learned was cold, that is to say, it could be checked up by careful examination of a pithed frog or a heart–lung preparation. Every effort was made to eliminate variables such as emotions" (Winnicott, 1957g, p. 35). Although Winnicott completed his studies at Cambridge, he received only a mediocre third-class Bachelor of Arts degree. In all likelihood, he devoted little of his time to the study of "cold" physiology; instead, he hired a piano, which he played "unceasingly" (Clare Winnicott, 1978, p. 26), and he sang heartily in a good tenor's voice. As such, his college room became a very popular meeting-ground. In addition to his B.A. degree from the University of Cambridge, he later received an M.A. degree as well, granted as a ritualistic honour to Oxbridge graduates without the need for further study.

As Britain entered the First World War, several of the colleges at the University of Cambridge became transformed into temporary military hospitals, and by 1916 Winnicott began to work with patients who required acute medical treatment. As a medical trainee, he received a special exemption from military service in order to pursue his studies, but many of his friends enlisted for active duty and subsequently died in combat. Winnicott's second wife has remarked that "Many close friends were killed early in the war and his whole life was affected by this, because always he felt that he had a responsibility to live for those who died, as well as for himself" (Clare Winnicott, 1978, p. 27; Donald Campbell, personal communication, 2 May 1994). Winnicott did what he could in the makeshift military hospitals to help the wounded soldiers. He also utilized his considerable musical talents to entertain the patients, and he would enliven the proceedings by singing comical songs, such as "Apple Dumplings!", a hit tune from 1917, on the ward on Saturday nights (Clare Winnicott, 1978).

Winnicott turned twenty-one years of age in April of 1917, and, like so many other young Englishmen of his generation, he was swept along in the rising tide of nationalistic fervour and decided that he must do something more active for his King and for his country, even though as a medical student he could have remained shielded from conscription. Many of his friends died tragically in combat, but he survived the war. For a time, he worked as an orderly for the St. John's Ambulance Service (Khan, 1987); then, because he had spent virtually all of his childhood in Plymouth, looking out on the English Channel and swimming in its waters, Winnicott enrolled in the Royal Navy and received a position as Surgeon–Probationer—the sole medical officer on a destroyer. He also claimed to have joined the Navy, rather than any of the forces on land or in the air, because the blue of the Navy uniform matched the colour of his eyes (Little, 1985). Winnicott's appointment on the ship seems to have been arranged "to reassure the sailors' mothers that their boys had a doctor on board" (quoted in Anonymous, 1961, p. 137).

The vessel did become embroiled in fighting enemy forces, and *Mr* Winnicott, not yet a qualified doctor, did his best to treat the various casualties, assisted by a very experienced medical orderly (Clare Winnicott, 1978). He cheerfully admitted that at this time in his career he could not distinguish between syphilis and gonorrhoea (Anonymous, 1961). No doubt the naval experience taught him a great deal, not least the art of communication with men from very different socio-economic backgrounds—a skill that aided Winnicott considerably in his subsequent clinical practice. One Scottish engineer on the destroyer found it hard to believe that Winnicott's father earned his living as a *merchant*, in view of Winnicott's own posh accent, his delicate breeding, and his fine comportment.

Though Winnicott provided regular medical care for his fellow shipmates, he also enjoyed much leisure time on the destroyer, and during these periods of repose he read the novels of Henry James and George Meredith with great avidity. Winnicott's predilection for the writings of Henry James, in particular, proved unwittingly fortuitous, because decades later, he would come to treat a very fragile woman who devoured the works of James "voraciously" (Winnicott, 1963i, p. 83). Undoubtedly, Winnicott's great familiarity with these classic novels must have proved quite valuable in the clinical sessions with his patient.

Shortly before the war ended, Winnicott left the Royal Navy, and he resumed his medical training at St. Bartholomew's Hospital Medical College of the University of London—the oldest and among the most venerable teaching hospitals in England, founded in 1123 by the Augustinian monk Rahere. Records indicate that Winnicott matriculated at the medical school of St. Bartholomew's Hospital on Friday, 2 November, 1917, entering the field of medicine at a relatively primitive time when "People just died like flies of dysentery and other things" (Winnicott, 1969e, p. 203). During this period, Winnicott lived in "some very good digs" in the slums of North Kensington, at 62, Oxford Terrace, Paddington, in West London, with a number of young friends, including a poet whom Winnicott (1966d, p. 6) recalled as "very tall and indolent and always smoking". The poet seemed to spend most of his time in bed, lolling in a regressive state. Winnicott's association with this poet may have helped him to develop both an understanding and an appreciation of the regressed psychiatric patients with whom he would later work as a psychoanalyst.

Before his death, Winnicott (1984c, p. 235) referred once again to this particular nameless young gentleman:

> I am reminded here of a friend of mine, a very fine person, who did a great deal in his medical career and who was very much respected in his private life. He was rather a depressive individual. I remember at a discussion on health he surprised a company of doctors all fully committed to the

elimination of disease by starting off his contribution with the words, "I find health disgusting!" This was serious. He went on (mobilizing his sense of humour) to describe the way in which a friend of his with whom he lived when he was a medical student got up early in the morning and had a cold bath and did exercises and started the day full of glee; he himself, by contrast, was lying in bed in a deep depression, unable to get up except on the basis of a fear of the consequences.

It would be quite reasonable to presume that the jolly friend may have been Winnicott himself, whose enthusiasm for his medical studies must have stood out in stark contrast to the melancholy of his more indolent friend.

Winnicott thrived in London, and he dated quite a number of young women, almost marrying on several occasions (Clare Winnicott, 1978). One of his fiancées, Fiona Ede, was in fact the sister of Winnicott's friend from school, H. Stanley Ede; but this match did not endure (Charles Rycroft, personal communication, 29 November 1993; Joseph Buist Loudon, personal communication, 11 January 1995). As a matter of some small interest, Miss Ede never married at all, but she did enjoy a rich life as a private secretary to the internationally renowned opera singer Joan Sutherland (cf. Braddon, 1962), whom she accompanied on many of her world travels, though she spent most of her time tending to secretarial duties in England.

Winnicott also treated himself to skiing holidays, visits to the opera, singing, and dancing, not to mention writing pieces for the hospital magazine, which included some sardonic poems (Winnicott, 1920a, 1921a), a report on the Amateur Dramatic Club at the hospital (Winnicott, 1920b), and an even more sober piece about the out-patient department (Winnicott, 1921b). In spite of his active social life, he applied himself more fully to his studies in London than he had done in Cambridge. According to his widow, Winnicott "soaked himself in medicine and fully committed himself to the whole experience" (Clare Winnicott, 1978, p. 27).

At St. Bartholomew's Hospital, Winnicott studied with Dr Thomas Jeeves Horder (1871–1955), later to become Lord Horder, the first Baron Horder of Ashford, one of the most celebrated and outstanding physicians of the twentieth century, renowned for his clinical research (e.g. Horder, 1915), for his superb teaching (e.g. Horder, 1953), and for his extraordinary diagnostic and clinical skills (Michael Fordham, personal communication, 13 February 1994). Dr Horder may have stimulated Winnicott to study more diligently, and he certainly laid stress on the value of listening to patients with great care. Most medical practitioners, then and now, conduct a clinical interview by asking a few pointed and closed-ended questions—for example, "Does it hurt when I press here?". Horder, in contrast, prided himself on his ability to let the patients tell their own stories, in their own words, and in their own time. He believed that this approach would provide the physician with a much greater amount of clinical information. Without doubt, Winnicott internalized this attitude in his subsequent psychoanalytic work with scores of individual patients.

Furthermore, Dr Horder placed considerable emphasis on the *relationship* between the patient and the doctor, at a time when most hospital physicians had precious little interest in such apparent frivolities. Uniquely, Horder wrote that young men should:

> Begin to cultivate this gift of sympathy early. Sit down on the lockers of the patients who are allotted to you and talk to them. The experience will surprise you—and it will probably surprise the patient! A good deal has been said about the doctor–patient relationship; but since it is the very soul of good doctoring its importance can never be exaggerated. [quoted in Mervyn Horder, 1966, p. 56]

Perhaps these particular values influenced Winnicott to enter the psychotherapeutic field rather than one of the more research-orientated branches of medicine such as bacteriology, endocrinology, or microbiology. With Dr Horder as a potent mentor, Winnicott soon chose to specialize in that area of the healing arts which relies almost exclusively on the establishment of a therapeutic alliance between doctor and patient—namely, clinical psychotherapy.

Horder also considered the physical comfort of his patients, and on a cold day, he would always warm both his hands and his stethoscope with tepid water before proceeding to a clinical examination of the patient's body. Interestingly, Robert Donat, the famous movie star of the 1930s who appeared in such memorable films as *The 39 Steps* and *Goodbye, Mr. Chips*, sought treatment from many distinguished medics, but none had impressed him more than Thomas Horder. In an after-dinner tribute, Donat once praised Horder as the only doctor he had consulted who ever engaged in the welcome practice of warming his cold, metallic stethoscope before placing it on the patient's chest (Mervyn Horder, 1966). One wonders how many current physicians would ever offer such a courtesy. Apparently, by urging them to warm their hands and their stethoscopes, Horder influenced a whole generation of physicians, including the late Dr Frederick Oliver Walker, an eye surgeon at St. George's Hospital in London, who had known Dr Horder from his days in the East End. Dr Walker continued the Horder tradition by failing students who did not have the sensitivity to warm their hands before examining a patient (Liza Honeyman, personal communication, 23 June 1994).

Winnicott keenly observed the minute details of his teacher's work, and he absorbed a great many of Horder's methods and sensibilities (interview with Clare Winnicott: Neve, 1983), always aware that a good doctor must combat not only the disease, but also the physical and the psychological needs of the person presenting for treatment. Several years after Winnicott's death, his widow reflected on Winnicott's relationship with Horder: "He always said that one of the most profound influences in his life was the teaching of the well known Physician Sir Thomas Horder (later Lord Horder) when D. W. was a medical student at Bart's. It was Lord Horder who taught him the value of taking a careful detailed case history, and of *listening* to the patient, and not simply asking questions" (Clare Winnicott, 1977, p. 1). As a matter of further interest, Horder would eventually become a vice-president of the psychodynamically orientated Institute for the Scientific Treatment of Delinquency (later known as the Institute for the Study and Treatment of Delinquency). Other vice-presidents included not only Sigmund Freud, but also Alfred Adler, Havelock Ellis, Edward Glover, Carl Gustav Jung, Ernest Jones, Emanuel Miller, and Otto Rank. Horder's inclusion among this distinguished group of psychologists would indicate his comfort with mental health matters and issues (cf. Cordess, 1992).

At one point during his medical training, Winnicott developed an abscess on his lung, necessitating that he spend three months as a patient in hospital. St. Bartholomew's Hospital may have boasted a fine teaching staff, but the building itself left much to be desired; and one of Winnicott's acquaintances described it as "a gigantic old ward with a high ceiling dwarfing the serried ranks of beds, patients and visitors" (quoted in Clare Winnicott, 1978, p. 28). Apparently, Winnicott chuckled as he realized the extent to which doctors and nurses neglected him amid the crowd of fellow patients; and he recommended that every doctor should undergo the experience of being a needy and dependent patient, in order to acquire a better appreciation of the fears of the ill person. Years hence, as a seasoned child psychiatrist and psychoanalyst, Donald Winnicott would spend many long hours visiting quite regressed men and women in hospital (cf. Little, 1985); on these occasions, he may well have relied on the memory of his own personal convalescence in St. Bartholomew's Hospital in order to improve his understanding of the abject helplessness of his patients.

Medical school not only provided Winnicott with a basis for his later professional activities, but during this period, he also had the opportunity to encounter the work of Sigmund Freud and the field of psychoanalysis for the first time—a discovery that would prove transformational. It seems that Winnicott used to remember his dreams quite well, but after the First World War he lost the capacity to do so, and this worried him. In an effort to seek some assistance with this personal predicament, Winnicott went to H. K. Lewis and Company, the leading medical bookshop and lending library in London, located on the corner of Gower Street and Gower Place, near the University College Hospital, in the centre of London, and he requested a book on dreams (Anonymous, 1961). The Librarian at H. K. Lewis's offered Winnicott a book by the philosopher Henri Bergson, but this proved of little immediate value. When he returned this volume, a member of the staff recommended instead a book written by the Swiss pastor and psychoanalyst Oskar Robert Pfister—presumably Pfister's (1913) textbook on psychoanalysis, which first appeared in English translation in 1915 under the title *The Psychoanalytic Method*. Shortly thereafter, in 1919, Winnicott read the English translation of Freud's magnum opus, *Die Traumdeutung*, better known to us as *The Interpretation of Dreams* (1900). Although Winnicott initially had planned to become a country doctor after he received his medical qualifications, the books by Pfister and Freud absolutely captivated him, and he knew at once that psychoanalysis would have to feature in his life in some way (Clare Winnicott, 1978).

When Winnicott wrote to his eldest sister Violet about his new-found passion for psychoanalysis, he described it as his "hobby" (Winnicott, 1919, p. 3), but his letter actually reveals a very profound understanding of Freud's work and a deep passion for the subject, quite rare for a twenty-three-year-old medical student. During the early 1920s, Winnicott's interest in psychoanalysis continued to grow, but he knew that before he could train in the technique of psychoanalysis he would first have to establish himself in medical practice.

Donald Winnicott learned very little formal psychiatry or indeed psychoanalysis as a medical student, but he did pay a good deal of attention to the specialist in charge of "mental diseases" at St. Bartholomew's Hospital, who used a rather crude form of hypnosis in his treatments. Winnicott (1919, p. 1) had already developed firm ideas about the efficacy of the newly discovered Freudian treatment, and he counselled his sister Violet:

> *Psychoanalysis is superior to hypnosis and must supersede it, but it is only very slow in being taken up by English physicians because it requires hard work and prolonged study (also great sympathy) none of which are needed for Hypnosis. Only yesterday I saw a man suffering from shell shock put under Hypnosis by the man who looks after mental diseases at Bart's. This man could never do Psychoanalysis because it needs patience and sympathy and other properties which he does not possess.*

The unflattering comment about the "man who looks after mental diseases" might refer to Sir Robert Armstrong-Jones, a senior staff member in "Mental Diseases" at St. Bartholomew's Hospital.

Needless to say, Winnicott had already grasped some of the vital aspects of psychoanalysis, including a recognition that a lengthy training would be required, drawing upon the practitioner's inner reserves and resources. At some point during the 1920s, he resolved that after he had completed his medical studies he would undertake the comprehensive clinical training at The Institute of Psycho-Analysis in London.

Winnicott finally graduated in 1920, thus becoming a licensed medical doctor; and he remained at St. Bartholomew's Hospital for a time as a House Physician, working for the Scottish doctor, Professor Francis R. Fraser. In the same year he qualified as a Member of the Royal College of Surgeons (M.R.C.S.) and as a Licentiate of the Royal College of Physicians (L.R.C.P.). These two diplomas, obtained by examination, provided Winnicott with the minimal medical qualifications that would have permitted him to practise legally as a physician in Britain, recognized by the General Medical Council. But he did not acquire either the degree of Bachelor of Medicine or the degree of Bachelor of Surgery from the University of London, the organization that accredited the training at the medical school of St. Bartholomew's Hospital. It seems that he had either failed these examinations or had never sat them in the first place. Without these medical degrees, he could not thus enrol for the higher degree of M.D. (*Medicinae Doctoris*), which would have offered him various opportunities in the hierarchy of academic medicine (Lawrence Goldie, personal communication, 14 September 1994). Eventually, he became a full Member of the Royal College of Physicians (M.R.C.P.) in 1922.

Ultimately, Winnicott chose to specialize not in neurology or psychiatry, as most students of the mind would have done, but, rather, in the discipline of paediatrics. Although psychological ideas certainly informed Winnicott's clinical work at this time, for whatever reason he still had neither undergone any personal psychotherapy nor pursued any psychoanalytic training. Instead, he became a fully fledged paediatrician, content for the time being to have read only "a book or two on psycho-analysis" (Winnicott, 1949d, p. 178). We actually know very little about Winnicott's working days as a House Physician; he did, however, report a number of incidents that provide a glimpse into the difficulties that he endured as a junior practitioner.

Winnicott (1949d) described the case of a fifty-year-old woman whom he treated during his tenure as a House Physician. The patient in question, a shorthand–typist called Miss H, suffered from a severe neurosis, which included bouts of extreme constipation, of an intensity that Winnicott had not previously encountered. Miss H also struggled with acute attacks of anxiety. Winnicott admitted that he had only read one or two books on psychoanalysis at this time—probably those by Sigmund Freud (1900) and Oskar Pfister (1913)—and on the basis of this rudimentary knowledge he facilitated rather a basic cathartic treatment in which the patient

> would lie and sleep, and then suddenly wake in a nightmare. I would help her to wake by repeating over and over again the words that she had shouted out in the acute anxiety attack. By this means when she wakened I was able to keep her in touch with the anxiety situation and to get her to remember all sorts of traumatic incidents from her very eventful early childhood. [Winnicott, 1949d, p. 178]

These early Freudian-style cases lingered in Winnicott's mind for decades, and he often found himself recounting them to colleagues for illustrative purposes. In a 1953 letter to the Kleinian psychoanalyst, Esther Bick, Winnicott (1953e, p. 51) summarized a particularly fascinating vignette from St. Bartholomew's Hospital:

> *I am reminded of a case of compulsive over-breathing which came my way when I was a House Physician in 1922; this went on for many hours and was leading to serious physical effects, but it disappeared when in the history-taking I and the patient discovered that it started during intercourse and as part of a phobia of intercourse.*

Not many medical doctors in 1922, or even today, would have had the capacity to evoke such intimate material in the course of a clinical encounter. Undoubtedly, these early successes with the "talking cure" helped to consolidate Winnicott's increasing commitment to psychoanalytic investigation.

One other situation that Winnicott reported upon from this time proved less salutary. With great frankness, Winnicott (1970b, p. 114) reflected:

> I personally have made mistakes that I hate to think about. Once, before the days of insulin, I drowned a diabetic patient in a stupid and ignorant attempt to apply instructions from

above. The fact that the man would have died anyway does not make me feel better. And I have done worse things. Happy is the young doctor who does not get exposed as ignorant before he has built up some position among colleagues that will see him through disasters.

Winnicott must have experienced a good deal of guilt about having drowned his patient. Certainly, this old case from the 1920s haunted Winnicott for roughly fifty years, and he continued to refer to it until as late as 18 October 1970, in a talk to a group of doctors and nurses at St. Luke's Church in Hatfield, delivered only weeks before his own death.

Dr Winnicott flourished in his work as a paediatrician, often dealing with some very difficult and unpalatable cases. His practice included the treatment of children who had become afflicted with polio or extreme summer diarrhoea in the course of various epidemics. At this time, antibiotic remedies had not yet become available, and as Winnicott (1969l, p. 196) later recalled, "Our wards were full of children with pus in the lungs or the bones or the meninges." In 1923, he received an appointment as House Physician at the Hospital for Sick Children at Great Ormond Street in London, in order to study an anticipated epidemic of summer diarrhoea. But a full-scale epidemic did not develop as predicted, and so Winnicott did not actually assume the appointment (Anonymous, 1961). Instead, in 1923, he undertook two other hospital appointments in London, one as Assistant Physician at the Queen's Hospital for Children in Hackney, in London's East End, where he would make important contributions to the psychological study of juvenile rheumatism (Winnicott, 1939), and the other at the Paddington Green Children's Hospital. At the Queen's Hospital for Children, known fondly as "The Queen's", he also worked for three sessions each week as Physician in Charge of the London County Council Rheumatism Supervisory Centre treating patients with rheumatic fever and subsequent rheumatic heart disease, a common affliction at that time. Winnicott (1969l) also had to contend with patients suffering from chorea. He worked in this field for some ten years, until 1933. In contrast, his practice as Consultant at Paddington Green became the core of his clinical experience, and he would remain there for forty years, retiring reluctantly in 1963 (Winnicott, 1963j). He referred to his clinic at the Paddington

Green Children's Hospital as his "Psychiatric Snack Bar" (quoted in Clare Winnicott, 1978, p. 28), a place where large numbers of patients could receive a little psychological sustenance. Evidently, Winnicott's psychological slant had helped him to obtain the post at Paddington Green, a hospital already known for its "special climate" (Winnicott, 1988, p. 9, fn.), created by Dr Leonard George Guthrie (1859–1918), a former Senior Physician at Paddington Green and the author of *Functional Nervous Disorders in Childhood* (Guthrie, 1907), one of the first textbooks on the emerging discipline of child psychiatry. Guthrie began his career as a paediatrician, and he assumed his appointment at the Paddington Green Children's Hospital in 1910 (Winnicott, 1949e). During the early days of his professional practice, Winnicott also published a number of medical papers based on his clinical work, including articles on conditions such as varicella encephalitis (Winnicott & Gibbs, 1926), enuresis (Winnicott, 1930), haemoptysis (Winnicott, 1931b), pre-systolic murmur (Winnicott, 1931c), and papular urticaria (Winnicott, 1934).

Though the special climate at the Paddington Green Children's Hospital nurtured Winnicott's blossoming interest in the psychological aspects of paediatrics, most of his colleagues in the 1920s had little patience for exploring the emotional components of children's illnesses. To cite but one example of Winnicott's progressive ideas, influenced in large measure by his forays into the psychoanalytic literature, let us recall that at that time, most traditional paediatricians tended to treat childhood depression by recommending that the youngsters be confined to their beds for *weeks* or even *months* at a time. Winnicott regarded this imprisonment in bed as an abomination, and he risked his reputation by saying so (Gillespie, 1971b). One distinguished paediatrician who sympathized with the psychological approach would later recall that Donald Winnicott's "ideas were on the whole rejected by his contemporaries in paediatrics and I am afraid that he suffered a real, though unintended, persecution at their hands" (Tizard, 1971, p. 226).

As the years progressed, Winnicott spent less time working primarily as a paediatrician, and he toiled instead as a psychoanalytic child psychiatrist; yet although the extent of his psychological interests continued to mushroom, he always maintained a passion for paediatric work. In fact, he even described himself as a "psychiatrist who has clung to pediatrics" (Winnicott, 1948b, p. 229), expressing contempt for a child psychiatrist who once had told him, "I can't bear children's bodies" (quoted in Anonymous, 1961, p. 137). And when Winnicott (1958a) produced the first volume of his collected papers for psychoanalytic colleagues, he chose as his subtitle *Through Paediatrics to Psycho-Analysis*, rather than *From Paediatrics to Psycho-Analysis*, thus marking his continued allegiance to the subject. Because of his thorough grounding in the physiological underpinnings of paediatrics, Winnicott (1969l) could take took advantage of the advances in pharmacology. Apparently, the advent of penicillin transformed the nature of paediatric work, and with drugs at hand to help care for children's bodies, Winnicott could thereby focus his attention on the minds of his young patients more thoroughly.

Even so, his deep saturation in paediatric practice saved the lives of many of the young patients whom he treated primarily for psychological problems. His former Registrar, John Davis (1993a), recalled that Winnicott once asked him to conduct a physical examination of a little girl who presented with headache symptoms, explaining to Davis that his own knowledge of organic medicine had become "a little rusty" (Davis, 1993a, p. 96). Dr Davis did indeed discover papilloedema, a sign of raised pressure in the skull caused by a cerebral tumour. An ordinary psychiatrist would easily have missed the physical cause of the headaches, but because of his paediatric experience, Winnicott had the sophistication to seek appropriate consultation from a younger and more medically agile colleague. Eventually, Winnicott arranged for the removal of the tumour, and the youngster lived. Winnicott did of course retain his interest in the medical side of paediatrics, but he had the wisdom and the humility to focus his energies on the psychological approach to childhood illness instead. By 1963, the year of his retirement from "The Green", he wrote to a colleague, a certain Dr Cave, declining an invitation to give a lecture on the *physical* development of children, on the grounds that "I have now been so long in child psychiatry" (Winnicott, 1963k).

CHAPTER FOUR

Psychoanalytic training

Not only did Winnicott join the staff of two prestigious children's hospitals in 1923, but in that same year he also became a married man. On 7 July 1923, he wed Miss Alice Buxton Taylor, a woman thirty-one years of age— some four years older than the bridegroom—in the parish Church at Frensham, Surrey. Alice, the beautiful and artistic step-daughter of a distinguished medical practitioner, worked as a potter (Phillips, 1988; Michael Fordham, personal communication, 13 February 1994). Masud Khan (1987) noted that she had a fine operatic singing voice, but others could not confirm this. Dr Michael Fordham, the pioneering Jungian analyst, remembered Alice Winnicott with great fondness (Fordham, personal communication, 13 February 1994). At first, the marriage seems to have brought some degree of satisfaction to Winnicott. He certainly acknowledged her in the Preface to his first published book, *Clinical Notes on Disorders of Childhood*: "I am grateful to my wife for her help in manuscript- and proof-reading, and for her constant and valuable interest in my work" (Winnicott, 1931a, p. v). The marriage would endure for twenty-five years, but unhappily the bride suffered from substantial psychiatric difficulties, which included hallucinatory and delusional material. Winnicott's student, Masud Khan, noted that Alice Winnicott "went mad, and taking care of her took all his youth" (Khan, 1987, p. xvi; cf. Grolnick, 1990). Winnicott arranged for his wife to be psychoanalysed by a colleague, Dr Clifford Scott, an eminent student of Melanie Klein, though we know virtually nothing about the details of the treatment (Grosskurth, 1986). The marriage ended in a separation in 1949, at Winnicott's instigation. This marriage must have caused Winnicott a great deal of sadness; yet even so, he may well have learned a considerable amount about psychosis from his daily contact with Alice.

It might be helpful to speculate on the unconscious factors that had compelled Winnicott to marry a woman with severe psychological difficulties. It would not be unreasonable to suspect that Winnicott harboured extensive rescue phantasies in relation to his depressed mother, Elizabeth, and he then enacted these wishes in his marriage by looking after a woman with profound vulnerabilities. Eventually, the strain of a partnership based on clinical care-taking became unbearable (cf. Eber & Kunz, 1984).

It seems evident that the couple began to experience marital difficulties at a very early stage, and at some point in the latter part of 1923 Winnicott decided that he would undergo psychoanalytic treatment. Although he had maintained a professional interest in the work of Freud and his followers since his medical school days, Winnicott admitted quite candidly that he began treatment for private reasons: "Through having personal difficulties I came into psychoanalysis at an early stage of my work as a children's doctor" (Winnicott, 1988, p. 2). In an effort to remedy the situation, he went to Dr Ernest Jones (1879–1958), the dean of psychoanalysis in Britain, for a professional consultation. Winnicott (1957h, p. 1) reminisced, "Well I do remember my first meeting with him, in 1923, when I went as a rather inhibited young man asking whether anything could be done about it. He alarmed me by giving me an advance list of my symptoms." More than thirty-five years later, Winnicott would recollect that, "I went to him as a young man because I was ill", and that Dr Jones impressed him because "He knew more about my illness than I did" (quoted in Jones & Ferris, 1959; cf. Winnicott,

1962e). Winnicott (1957h, p. 1) noted also that after his appoint-ment with Ernest Jones, "I forgot to pay my consultation fee".

Let us pause for a moment to study the words that Winnicott used to characterize his plight. It is one thing to describe himself as an "inhibited" man experiencing "personal difficulties", but it is quite another matter for Winnicott to have referred to himself as "ill". It would be folly to speculate too deeply about the type of illness with which Winnicott had to contend, because we have no concrete evidence whatsoever on which to base any hypotheses. As far as we know, his personal problems did not require hospi-talization or formal psychiatric treatment; but he did spend at least fifteen full years undergoing psychoanalysis—a very long time by any criteria—thus suggesting that he might have re-garded his own difficulties as considerable.

It may be that Winnicott struggled, in part, with a variety of psychosexual conflicts. In a shameful breach of confidentiality, Winnicott's first analyst, James Strachey, had certainly hinted to his own wife, Alix Strachey, that Winnicott suffered from erectile difficulties or even deeper terrors of the female genitalia. Alix Strachey (1924, p. 166), in reply, wondered whether Winni-cott would "f–ck his wife all of a sudden". And Masud Khan's biographer, Judy Cooper, has reported that Rajah Khan, one of Winnicott's patients, once appeared at a conference devoted to the work of Winnicott, sponsored by The British Psycho-Analyti-cal Society, and announced: "Did you know that Winnicott was totally impotent?" (quoted in Cooper, 1993, p. 35).

In later years, Winnicott (1957g) even presented a paper to the Society for Psychosomatic Research at University College, London, in which he spoke explicitly of the possible connection between cardiac disease, impotence, and frigidity. Many mem-bers of the audience would have known that Winnicott had himself suffered from coronary illness at this time, and they might have speculated that his clinical observations derived from personal experiences.

One has difficulty in evaluating such evidence, but in view of the broken confidence by James Strachey, numerous rumours and suspicions among psychoanalysts, as well as Winnicott's failure to father any children by either of his two marriages, a presumption of impotence would not be unreasonable. Fortunately, whatever the nature of Winnicott's psychological struggles, he received a great deal of help and relief—at least in a large number of areas—from his analytic treatment, and he went on to live a remarkably creative and highly stable life. And though he had difficulties with his first wife, Alice, his subsequent marriage to Clare Britton proved highly enjoyable and very romantic.

At Jones' recommendation, Winnicott embarked upon a course of personal analysis with James Strachey (1887–1967), one of the most promising and colourful members of the fledgling English psychoanalytic movement. Strachey had only just become an Associate Member of The British Psycho-Analytical Society, having been formally elected at the Annual General Meeting on 4 October 1922 and thus fully able to take on private patients (Bryan, 1923). To the best of our knowledge, the analysis began in 1924 and lasted for roughly ten years, terminating in 1933 (cf. Meisel & Kendrick, 1985). In 1927, some years after the analysis had commenced, Winnicott enrolled as a training candidate at The Institute of Psycho-Analysis in London (King, 1991a); he eventually became the first male to qualify as a child psychoanalyst in Britain (Jones, 1937).

Also at this time, in 1924, Winnicott started his private practice at 33, Weymouth Street, in the heart of London. Sir Frederick Winnicott's money helped Winnicott to establish his first office (Clare Winnicott, 1977). The pioneering psychoanalyst, Dr Estelle Maud Cole, a former Medical Officer of the Psychological Clinic at Brunswick Square in London and the author of a number of rudimentary psychoanalytic papers (e.g. Cole, 1921, 1922), maintained an office nearby at 12, Weymouth Court, on Weymouth Street, though we have no information that Winnicott ever met with her extensively. Winnicott's widow reported that he actually worked out of an office in Harley Street, London's exclusive enclave for private, monied medicine, but I can find no evidence at all for this assertion. Presumably, Clare Winnicott (1977, 1978) referred to the Weymouth Street office as Harley Street for the sake of simplicity, as Harley Street has a better reputation. Eventually, he opened an office quite nearby, at 44, Queen Anne Street, where he maintained his private practice for a very long time. He then moved his practice to 47, Queen Anne Street, before settling it permanently in his Belgravia home in the early months of 1952.

At first Winnicott had rather few paying patients, and he seemed "very ashamed of the fact" (Clare Winnicott, 1977, p. 2)—and so, to impress the porter, Winnicott provided travel fare for some of his more indigent patients from the Paddington Green Children's Hospital to come for consultations to his private consulting room. Winnicott's widow later recalled, "Of course, this procedure was not entirely on behalf of the porter, because he selected cases in which he was particularly interested and to which he wanted to give more time so that he could begin to explore the psychological aspects of illness" (Clare Winnicott, 1978, pp. 28–29). This vignette indicates Winnicott's passion for his work and his compassion for his patients. It would have been all too easy for him to have devoted little time and energy to his more impoverished patients, but because of his interest in their private lives he treated each new case as a special research opportunity. Winnicott's passion for paediatrics and psychoanalysis proved rather unusual, and he recalled, "At that time no other analyst was also a paediatrician, and so for two or three decades I was an isolated phenomenon" (Winnicott, 1962e, p. 172).

Years later, Winnicott (1969k, p. 189) would reminisce about the early days of paediatric practice, reflecting that at the start of his career he would invariably give "one, two, or three bottles of something or other, or pills, to every patient. Eventually I dropped the whole thing and dropped prescribing altogether; but this of course meant that I had to deal with the patients in a much more personal way and I had lost the short-cut to happiness". Winnicott's budding analytic experience on James Strachey's couch in Bloomsbury facilitated his historical conversion from orthodox paediatric care to a more psychodynamically orientated approach.

Winnicott's psychoanalytic treatment with James Strachey seems to have proved quite useful in a number of respects. It may well have sustained him through his considerable marital difficulties; furthermore, this decade spent on Strachey's couch permitted him to evolve from a young paediatrician into a fully qualified psychoanalyst. James Beaumont Strachey, the thirteenth and youngest child of Lieutenant General Richard Strachey, a distinguished soldier and mathematician, first discovered psychoanalysis as a student at the University of

Cambridge, in the early years of this century (Hartman, 1976; Sherman, 1983; Meisel and Kendrick, 1985). Strachey's involvement in both the Society for Psychical Research and in the Bloomsbury Group—two of the first British societies to study Freud seriously—intensified his interest in psychoanalytic theory. He soon developed the wish to train as a psychoanalyst himself; and to do so, Ernest Jones had advised him to study medicine as the ideal preparation for his subsequent psychotherapeutic work. But Strachey, the younger brother of the noted writer Lytton Strachey, relished good literature too much to enjoy the stodgy medical curriculum at St. Thomas's Hospital in London, and so he left medical school after only three weeks, having had quite enough of "dissecting frogs' legs" (Winnicott, 1969a, p. 130). Instead, he went to Vienna in 1920 with his new wife Alix, and they each underwent a personal analysis with Sigmund Freud. In those days, a period of treatment on Freud's couch provided aspiring analysts with a golden passport and offered them more insight into the nature of psychoanalytic practice than any medical training would have done. As a result, both James and Alix Strachey soon became important figures in the international psychoanalytic community.

James Strachey wrote very few professional papers (e.g. Strachey, 1930, 1931, 1934, 1939); instead, he spent most of his time translating Freud's German works into English, and he served as both the senior editor and translator of the authoritative twenty-four volume collection, *The Standard Edition of the Complete Psychological Works of Sigmund Freud* (Freud, 1953–1974). He did, however, produce one paper on psychotherapeutic technique that has become an undisputed classic in the psychoanalytic literature, entitled "The Nature of the Therapeutic Action of Psycho-Analysis", published in 1934, shortly after the completion of Winnicott's treatment. In this important essay, Strachey attempted to explore how the analytical process actually operates, as well as how the analyst achieves beneficial results—two crucial questions that would also preoccupy Winnicott in later years. Strachey (1934, p. 143) introduced the concept of the "mutative interpretation"—an interpretation that would illuminate the internal world of the patient and consequently promote psychological change and emotional maturation. In other words, a mutative interpretation should result in a *mutation*, or transformation of some sort. Strachey further hypothesized that the best mutative interpretations would also be *transference* interpretations—namely, remarks that derive from the analyst's insights into the relationship between patient and analyst. If the psychoanalyst observes the analysand behaving in a certain way during treatment, this will invariably provide clues regarding that person's experiences during early childhood. And, according to Freudian theory, symptoms will begin to erode and changes will ensue when the clinician interprets the transference insightfully, because a wise and meaningful transference interpretation will make the patient feel understood and appreciated at quite a deep level.

Winnicott seems to have derived great benefit, both personally and professionally, from Strachey's emphasis on mutative transference interpretations as the most curative components in psychotherapeutic work. I suspect, however, that he may have profited even more from another subsidiary concept in Strachey's paper—specifically, the notion of the psychoanalyst as an "auxiliary super-ego" (Strachey, 1934, p. 138). The idea of an auxiliary superego may be absolutely meaningless to practitioners not steeped in psychoanalytic vocabulary; but basically, stripped of its complexity, this refers to the analyst's unique opportunity to serve as an ideal role model for the patient. Imagine that an analysand had suffered in childhood at the hands of a volatile parent who would scream and shout. In consequence, this person may have developed a punitive superego or conscience, as a direct result of having internalized the parent's emotional and behavioural repertoire. The psychoanalyst, in contrast, will never shout or scream at the patient as the parent had done, and thus the patient will be both relieved and privileged to relate to the non-persecutory and non-punitive superego of the analyst. Such exposure to a less disturbed personality will be extremely liberating, and Strachey realized that the internalization of this sort of auxiliary superego could in fact facilitate the cure. Winnicott would eventually extend Strachey's idea of the analyst as an auxiliary superego; and he would even inaugurate a great debate on the ways in which the psychoanalyst could become an auxiliary *parental* figure.

As for the specific quality of Winnicott's analysis with James Strachey, we can only conjecture. Winnicott remained in treatment with Strachey for approximately ten years, attending daily at Strachey's consulting room at 41, Gordon Square, in the heart of Bloomsbury, in Central London. We know that Strachey had sub-let a number of the floors of his very large house for financial reasons (Woolf, 1928), so Winnicott may have seen a goodly number of strangers entering and leaving the building during the many years of analysis; and perhaps such sightings may have given rise to any number of phantasies about Strachey's private life. One certainly wonders whether Winnicott ever saw Virginia Woolf, who lived immediately around the corner at that time, at 52, Tavistock Square, having moved there on 13 March 1924, around the period that Winnicott's treatment had begun. Other "Bloomsberries" also resided close at hand, including Strachey's brother, the writer Giles Lytton Strachey, who lived at 51, Gordon Square, and John Maynard Keynes, the economist, who inhabited 46, Gordon Square.

In all probability, Winnicott went to Strachey for treatment on six days of the week, Monday to Saturday, as befitted the custom of the time. A ten-year treatment would be regarded as a very long period of psychoanalysis by contemporary standards, but it was almost unheard-of in the 1920s, when most training analyses lasted for only one or two years. For example, Dr Raymond de Saussure, a pioneer of psychoanalysis in Switzerland, underwent analysis with Sigmund Freud in Vienna; his treatment, begun in 1920, lasted only five months (Swerdloff, 1965b). Winnicott's perseverance suggests that he may have found the treatment useful and that the nature of his "illness" required a very prolonged journey of discovery in Strachey's care.

Interestingly, in the first year of his treatment, Winnicott seems to have delayed in paying his bill. Strachey charged him the significant sum of 7 guineas per week—a rather substantial fee (Alix Strachey, 1925); and on at least one occasion Winnicott presented Strachey with a cheque, but he "forgot" to sign it— perhaps a manifestation of hostility towards his analyst (Strachey, 1924a). Strachey seems to have worried not only about his fee, but also about Winnicott's stability; and in yet another brazen breach of confidentiality, he actually wrote to his wife Alix: "Where shall we be if Winnie cracks up? In the Bum-bailiff's hands, I fear" (Strachey, 1924b, pp. 119–120). On the positive side, Winnicott did concede that during the course of the analysis he experienced "a long series of these healing dreams which, although in many cases unpleasant, have each one of them marked my arrival at a new stage in emotional development" (Winnicott, 1949b, p. 71).

Furthermore, in order to understand the complexity of this situation more fully, we must remember that James Strachey, although married, seems to have preferred homosexual to heterosexual activity—at least during his younger years. As an undergraduate student at the University of Cambridge, Strachey (letter to Duncan Grant, 9 March 1907, cited in Meisel & Kendrick, 1985) became infatuated with the homosexual poet Rupert Brooke and confessed his love to him. Undoubtedly, Donald Winnicott, a fellow Cantabrian, either knew of Strachey's much-discussed homosexual orientation or he may have sensed it unconsciously, especially in view of Strachey's foppish appearance and effeminate posture. Strachey certainly betrayed his feminine identifications in a number of different spheres; he even authored a paper about the Egyptian King Akhenaten, whom he characterized as having "an unusually large feminine component in his constitution" (Strachey, 1939, p. 42).

Many of the members of the psychoanalytic community knew that though Strachey enjoyed great compatibility with his wife Alix, the pair did not become drawn to one another on the grounds of genital attraction. Theodor Reik, one of Freud's disciples who knew Strachey in Vienna, once greeted the Englishman on the occasion of his wedding anniversary. But Reik erred, and instead of congratulating Strachey on his *anniversary*, he uttered: "Well, Strachey, how was your adversary?" (quoted in Swerdloff, 1965a, p. 44)—a most telling parapraxis. And Michael Balint, a leading British analyst of Hungarian birth, remembered Strachey as "a bit of a tender soul" (quoted in Swerdloff, 1965c, p. 74), rather a euphemistic expression. Thus, it may be that Winnicott experienced considerable homosexual anxiety in his first months of intimate treatment with Strachey, and one wonders whether the latter possessed the clinical and psychical resources to deal with a case of impotence in a predominantly heterosexual patient. In view of Winnicott's sustained childlessness, his lack of professional interest in adult genital sexuality, and his preoccupation with impotence, I suspect that Strachey did Winnicott a great disservice by not analysing fully, if at all, these aspects of his character structure. If Strachey really did possess even a mildly substantial homosexual character structure, then one could regard his neglect of these areas of Winnicott's own personality as a woeful instance of malignant countertransference.

On the whole, however, Winnicott derived much sustenance and solidity from his lengthy encounter with his stalwart analyst. James Strachey stood by Winnicott through many transformative and emotive life events, such as the early years of his marriage, the development of his private practice, the launching of his lengthy training in adult and child psychoanalysis, the award of a Knighthood to his father in 1924, and, in particular, the death of his mother Elizabeth in 1925.

John Frederick Winnicott received his Knighthood in 1924. As far as we can tell, Donald Winnicott did not attend the ceremony, though no doubt this new empowerment of his already potent father would have generated considerable oedipal rivalries, and it seems likely that Winnicott might have discussed his competitive feelings towards his father at great length in his analysis with James Strachey.

Shortly after the start of Winnicott's analysis with Strachey, Donald's mother died tragically in 1925, at the family home at Rockville, after a catarrhal pulmonary illness that lasted for seventeen days. She had only recently begun to enjoy the title of Lady Winnicott, conferred through her husband's Knighthood in 1924. We have no clear idea of how Donald Winnicott responded to the death of his mother, but in any case James Strachey would undoubtedly have helped Winnicott to endure the pain of this bereavement during the many long hours of analysis. The death of his depressive mother may have brought some relief to Winnicott as well, for he hardly ever mentioned her again in later years, and he may have derived some satisfaction from the knowledge that her suffering had now come to an end.

Some years after the analysis ended, Strachey (1940, p. 18) encapsulated his philosophy of treatment in a private letter to his associate, Dr Edward Glover:

> It ought naturally to be the aim of a training analysis to put the trainee into a position to arrive at his own decisions upon moot points—not to stuff him with your own private dogmas.

In view of Winnicott's subsequent decades of fertile and original clinical research, we can be assured that, in his case, at least, Strachey had succeeded in his quest.

After the termination of the analysis, Winnicott maintained a pleasant relationship with Strachey (cf. Winnicott, 1951d). The interactions between the two men became infinitely more collegial, and Strachey abandoned his traditional analytic neutrality and reserve; and he and his former patient corresponded on an intermittent basis. Some twenty-four years after the termination of Winnicott's analysis, Strachey (1957) wrote from his retirement home at Lord's Wood, in Marlow, Buckinghamshire:

> By the way we both hope very much that one of these days you + your wife will turn your horses' heads in this direction + look in on us. We practically never bridge from here + a telephone call at short notice would almost always be warning enough for us to scratch up a meal. It would be very nice to see you.

Several years later, Strachey asked Winnicott for a favour. Addressing him as "Dear Donald", Strachey (1960) enquired: "I wonder if you have any drag at the Royal Society of Medicine?" Apparently, the Library at the Royal Society of Medicine had created difficulties for Strachey's research assistant, Mrs Angela Harris, and had curtailed her library privileges; and this restriction interfered with progress on Strachey's editorial work for *The Standard Edition of the Complete Psychological Works of Sigmund Freud*. Strachey turned to Winnicott, a respected medical doctor, for assistance. Strachey's letter of Friday, 8 January, 1960, must have reached Winnicott either on Saturday, 9 January, or more probably, on Monday, 11 January, and Winnicott replied almost instantly, on this last date. Winnicott (1960h) responded more formally to "Dear James Strachey", answering,

> I am appalled to think that work on the Standard Edition should be held up by the R.S.M., and at the earliest possible moment I will interview the Librarian.

Most contemporary psychoanalysts would be more reluctant, I trust, to turn to former analytic patients for favours of this nature, and though at some level Winnicott may have enjoyed helping his old analyst, he may have experienced some resentment as well.

The pleasant atmosphere that characterizes this post-termination correspondence may also have disguised certain rather less salubrious sentiments. Long after the analysis, Winnicott did, in fact, confide to both his second wife, Clare Winnicott (interview, 13 November 1981, in Anderson, 1982b) and to a close colleague and patient, Dr Margaret Little (interview, 1 November 1981, in Anderson, 1982b), that the treatment did not help him as much as it should have done. Winnicott (1952b, p. 33) told his senior colleague, Ernest Jones, that Strachey had not always assisted him: "He did, however, say two or three things that were not interpretations at a time when interpretation was needed. Each one of these has bothered me and at some time or other have come out in an unexpected way." In particular, Strachey advised Winnicott to establish contact with Mrs Melanie Klein, the brilliant and dynamic leader of child psychoanalysis, with whom Winnicott would endure a rather stormy relationship for nearly three decades. As he (Winnicott, 1962e, p. 173) reminisced:

> It was an important moment in my life when my analyst broke into his analysis of me and told me about Melanie Klein. He had heard about my careful history-taking and about my trying to apply what I got in my own analysis to the cases of children brought to me for every kind of paediatric disorder. I especially investigated the cases of children brought for nightmares. Strachey said: "If you are applying psycho-analytic theory to children you should meet Melanie Klein. She has been enticed over to England by Jones to do the analysis of someone special to Jones; she is saying some things that may or may not be true, and you must find out for yourself for you will not get what Melanie Klein teaches in my analysis of you."

We shall explore the particular aspects of Winnicott's relationship with Melanie Klein in due course.

Dr James William Anderson (1982a), an American psychoanalyst who has written astutely about Winnicott's life history, has characterized Winnicott's encounter with Strachey as highly ambivalent. After all, Strachey underlined the vital importance of interpretation as a clinical tool, whereas Winnicott (1962d) would eventually become very suspicious of colleagues who interpreted too much. Nevertheless, Strachey provided Winnicott with a basic introduction to psychoanalysis, and he transmitted Freud's theories to him in a very direct way. Winnicott (1952e, p. 33) told Ernest Jones that, "In 10 years' analysis Strachey made practically no mistakes and he adhered to a classical technique in a cold-blooded way for which I have always been grateful." After Strachey died in 1967, Winnicott wrote the principal obituary for *The International Journal of Psycho-Analysis*, in which he described his former analyst with his unparalleled succinctness as "not a great man", but he conceded that "He will always be my favourite example of a psycho-analyst" (Winnicott, 1969a, p. 131).

CHAPTER FIVE

Melanie Klein and Joan Riviere

J ames Strachey not only conducted Winnicott's first analysis, but, as we have indicated, he also urged the young paediatrician to seek the acquaintance of Melanie Reizes Klein (1882–1960), a formidably talented psychoanalytic practitioner who would influence Winnicott profoundly. After she became excited by Freud's writings, Mrs Klein trained as an analyst in Hungary and in Germany; indeed, she pioneered the field of child psychoanalysis almost single-handedly, encouraged by two of Freud's closest colleagues, Sándor Ferenczi and Karl Abraham. After a very brief but highly successful lecture tour in London in 1925, Klein emigrated to England permanently in September of 1926, at the invitation of Ernest Jones, who greatly respected the quality of her clinical and theoretical work. Furthermore, Jones also needed a talented child psychoanalyst to treat his young children; and Mrs Klein seemed to be the ideal candidate for this important position, as it would have proved impossible for Jones to entrust his family to any of his younger and more inexperienced British colleagues (cf. Brome, 1982; Grosskurth, 1986). After her arrival in London, Klein did eventually undertake the treatment of Jones's children, Mervyn and Gwenith, and of Jones's wife, Katherine, as well.

It seems that Winnicott did not meet Mrs Klein straight after her emigration, though he claimed that he had known of her work as early as 1927 (Winnicott, 1988). Their relationship blossomed in earnest in 1932 after Winnicott had read Alix Strachey's translation of Klein's (1932) masterwork, *Die Psycho-analyse des Kindes*, which had only recently been published in English as *The Psycho-Analysis of Children*. Winnicott took this ground-breaking volume with him on holiday to Dartmoor. He rarely ever read the psychoanalytic literature with any verve or thoroughness, but Klein's book captivated him so much that as soon as he had finished it, he immediately read it once again (Winnicott, 1953d; Grosskurth, 1986). We do not know whether Winnicott had seen the typescript of Mrs Strachey's work before this time, but he certainly knew quite a great deal about it long before its appearance, because in 1931 he inserted a footnote into his own textbook on paediatrics: "See the detailed description of cases of anxiety in Melanie Klein's forthcoming book on Psycho-analysis of Children. (Hogarth Press.)" (Winnicott, 1931a, p. 103, fn. 1). Winnicott found Klein's work attractive from a professional point of view, because her work helped him to acquire a better understanding of his child cases; but his thrill at reading *The Psycho-Analysis of Children* might also have been increased by the fact that his analyst, James Strachey, had recommended Klein to him. Furthermore, Strachey's wife, Alix, had translated the volume from German into English; therefore, Winnicott's reading of Melanie Klein's seminal text offered him a sublimated opportunity for contact not only with his analyst, but with his analyst's wife, and with his analyst's close colleague, as well.

Shortly before Winnicott met Klein in person, his own mother had died. As we have already indicated, we have no firm idea how Donald Winnicott, only twenty-nine years of age, reacted to the death of his mother. At any rate, one certainly wonders whether the close conjunction of the death of Mrs Winnicott and the subsequent appearance of the large-bosomed Mrs Klein might help to explain Winnicott's attraction to Klein on a more infantile level. Irrespective of his deeper motivations, Winnicott certainly regarded Klein's clinical work and her psychological theorizing with the utmost admiration during this critical stage of his professional development.

Klein's observations on the earliest psychic life of the child excited Winnicott a great deal, and her ideas offered him both confirmation of his own forward-thinking observational research, and inspiration for his subsequent studies. He satisfied his desire for contact with Klein by engaging her as a clinical supervisor for his child analytic cases, and he recalled that: "I took her a case written up in great detail, and she had the goodness to read it right through, and on the basis of this one pre-Klein analysis that I did on the basis of my own Strachey analysis I went on to try to learn some of the immense amount that I found she already knew" (Winnicott, 1962e, p. 173). Klein proved so adept and impressive as a supervisor that, "On Saturday evening, if she so wished, she could go over every detail of the week's work with each patient, without reference to notes. She remembered my cases and my analytic material better than I did myself" (Winnicott, 1962e, p. 173). He also reported one instance when Klein rescued him from a tricky situation. He noted that: "I remember on one occasion going to her for a supervision, and of a whole week's work I could remember nothing at all. She simply responded by telling me a case of her own" (Winnicott, 1962e, p. 173). Winnicott also praised Klein for her lack of rigidity. All told, he seems to have spent approximately six years in clinical supervision with Melanie Klein, from 1935 until 1941 (Rodman, 1987b).

Most students of psychoanalytic history regard Melanie Klein's greatest contribution to be her elucidation of the first year of life, and we owe her a tremendous debt for helping us to understand the intensity of the erotic and sadistic forces that govern the minds of young babies. Furthermore, she undertook an important revision of earlier Freudian theory by stressing that the Oedipus complex occurs during the first year of life, in contrast to the views of more orthodox practitioners, who located this psychic configuration at the age of four or five years. Winnicott needed Klein to guide his understanding of the early years of childhood, because many of his paediatric patients had not yet reached the age of four or five. Traditional Freudian theory revolves around the trio of mother, father, and baby; whereas Kleinian theory focuses more particularly on the infant's relationship to the mother's breast. This critical shift helped Winnicott to broaden his comprehension of the child's earliest terrors and preoccupations.

Classical Freudians tend to interpret anxiety as a fear of castration caused by the angry father's threat to mutilate his son's genitals in retaliation for the son's incestuous wishes towards his mother. Winnicott never denied the existence of castration anxiety, but he used Klein's theories to discover certain *pre-oedipal* anxieties far more primitive than the fear of castration. He examined the more petrifying agony of being dropped from the arms of the breast-feeding mother, falling interminably in a chaotic abyss, experiencing disintegration, unthinkable anxiety, and dread of death (Winnicott, 1968a).

Klein's work cannot be portrayed with any adequacy in this brief summary; readers who wish to learn more about the complexity of Mrs Klein's theories would do well to consult her own works in greater detail (e.g. Klein, 1946, 1950, 1957, 1959, 1961). For our purposes, it will suffice to recognize that while psychoanalysts have always considered childhood experiences as the foundation of later personality development, Klein actually rooted disturbances of psychological functioning in the very *earliest months* of life. This discovery, based on her careful empirical observation of children in analysis, stimulated Donald Winnicott to embark on his own study of how each nuance of the mother's early touches and moods would shape and mould the baby's mental life.

Winnicott admired Klein so much that he actually wished to undergo a further analysis, with her, in spite of his many long years with Strachey. One might understand Winnicott's wish for a second analysis as an attempt to learn more about Kleinian theory from a highly personal perspective; but also, by this time, his wife, Alice Winnicott, had begun to act increasingly psychotic in her behaviour, and Winnicott undoubtedly wanted more psychotherapeutic assistance during this troubling period. To his great chagrin, Klein refused to accept him for treatment, because she needed Winnicott to psychoanalyse her own son, Erich. Mrs Klein even wanted to supervise her son's analysis, but

Winnicott did not approve of this intrusive suggestion (Gross-kurth, 1986; cf. Winnicott, 1962e). Eager to learn about Kleinian analysis on a first-hand basis, Winnicott underwent another bout of analytic treatment, for roughly five years, with Klein's confidante and associate, Joan Riviere. This analysis gave him a privileged insight into the world of Kleinian ideology, but, sadly, it proved a rather disappointing experience by all accounts (e.g. Khan, 1988; Padel, 1991). The analysis may well have been doomed from the start because Winnicott had wanted Mrs Klein as his psychoanalyst, and he may have regarded Mrs Riviere as a mere consolation prize.

Joan Hodgson Verrall Riviere (1883–1962), the daughter of a well-to-do solicitor, probably first encountered psychoanalysis at the Society for Psychical Research (Strachey, 1963; cf. Hughes, 1991). She began personal psychoanalysis with Ernest Jones and then completed her education in 1922 by undergoing a second analysis in Vienna with Sigmund Freud (Hartman, 1976). Freud appreciated the talents of his British analysands such as Strachey and Riviere, and he set them to work on translations of his German-language books and articles. Indeed, Mrs Riviere had already begun to undertake translation work prior to her analysis with Freud. Long before James Strachey produced the *Standard Edition* of Freud's psychological writings, Mrs Riviere supervised the editing and translation of three of the five volumes of the *Collected Papers* of Sigmund Freud (1924a, 1924b, 1925), still favoured by many older psychoanalysts for having captured so well what one historian has described as "Freud's virile and witty German speech" (Gay, 1988, p. 741).

Riviere wrote many outstanding essays on a variety of psychoanalytic topics (e.g. Riviere, 1929, 1932, 1936b), including a vital contribution on working with "specially refractory cases" (Riviere, 1936a, p. 305). This essay, "A Contribution to the Analysis of the Negative Therapeutic Reaction", may well have influenced Winnicott somewhat in his own personal quest to work with very difficult patients, whom many practitioners regarded as untreatable.

Joan Riviere certainly had several loyal associates (Segal, 1991), and she had exerted a marked impact upon students at The Institute of Psycho-Analysis (Hughes, 1991). One of her patients, the noted psychoanalyst Dr Susan Isaacs, even dedicated her book on *Social Development in Young Children: A Study of Beginnings*, to her. The dedication reads quite movingly: "TO JOAN RIVIERE WHO HAS TAUGHT ME TO UNDERSTAND MY OWN CHILDHOOD" (Isaacs, 1933, n.p.). Nevertheless, in spite of the admiration that she received, Joan Riviere also alienated many colleagues and trainees with her forceful personality. Dr Edward Glover (1969, p. 499), one of the deacons of the pioneering era of British psychoanalysis, reported on Riviere's editorial work for *The International Journal of Psycho-Analysis*, noting: "Woe to the luckless contributor who was bold enough to deck his submitted article in slipshod English or seek to cover a shaky thesis in terminological obscurities." Marion Milner, a distinguished analyst in her own right, renowned for her warmth and for her good nature, remembered Riviere as a "bully" (quoted in Grosskurth, 1986, p. 396). And Dr Charles Rycroft (personal communication, 29 November 1993), another colleague from The British Psycho-Analytical Society, found Riviere "terrifying"—a quality exacerbated by her very tall physical stature. In fact, Riviere behaved in a grossly unprofessional manner by making caustic remarks about Winnicott's personality during the course of public meetings of professional organizations. Winnicott once told an associate: "I can't say I had analysis with Joan Riviere; it is true, however, that she did analyse me for some ten years. And she kept on analysing me during discussions at the Scientific Meetings" (quoted in Khan, 1988, p. 48). On one particularly murky occasion, she actually announced to the audience at the Medical Section of the British Psychological Society, that Winnicott "just makes theory out of his own sickness" (interview with M. Masud R. Khan, 15 October 1981, quoted in Anderson, 1982b, p. 1). This information about Joan Riviere's castigation of Winnicott derives from an interview with Winnicott's former patient, Masud Khan (15 October 1981, in Anderson, 1982b), and from a passage in Khan's last book, *When Spring Comes: Awakenings in Clinical Psychoanalysis* (Khan, 1988). Many members of the psychoanalytic profession may regard the rather volatile Khan as a somewhat unreliable witness (cf. Cooper, 1993), and, indeed, one must treat his remarks with at least a certain caution; nevertheless, his reminiscences of conversations with Winnicott may indeed capture something of the flavour of the bitterness that existed between him and Joan Riviere.

Towards the end of her life, Riviere sent an extremely critical letter to Winnicott after he had taken the trouble to notify colleagues of her impending seventy-fifth birthday. At that time, Winnicott served as President of The British Psycho-Analytical Society, and it fell upon him to inform fellow analysts of this special event in the life of one of the most celebrated of British analysts. Joan Riviere's (1958a) vitriolic letter of 12 June 1958 to Winnicott, her former analysand, merits full quotation:

> *Dear Dr Winnicott*
>
> *I felt very angry when you calmly told me you had sent round notices about my birthday, in spite of your promise to me to do nothing without my agreement. Now this morning I have had two letters from people about it + another congratulating on telephone!—It is absolutely inconceivable that you should be so irresponsible + choose to do as you wish + decide that "it doesn't matter" what you promise or what I wish.*
>
> *My birthday does not take place for a month! + this party not for four months! What sort of excuse have you for rushing out notices at this date? Can't you see you are simply making me look a fool (+ yourself).*
>
> *I shall certainly not conceal from people that I am no party to it + don't like it + I warn you that if you attempt to get up any present for me, I shall refuse it.*
>
> *Yours sincerely*
>
> *Joan Riviere*
>
> *I enclose notes about your paper which you may want.*

Riviere's anger and anxiety clearly resulted in her distorting at least one fact: she had berated Winnicott for sending out notices so far in advance—one full month before her birthday; but in fact, Riviere was born on 28 June, and thus the anniversary of her birth was only two weeks and two days away at the time that she wrote this fiery missive to her former patient. Winnicott may well have felt hurt after having received the news of her displeasure, but he maintained his composure, replying to his former analyst, "For some reason or other you are, I think unduly sensitive" (Winnicott, 1958j, p. 118).

In fairness, Riviere's letter implies that Winnicott had promised that he would not send out any birthday notices, so he
does seem to have gone against his word. Nonetheless, Riviere's
acerbic tone strikes one as quite inexcusable, regardless of her
advanced age and bad physical state at the time. Fortunately,
the situation does seem to have righted itself eventually, and
Mrs Riviere did nevertheless enjoy her seventy-fifth birthday
party. On 7 December, Riviere (1958b) wrote Winnicott a rather
different letter:

> *Dear Dr Winnicott*
>
> *I want to send a word of my most grateful appreciation to
> you + others, whose names I do not know, for the most de-
> lightful + enjoyable evening you all arranged for me as a
> birthday present. It could not have been better, I think + it will
> be a most memorable occasion to me.*
>
> *With my most grateful thanks.*
> *Yours sincerely*
>
> *Joan Riviere*

What can have accounted for the extraordinary interchanges
between Joan Riviere and Donald Winnicott, and why did she
humiliate her analysand at public gatherings? We may never
know the full extent of this unpleasant relationship, but we do
know that as Winnicott became more independent and as he
began to speak critically about the work of Melanie Klein and her
followers, Riviere behaved in an increasingly hostile manner.
From the outset, Klein concentrated on the worthy study of
the child's unconscious phantasy world—that is, the *inner world.*
Winnicott certainly appreciated the inner world, but he chose to
study how the *outer world* of the family environment would either
facilitate or inhibit the growth of the child's mind, and the early
Kleinians felt extremely threatened by those who would shift
attention away from the internal world (cf. King & Steiner, 1991).

During Winnicott's treatment with Riviere, he informed her of
his plan to write a book: "I said to my analyst, 'I'm almost ready
to write a book on the environment'. She said to me 'You write a
book on the environment and I'll turn you into a frog!' Of course
she didn't use those words, you understand, but that's how
what she did say came across to me" (quoted in Padel, 1991, p.

336). Winnicott had certainly chosen some very interesting imagery to describe his perception of Joan Riviere. In traditional fairy tales, men and women, or princes and princesses, become routinely transformed into frogs by evil, wicked witches. By claiming, however jocularly, that Mrs Riviere had threatened to turn him into a frog, Winnicott thereby found himself betraying his view of her as a witch-like figure.

Not surprisingly, Dr John Bowlby had a similar experience as a result of his analytic treatment with Mrs Riviere, which lasted from 1929 until 1939. Bowlby remarked that though his analyst respected his research work, he "suspected that she did not regard it as psychoanalysis, since she held strong views that psychoanalysis was in no way concerned with external events" (interview, 24 January 1986, quoted in Hughes, 1991, p. 32). Bowlby also mentioned that he regarded his analysis with Riviere as "too long" (quoted in Hughes, 1986, p. 32); and Bowlby's son, Sir Richard Bowlby (personal communication, 21 May 1994), confirmed that his father and Mrs Riviere simply could not get on, though she seems to have been a nice woman with whom John Bowlby would occasionally dine after the conclusion of his treatment (Hughes, 1991). On a related note, Joan Riviere's physician, Dr Annis Calder Gillie (later to become Dame Annis Gillie), highlighted Riviere's extremely strong emphasis on the internal world when she recalled that Riviere always searched for a psychological origin for any illness, whereas even Melanie Klein, who also sought treatment from Dr Annis Gillie, would accept the reality of a viral infection (interview, 13 March 1983, in Grosskurth, 1986).

It may seem comical to contemporary psychotherapists that Joan Riviere should have objected to a book on the environment (in other words, a book on the influence of the mother); but during the 1940s, with Britain at war, hostilities predominated as each faction within the psychoanalytic community fought for supreme control of a particular slice of human psychology. One also wonders to what extent Winnicott's own fears of the formidable Mrs Riviere may have inflamed their interactions. After all, Riviere overshadowed Winnicott, quite literally, as a result of her great physical presence. In Phyllis Grosskurth's (1986) comprehensive biography of Melanie Klein, one finds a photograph of

Melanie Klein's seventieth birthday dinner, held in 1952 at Kettner's restaurant in the Soho section of London. Both Mrs Riviere and her former patient, Dr Winnicott, attended the meal organized by Dr Ernest Jones. Fascinatingly, Riviere and Winnicott stand side by side in the photograph, and she appears taller than he by several inches, suggesting that she may have intimidated Winnicott on every level, including the physical dimension. Even Freud's tiny grandson, Heinz Rudolf Halberstadt, noted Riviere's formidable height: one day, after bursting into Freud's consulting room during one of Riviere's analytic sessions, little Heinz referred to Joan Riviere as the "tall auntie" (quoted in Freud, 1923, p. 274). One cannot underestimate the potential effect of Riviere's height on Winnicott's relationship with her.

Winnicott's involvement with the Kleinians became so very unsatisfying that he abandoned all hope of being appreciated by them, and he focused his energies, more creatively, on his own writings. Yet the strained interactions between him and the Kleinians would always rankle to a certain extent. He struggled to locate himself in the developing organizational infrastructure of The British Psycho-Analytical Society, but unfortunately he did not feel completely at home with either Melanie Klein or with her principal adversary, Anna Freud. Gradually, Winnicott dealt with the internal psychoanalytic disputes by declaring himself an independent thinker rather than a dutiful supporter—thereby incurring the wrath of Klein, Riviere, and many others besides and suffering the fate of someone "so off the beaten track and so different from the ordinary analyst" (James, 1991).

In 1956, many years after the formal separation between Winnicott and the Kleinians, he wrote to his former psychoanalyst, Mrs Riviere, about his sadness that she and Klein would not recognize his work:

> *After Mrs Klein's paper you and she spoke to me and within the framework of friendliness you gave me to understand that both of you are absolutely certain that there is no positive contribution to be made from me to the interesting attempt Melanie is making all the time to state the psychology of the earliest stages.* [Winnicott, 1956f, p. 94]

The remarks made by Klein and Riviere—his clinical supervisor and his analyst, respectively—must have devastated

Winnicott. In a further attempt to gain her favour, Winnicott (1956f, p. 94) further pleaded with Riviere:

> If I am any good at analysis myself it is largely due to her work and also to yourself.

He then continued:

> You have expressed to me often that you value my state-ments of the mother–infant relationship, and I want to ask you whether you could carry the matter a little further and consider whether perhaps there is not something in the theory at this point that I can contribute. If I contribute to psychoanalytic theory it is not of course necessary for me to be accepted by either yourself or Melanie Klein, but I do in fact mind tremendously if I really have a positive contribution to make, however small, and if this cannot find acceptance either with you or with Melanie. [Winnicott, 1956f, p. 96; cf. Winnicott, 1952c]

Still, in spite of the considerable difficulties between himself and Riviere, and in spite of his sense of having been rejected, Winnicott remembered his second analyst affectionately as a fine clinician, who helped him to see more clearly after having been in a deep ditch for a long time (Jennifer Johns, personal communication, 30 August 1989, cited in Hughes, 1991). He even recommended her to a friend as a good choice for a clinical supervisor (Grosskurth, 1986).

Winnicott remained in treatment with Riviere for approxi-mately five years, attending for daily sessions at Mrs Riviere's home at 4, Stanhope Terrace, in West London—conveniently situated close to the Paddington Green Children's Hospital, where he worked. Winnicott always knew how to excuse people for their shortcomings and how to recognize their positive quali-ties; and though Riviere could be a very trying person, he used her for what she could offer him (cf. Winnicott, 1967c).

Interestingly, Winnicott's two analysts had many features in common. Strachey and Riviere had both studied with Freud; both had translated his works into English; and neither had qualified in medicine, unlike many of the early British practition-ers of psychotherapy such as David Eder, Edward Glover, Ernest Jones, and John Rickman. In their own way, James Strachey and

Joan Riviere served as models for Winnicott, because, like them, he became a devotee and student of Freud; and though he never translated Freud from German into English, he performed another kind of Freud translation by communicating Freud's ideas to the general public in *ordinary* English. Shortly after his analysis with Riviere had ended, Winnicott began to deliver many popular radio broadcasts for non-specialists, explaining psychological knowledge in very simple, graspable terms. Furthermore, although Winnicott, unlike Strachey or Riviere, did have a medical degree, he worked hard to de-medicalize psychoanalysis and to present it as a form of exclusively psychological therapy (cf. Winnicott, 1943b, 1944c, 1944d). In this regard, he bravely fought against the passion for cruel somatic treatments, such as pre-frontal leucotomy and other forms of psychosurgery, that flourished in Britain during the middle of the twentieth century (cf. Partridge, 1950).

Winnicott would eventually surpass both Strachey and Riviere in brilliance and in productivity, but these two early Freudians forged a path for him at a germinal stage in his career; and to a certain extent they became role models to Winnicott in their allegiance to a non-medical Freud, who could be read and understood by all manner of English-speaking people. In this way, they proved valuable as analysts; and after Winnicott completed approximately fifteen years of personal treatment on their respective couches, his creative capacities mushroomed extensively.

It may be helpful at this point to study Winnicott's relationship to Freud. To the best of our knowledge, the two men never met. After Freud arrived in London on 6 June 1938 to escape from the Nazis, he kept a detailed diary of visitors, and Winnicott's name does not appear therein (Molnar, 1992, and personal communication, 11 September 1991). No doubt the young Dr Winnicott, only recently qualified as a psychoanalyst himself, did not wish to impose himself on the ailing Professor Freud. Nevertheless, Freud would always remain the single greatest influence on Winnicott—much more so than Darwin, Horder, Strachey, Riviere, or even Klein. In 1986, a shrewd antiquarian bookseller managed to purchase some books from Winnicott's professional library, and I, in turn, bought three volumes by Freud from Winnicott's collection. These three books all bear Winnicott's initials, inscribed on the flyleaf in pencil, in his characteristic handwriting. Although they had clearly belonged to Winnicott, they contain absolutely no scribbles or annotations of any kind; and though they are more than forty years old, the Freud books remain in such good condition that they appear never to have been read. Of course, Winnicott may have studied these volumes in other editions—many analysts own multiple copies of Freud's works—but other evidence suggests that though Winnicott pledged himself fully to Freud's profession, he actually read relatively little of Freud's own writings.

First of all, we know that Winnicott probably never studied Freud in German—at least not in any depth. He told one of his correspondents that "I read German very slowly and I am not able to get the full volume of something in German without a good deal of work" (Winnicott, 1964e). When Winnicott began to study psychoanalysis, many of Freud's writings had not yet appeared in translation, and Winnicott's poor knowledge of German would not have allowed him to grasp the full measure of Freud's writings at a crucial and formative stage of his career. Winnicott seems to have read a comparatively small amount of Freud; and his first analyst, James Strachey, actually departed from his classical posture of analytic neutrality and encouraged Winnicott actively to read Freud's work, reminding him that, "after all the part that you need to read is not very voluminous" (quoted in Winnicott, 1952b, p. 33). But though Winnicott certainly never acquired a Talmudic comprehension of Freud, as some analysts have done, he did strive to acquire knowledge wherever he could, not only from his erudite analysts, but also from personal conversations with his friend Dr John Rickman, another Briton who had trained with Professor Freud in Vienna. Rickman told Winnicott about Freud's little-known interest in birth experience—an area of investigation that Dr Winnicott would soon claim as his own (Winnicott, 1988).

Though Winnicott could not cite chapter and verse, he happily admitted: "Let me say at once that I have derived most of my concepts from those of Freud" (Winnicott, 1971c, p. 1). Perhaps Winnicott best captured his relationship to Freud in a letter that he wrote to a colleague, Dr Clifford Scott, during Winnicott's first term of office as President of The British Psycho-Analytical Society:

I feel odd when in the president's chair because I don't know my Freud *in the way a president should do; yet I do find I have Freud in my bones.* [Winnicott, 1956e, in Grosskurth, 1986, p. 401]

During Winnicott's second term of office as President nearly a decade later, he affirmed his allegiance to Freud by offering to raise money so that the talented sculptor Oscar Nemon could cast his large statue of the father of psychoanalysis in bronze; this now stands proudly on a patch of grass next to the Swiss Cottage Centre, in North-West London, not far from Freud's final home at 20, Maresfield Gardens, Hampstead. (At the time of this writing, plans seem to be under way to move the statue in front of the Tavistock Clinic, even closer to Freud's old house.) Not only did Winnicott lead the fund-raising campaign for the bronzing enterprise (Rodman, 1987c), he even sold off miniature statuettes of it to collect money for the project (Malcolm Pines, personal communication, 3 October 1994). Winnicott's secretary, Mrs Joyce Coles, has reported that her employer derived much pleasure from the thought that generations of little children would have the opportunity to enjoy playing on Nemon's splendidly crafted sculpture, even clambering onto Freud's head! (Clancier & Kalmanovitch, 1984). Melanie Klein may have inspired Winnicott, but Sigmund Freud stabilized him, and all of Winnicott's subsequent work can be conceived of as a vital extension of Freudian orthodoxy.

CHAPTER SIX

Professional maturity

I n 1934, Winnicott qualified as an adult psychoanalyst, and as an Associate Member of The British Psycho-Analytical Society; and in 1935, he received his certification as a child psychoanalyst. Nina Searl and Ella Freeman Sharpe, two early pioneers, had supervised the treatment of his adult patients during his lengthy training, and Melanie Klein, Melitta Schmideberg (the daughter of Mrs Klein), and Nina Searl supervised his work with children (King, 1991a). His first patient in child analysis proved rather a handful—a delinquent boy who bit Winnicott on the buttocks on several occasions (Winnicott, 1956c). By 1936, he became a Full Member of the Society, having presented his membership paper on "The Manic Defence" on 4 December 1935 (Winnicott, 1935); and in 1940, after a long apprenticeship, he was appointed as a Training Analyst at The Institute of Psycho-Analysis—that is, he could now undertake the personal treatment of analysts in training. Melanie Klein even anointed him as an approved Kleinian Training Analyst for a time—one of only five such people in the early days of British psychoanalysis (King, 1991a).

Winnicott must have enjoyed a very solid reputation as a psychoanalytic practitioner in the mid-1930s, because not only did Melanie Klein entrust her son Erich to him for treatment, but Ernest Jones (1937) also referred his young daughter Nesta May to him for a child analysis, in order to help her cope with her pathologically jealous feeling towards her brother Mervyn. Previously, only Melanie Klein had had the honour and the privilege of treating members of the family of Dr Ernest Jones, the long-established President of The British Psycho-Analytical Society. Edith Tudor-Hart's studio photograph of Winnicott from this period (reprinted in Clancier & Kalmanovitch, 1984) reveals a man of purpose, stature, and intensity; and Basil's portrait photograph of him, also from this time, offers us a glimpse of a man of benevolent fortitude.

Winnicott must have felt quite proud for having completed the exhaustive and exhausting training in both adult and child psychoanalysis and to have received such approval from no less a figure than Ernest Jones. In subsequent years, Jones would refer other patients to him (cf. Kubie, 1957). Jones seems to have remained a consistent admirer of Winnicott's work, and after the latter had sent him two of his newly published books on baby and child care (Winnicott, 1957a, 1957b), the elder states-man of British psychoanalysis replied: *"Thank you very much for the two books which I am glad to have since I appreciate very highly your writings and ideas. I hopw* [sic] *that they will come in before very long for the two members of my family in the fertile age, Nesta and Lewis's wife"* (Jones, 1957). In this way, Jones communicated to Winnicott that his treatment of the young Nesta May of two decades previously had begun to bear fruit, and that Nesta had started preparations to have children of her own. Ernest Jones, a very patrician figure in his own right, had perhaps come to represent a father figure for Winnicott, as Jones did resemble Frederick Winnicott in many respects; therefore, Winnicott must have craved Jones's approbation, and shortly before the latter died, Winnicott (1957l) wrote to Jones's wife, Katherine, that, "Dr Jones and all his family have meant a great deal to me."

Winnicott had also published an innovative and important paediatric textbook, *Clinical Notes on Disorders of Childhood*, which appeared in 1931 as part of the "Practitioner's Aid Series", designed for busy general medical doctors. This landmark volume helped to explain the psychological roots of certain childhood diseases. The textbook sold for 10s/6d, and it has since become a classic in the history of paediatrics, and in psychoanalysis. In the Preface to this book Winnicott even acknowledged his indebtedness to Sigmund Freud, who offered him "an increasing ability to enjoy investigating emotional factors" (Winnicott, 1931a, p. v). The author also expressed his appreciation to his former chief at St. Bartholomew's Hospital, Professor Francis R. Fraser, and to more recent colleagues, including Dr Reginald Miller, Dr Elizabeth O'Flynn, Dr Herbert Perkins, and his colleague from the Paddington Green Children's Hospital, Dr E. C. Coker.

The Preface to the book begins with an apologia by Winnicott (1931a, p. v): "This book proceeds from the heart of a clinician rather than from the brain of a library student; hence some of its merits and demerits." This remark offers an accurate summary of the kind of writing that he had provided and would continue to provide over the next forty years—namely, a set of works grounded extensively in clinical paediatric and psychiatric practice. He used very few references in his writings; instead, he focused almost exclusively on detailed case material, and this sharp attention to the minutiae of his interactions with patients would become not only one of Winnicott's professional trademarks, but also one of his many lasting legacies for the psychoanalytic community.

Clinical Notes on Disorders of Childhood seems to be the first volume to have appeared in the "Practitioner's Aid Series"; this strikes one as rather appropriate, because Winnicott's book proved to be a marvellously helpful addition to the medical literature, and it remains of great value to this day, full of rich case descriptions, and valuable insights into the nature of paediatric practice. The book includes chapters on history-taking, physical examination, and the proper reading of temperature charts, with further sections on problems of the nose and throat, heart disease, rheumatic fever, growing pains, arthritis, fidgetiness, chorea, diseases of the nervous system, mental defect, fits, convulsions, enuresis, speech disorders, as well as the more fully psychological problems such as anxiety, sexual enlightenment, and masturbation. Although primarily a guidebook for paediatricians, Winnicott could not restrain himself from including a number of brief references to the work of Sigmund Freud, Melanie Klein, and Ernest Jones, as well as brief comments on the work of Susan Isaacs (1930)—a brilliant child psychologist who would eventually train as a psychoanalyst. He also cited the recently published essay by his own analyst, James Strachey (1930), on "Some Unconscious Factors in Reading".

Winnicott inserted many of his recently acquired psychoanalytic insights as footnotes to his book, no doubt in an effort to communicate his enthusiasm for the Freudian approach, but also to protect himself from the protests of his more organically orientated paediatric colleagues, who would have balked at a book containing too many references to the controversial theories of the psychoanalysts. In his insightful chapter on "Arthritis Associated with Emotional Disturbance", he wrote: "The natural process of cure is already well on the way, and this is better than any treatment (unless psychoanalysis is available to make the natural process more complete and satisfactory)" (Winnicott, 1931a, p. 84, fn. 1). And in his chapter on "Convulsions, Fits", Winnicott described the case of a boy of only six and one half months of age, who developed a psychogenic convulsion after biting his mother's breast. Once again, Winnicott included this vital vignette as a footnote rather than in the body of the text, as though the thought of a seemingly physical symptom resulting from an interaction between mother and infant at the breast might prove too radical for the medical doctors of the time. Winnicott did, however, seem courageous enough to refer to Freud's work on the Russian writer Fyodor Dostoevsky, in which he had speculated about a causal link between powerful emotional states and subsequent epileptic reactions.

In *Clinical Notes on Disorders of Childhood*, Winnicott also devoted an entire chapter to the important subject of "mental defect"—a set of conditions better known today as "mental handicap" or "learning difficulties". In 1992, Valerie Sinason, a Consultant Child Psychotherapist at the Tavistock Clinic in London, published a ground-breaking book, *Mental Handicap and the Human Condition: New Approaches from the Tavistock* (Sinason, 1992)—undoubtedly the best work on the psychoanalytic understanding and treatment of the various forms of mental handicap. Sinason's book traces in a creative and original manner the effects of trauma in childhood on the development of handicapped states in later life. Winnicott actually anticipated a number of Sinason's own contributions about the links between trauma and handicap, though of course he did not elaborate them in the sophisticated way in which Valerie Sinason deals with the subject. But he did have the courage to articulate that "mental development is most commonly retarded by latent or manifest anxiety. Where the anxiety situation has come to consciousness through psychoanalysis, the result has been a marked increase in ability to enjoy playing and learning" (Winnicott, 1931a, p. 155). This observation also presages the research findings of Sinason (personal communication, 10 December 1995), who has discovered that after psychoanalytically orientated psychotherapeutic treatment, certain handicapped patients will improve to such an extent that they show improved scores on standard intelligence quotient tests. Unquestionably, the expression of anxiety and the ability to talk about trauma in treatment opens up mental space in the mind of the handicapped patient, and as a result, the so-called stupidity of mental handicap becomes far less pronounced.

Finally, in his textbook Winnicott also wrote on the crucial topic of hostility towards infants. In a striking footnote of great clinical wisdom, he (1931a, pp. 125–126, fn. 1) commented that "This ambivalent attitude is well illustrated when a mother of twins shows great fondness for one baby and dangerously hates the other. The common manifestation of unconscious hatred is over-fondness, perceived by the child as love plus hate." In later years, Winnicott reminded us that hatred towards newborn babies causes grotesque psychological damage in patients, and that such hostility for babies also forms the prototype of the professional mistreatment of patients—a phenomenon that Winnicott (1949b) would describe so tellingly in his enduring essay on "Hate in the Counter-Transference".

After the publication of *Clinical Notes on Disorders of Childhood*, Winnicott received a very favourable review of the book in *The International Journal of Psycho-Analysis*, the leading Freudian periodical, by the British psychoanalyst, Dr Sybille L. Yates (1932). Without doubt, the psychologically sophisticated Dr Yates grasped the full import of Winnicott's work, and she summarized the book thus:

Recollections of the passage, usually tucked away at the end, which, in most books on the diseases of children, treats of the "nervous child", will cause one to read with more than relief Dr. Winnicott's vivid clinical histories. The pictures given in these histories of the distinct personalities of different neurotic children show that the "nervous child" of the textbooks is as much a myth as is the "economic man". The author draws attention to the fact, little realized outside the narrow circle of medical psychologists, that childhood is the time when, most frequently, bodily illness is the expression of emotional conflict. Consequently he emphasizes the necessity for the understanding of the whole child and the due consideration of psychological elements in the treatment of these disorders. [Yates, 1932, pp. 242–243]

Yates also commented upon Winnicott's observation on the link between convulsive states and feeding disorders in early infancy, an insight that remains both revolutionary and groundbreaking.

By 1935, only a few years after the publication of his first book, Winnicott had finally completed his lengthy and arduous studentship in paediatrics, child psychiatry, and psychoanalysis. At last, he could use the foundation stones of Freud and Klein to create his own unique contributions. Indeed, as Winnicott grew professionally, his admiration for Klein became less effusive, and, as we have already noted, he began to concentrate more on his own approach to infant psychology.

Of course, as mentioned previously, Klein and Winnicott both focused on the pre-oedipal aspects of the child's personality, but whereas the former preferred to study the internal phantasy world of the child, the latter concentrated more interest in the actual relationship between child and mother. Furthermore, Klein tended to paint a picture of infants which highlighted their enviousness, aggressiveness, greediness, and psychotic experiences, whereas Winnicott emphasized their health, their sense of neediness, and their wish to be loved. No wonder that Joan Riviere became enraged at Winnicott for his creative differences (cf. Cooper, 1991). Even Mrs Klein herself, once beholden to Winnicott for having treated her son Erich, ultimately came to lambast him as "that awful man" in the final years of her life (Barbara Dockar-Drysdale, personal communication, 13 July 1991). Charles Rycroft (1994, p. 2), an acute observer of the debates between Mrs Klein and Dr Winnicott, reminisced that their relationship could be characterized as an "exercise in mutual non-comprehension"—a very sad indictment indeed, in view of the extraordinary capacities of these two towering figures.

The Kleinian bitterness towards Winnicott and his burgeoning independence reached such proportions that during the late 1960s certain tutors on the Child Psychotherapy course at the Tavistock Clinic (a proverbial home for the Kleinians) expressly forbade their students to attend Winnicott's public lectures, even though Melanie Klein had died some years previously. Mrs Frances Tustin (personal communication, 22 February 1994), a renowned child psychotherapist, who studied at the Tavistock Clinic with the Kleinian analyst Esther Bick, confessed that "I in my training was brought up not to read Winnicott". Another of those trainees, now a seasoned professional, laughed as she recalled how she visited Winnicott *in secret*, as though he epitomized some dreadful subversive underground movement. It must be said, however, that in spite of the catty remarks levelled against Winnicott, he did receive a series of invitations to teach the Child Psychotherapy trainees at the Tavistock Clinic (Bick, 1958b; cf. Bowlby, 1958), and he maintained a cordial correspondence with Esther Bick (e.g. Winnicott, 1953e). Winnicott also seems to have provided a supply of training patients for students at the Tavistock Clinic (Bick, 1958a). In contrast, Winnicott always remained above the narrow-mindedness of some of his Kleinian colleagues, and in his old age, he often referred to Klein with great respect (Winnicott, 1962e), though two years after Melanie Klein's death he did indulge in a more candid remark, spoken in the relative safety of the Los Angeles Psychoanalytic Society, far away in California. On this occasion, in a talk to a group of psychoanalytic candidates in training, Winnicott (1962e, p. 177) said that "Klein claimed to have paid full attention to this environmental factor, but it is my opinion that she was temperamentally incapable of this" (cf. Winnicott, 1969h).

Many writers and teachers exerted a very great influence on Winnicott's development, as we have established; but perhaps Winnicott's greatest source of inspiration and knowledge during his mature years came from his own work with the patients themselves. He wrote that many of his clinical ideas emerged by "simply following the lead given me by careful history-taking in innumerable cases" (Winnicott, 1936, p. 34, fn. 2). Perhaps the best expression of Winnicott's gratitude to the people he treated can be found in the dedication to his posthumously published book *Playing and Reality*, which reads, quite simply: "To my patients who have paid to teach me" (Winnicott, 1971a, n.p.).

We know very little about Winnicott's domestic life during the 1930s and 1940s. By 1932, he and Alice Winnicott had moved from Surbiton in Surrey to Sydney House, at 7, Pilgrim's Lane, Hampstead, London—an extremely commodious home sandwiched rather privately between Hampstead High Street and Hampstead Heath. The beautiful foliage and the hilly terrain of the nearby heath no doubt reminded Winnicott of the Devon countryside and moors, and this feature may have influenced his purchase of Sydney House. Pilgrim's Lane had housed many interesting personalities over the years, including William Johnson Cory, an Assistant Master at Eton College from 1845 until 1872 and author of the words to the Eton Boating Song.

Although Winnicott no longer had to endure the long commute from Surrey to London, he cannot have spent very much time at home. His numerous surviving case records indicate that he devoted an inordinate amount of time to his hospital patients and to his private practice on Queen Anne Street. It may be that the fragile Alice Winnicott had begun to exert numerous emotional demands, and he may have preferred office work to domestic life. He certainly seems to have seized every available work opportunity that presented itself, and Alice may well have suffered, too, from her husband's impotence and from his relative neglect.

Winnicott spent a certain amount of time in the company of his old friend from The Leys School, H. S. Ede, known to all his friends as "Jim", who lived near the Winnicotts at 1, Elm Row, Hampstead. As an art historian and collector, Ede knew virtually all the fashionable people in the world of art and entertainment, and even the quickest perusal of his visitors' book from the 1930s reveals that he received calls at home from some of the most interesting and glamorous personalities, including the actors John Gielgud and Ralph Richardson; the writers John Betjeman and Graham Greene; artists such as Vanessa Bell, Georges Braque, Duncan Grant, Henry Moore, and Ben Nicholson; choreographers and dancers, including Frederick Ashton, George Balanchine, Alexandra Danilova, Serge Lifar, Bronislava Nijinska, and Lydia Sokolova; the pianist Vera Moore; the socialite Lady Ottoline Morrell; the composer Constant Lambert; art critics and historians such as Kenneth Clark, James Pope Hennessy, Lincoln Kirstein, Herbert Read, Adrian Stokes; and many others besides.

Donald Winnicott and his wife often had the opportunity to meet this glittering array of talent. For instance, on 7 February 1932 the Winnicotts went to a party at Ede's house, and on this occasion the guest list included the celebrated pianist Vera Moore, who also had the distinction of being the mistress of the famous artist Constantin Brancusi; George Eumoropoulos, a collector of Chinese art; Helen Sutherland, also an art collector; and Dugald S. MacColl, a sometime Keeper at both the National Gallery at Millbank, and at the Wallace Collection. These gatherings at Ede's house, which also included frequent teas, must have provided Winnicott with a very necessary respite from his rather demanding work in paediatrics and psychoanalysis.

Donald Winnicott also visited the Ede household on more quiet, private occasions, and both he and Alice became extremely attached to Elisabeth and Mary Ede, the two charming daughters of Jim Ede. As Ede travelled quite a great deal, the two young girls often stayed at Pilgrim's Lane with the Winnicotts, and at one point Winnicott even offered to adopt the children—though Ede rebuffed this suggestion, as one might imagine (Elisabeth Swan, personal communication, 30 October 1994).

Jim Ede himself spent a great deal of his time with a poet and painter from Kent, David Michael Jones (1895–1974). Jones had suffered a number of breakdowns, and Ede felt that Winnicott might be in a position to help out; he thus arranged to introduce the two men. As early as 24 January 1932, Jones took tea with the Winnicotts at Ede's home, but the relationship between Winnicott and Jones seems to have intensified in the 1940s, after Ede had left England to live overseas. On 10 March 1943, Jones (1943a) sent a post-card to Ede, commenting, *"How jolly nice the W's are."* A few weeks later, on 27 March 1943, Jones (1943b) wrote to Ede, *"I did like the Winnicotes* [sic] *& shall certainly go & see them."* He also noted that, *"I enjoyed Mrs Winnicote's* [sic] *talk"*, mentioning that they happened to discuss such seemingly peculiar topics as stalactites and erosion, two subjects in which Alice maintained an interest. By the month of May, the relationship between Jones and the Winnicotts became increasingly involved, and Jones sent Ede a letter, which reported, really quite tellingly,

> *I had dinner with the Winnicots* [sic] *one night a little while back—which was nice & one day Dr Winnicot* [sic] *came here with my ointment—but actually I do believe he has a magic touch (!) as no irritation since he examined it—most remarkable!* [Jones, 1943c]

By 1944, Jones (1944) reported to Ede: *"I've not seen the Winnicots* [sic] *for many many months. I'll have to. You see—been ill most of the time."* This passage evidently refers to one of the many periods of breakdown that Jones spent in a supervised nursing home in Harrow under the care of a certain Dr Stevenson. Donald Winnicott seems never to have had a formal treatment relationship with David Jones, but the letters between Jones and Ede reveal how much social time Winnicott dedicated to Ede's ill friend. Winnicott's penchant for overworking had already begun to manifest itself, and the addiction would only intensify as the years progressed and as Winnicott became more celebrated and sought after as a psychoanalyst.

One cannot hope to provide a complete picture of Winnicott's life during this time without referring to the infamous theoretical controversies that beset the warring factions within The British Psycho-Analytical Society. In order to gain a fuller comprehension of Winnicott's frustratingly unpredictable relationship with Klein and Riviere, we must recall that much of the bitter wrangling among these analysts took place against a backdrop of a much more sinister and divisive set of arguments and disputes, known gingerly as "The Controversial Discussions" (King & Steiner, 1991). Between 1941 and 1945, The British Psycho-Analytical Society sponsored a series of scientific meetings to discuss the differing viewpoints of the two rival schools of Anna Freud and Melanie Klein. The two groups became embroiled in a stream of turbulent encounters, struggling valiantly to resolve such heated issues as the nature of the infant's psyche, the dating of the Oedipus complex, and the formation of the superego, not to mention the clinical and technical practices that devolved from the different theoretical positions. In particular, the participants grappled with Klein's observations about the phantasy life of the infant, ostensibly coloured by paranoid and persecutory anxieties. The Kleinians accepted this description as axiomatic, whereas Anna Freud's followers regarded it with suspicion.

Tensions became so pronounced that members of each group would often hurl psychiatric diagnoses at members of the rival group. Eva Rosenfeld (quoted in Rayner, 1991, p. 18), a refugee from Vienna, referred to this period as "the nightmare years". Dr John Bowlby (personal communication, 30 October 1986), a somewhat bemused participant, reminisced about the fatal evening when, after a psychoanalytic meeting, he had the dubious honour of driving both Miss Freud and Mrs Klein back to their respective homes in North London. Apparently, Anna Freud and Melanie Klein both sat in the back seat of Bowlby's car, thus leaving the passenger seat empty in the front. Neither lady would have dared to sit in front, with her rival in the rear—that would have appeared too overtly hierarchical. Instead, each woman chose a dignified equality of seating, thus permitting Dr Bowlby to serve as chauffeur. As Bowlby recalled, nobody uttered a word during the journey to North London, thus creating a very awkward situation for Bowlby himself.

The origins of "The Controversial Discussions" stem not only from theoretical differences between the Kleinian and Freudian factions, but, perhaps more fundamentally, from personal animosities and other private motivations. As we have already indicated, Melanie Klein held the position of undisputed queen of British psychoanalysis from 1926 until 1938, although her role was challenged after Anna Freud's arrival from Vienna. Both women had emigrated to England from German-speaking countries, and each struggled for the role of premier child psychoanalyst. Anna Freud bore the title of crown princess, as the daughter of Sigmund Freud; but Melanie Klein had already established herself in the London community over the previous twelve years, and she had developed a powerful and loyal band of followers (cf. King, 1988). And just as Britain entered into international warfare, so, too, did the members of The British Psycho-Analytical Society draw their battle lines. We know that the native English members of the Society experienced more than a certain amount of resentment as their rather Gentile professional group rapidly became transformed into an organization dominated by thickly accented Germanic–Jewish refugees from Nazi persecution. Regardless of their seasoning in Berlin and Vienna, indigenous Anglo–Saxons, such as Edward Glover, Sylvia Payne, Ella Freeman Sharpe, and others, must have found the substantial change in the demography of their psychoanalytic institution rather bewildering.

To their great credit, the local members made heroic efforts to accommodate the new Jewish arrivals in many respects, providing entry permits, accommodations, and referrals of patients. And yet the English analysts did experience some resentment and shock—quite an understandable reaction in view of the enormous change that had occurred in the composition of the psychoanalytic family. James Strachey (1940, p. 18) dashed off a very revealing letter to Edward Glover, written during a bout of fever, in which he lamented, *"Why should these wretched fascists and (bloody foreigners) communists invade our peaceful compromising island?"* Immediately after he had scribbled these words, Strachey may have felt a pang of regret or guilt, because he instantly qualified his calumny, noting, *"But I see I'm more feverish than I'd thought."* Only in a febrile state could the gentlemanly James Strachey dare to show the underbelly of his ostensibly friendly attitude towards the newcomers.

Winnicott played a rather minor role in "The Controversial Discussions", partly because he had only recently qualified as a psychoanalyst in his own right and he lacked the seniority of many of the more vocal contributors to the series of debates. Dr Charles Rycroft (personal communication, 29 November 1993) has suggested, quite astutely, that Winnicott's role as a younger sibling, sandwiched between two elder sisters—Melanie Klein and Anna Freud—mirrored precisely his own family constellation as the younger brother of two spinsterish sisters, Violet and Kathleen. And just as the youthful Donald Winnicott had escaped from his home in Plymouth to start a more independent and individuated life in Cambridge and then in London, so, too, did the more mature Dr Winnicott ultimately succeed in extricating himself from the partisan pull of Miss Freud and Mrs Klein. As the Second World War drew to a close, Winnicott and his like-minded confrères banded together in a rather loose way to form a so-called Middle Group—now known as the Independent Group—comprising such leading figures as Michael Balint, John Bowlby, Masud Khan, Pearl King, John Klauber, Margaret Little, Marion Milner, Charles Rycroft, and many others. The Middle Group created an intermediary space between the Kleinians and the Freudians, and though he had always refused to become their formal leader, Winnicott remains the most important and prolific proponent of this new breed of open-mindedness within The British Psycho-Analytical Society.

But Winnicott had more important preoccupations than a concern with local psychoanalytic politics. Shortly after Great Britain had become embroiled in the Second World War, he accepted a post as a Consultant Psychiatrist for the Government Evacuation Scheme in Oxfordshire, working particularly for the Oxfordshire Evacuation Hostel Scheme. This position would prove critical to Winnicott both personally and professionally. Not only did it enhance his working knowledge of extremely disturbed patients, but he also made the acquaintance of a beautiful and talented social worker, Clare Britton, with whom he then had an extra-marital affair (Lomax-Simpson, 1990; Irmi Elkan, personal communication, 6 October 1994).

At this time, Winnicott took responsibility for the mental health care of approximately 285 young children in five different hostels (Winnicott, 1948a). These boys and girls had been evacuated from their homes and separated from their parents, ostensibly to protect them from the bombing of London and other large cities. Winnicott visited these children each week, working with the hostel staff on a weekly basis as well (Clare Winnicott, 1984). Winnicott held this appointment from 1939 to 1946. As a matter of historical interest, the noted psychoanalyst, Eva Rosenfeld, a close friend of Anna Freud, worked with Clare Britton for a time in Oxfordshire, though it seems doubtful that she had any extensive contact with Winnicott during this period (Dyer, 1977).

Winnicott's work in Oxfordshire also gave him the chance to learn a great deal about the importance not only of intensive treatment, but of *residential care* and *residential management* as well. He soon recognized that some patients had suffered so much damage that a mere fifty-minute psychoanalytic session would not suffice; and he came to understand that certain individuals required psychotherapeutic care on a full-time basis.

Winnicott undertook other war work as well, though unlike some of his colleagues in The British Psycho-Analytical Society, such as Major John Bowlby, he did not enlist in the armed forces. Along with Melanie Klein and John Rickman, Winnicott served as a member of the advisory group to the Cambridge Evacuation Survey, supervised by the pioneering educationalist Susan Isaacs (Isaacs, Brown, & Thouless, 1941; cf. King, 1991b). Additionally, he worked with Edward Glover on a nation-wide survey for the Ministry of Health concerning the mental health of civilians between 1939 and 1943, known as the "Neurosis Survey" (King, 1991b). He also helped his Jungian colleague Michael Fordham (personal communication, 13 February 1994) with evacuation work in Nottingham, and he (Winnicott, 1941c) even found time to participate in the Child Discussion Group facilitated by Miss Theodora Alcock (1948), a psychologist who worked with 1,140 evacuated children from London between 1939 and 1945. Alcock (1963), known affectionately to her colleagues as "Theo", also helped to popularize the use of the Rorschach Test in Britain; and in her role as a tutor for trainee psychologists at the Tavistock Clinic, she would review the Rorschach protocols of Nazi war criminals as a teaching device (Mary Boston, personal communication, 28 September 1994).

In view of Winnicott's deep immersion in war work, one wonders whether he had time to visit his father and his sisters, who spent these years in Plymouth, dodging the German bombs. Tragically, repeated enemy air raids in 1941 and 1942 destroyed much of the city centre of Winnicott's beloved Plymouth, and he must have felt utterly crushed when he saw the carnage for the first time. The devastation caused by the Blitz included the burning of the Winnicott Brothers premises on Frankfort Street. The elderly Sir Frederick, still alive at this time, arranged to have the business moved temporarily to Plymouth's Bedford Terrace.

Winnicott knew that the process of evacuation would be very traumatic for the London youngsters; and in collaboration with

John Bowlby and Emanuel Miller (an eminent child psychiatrist, and also the father of the distinguished theatrical director, broadcaster, and physician, Dr Jonathan Miller), he wrote an important letter to the *British Medical Journal*, warning that if the authorities pressed forward with their evacuation projects, then in all likelihood these children would develop a plethora of crippling symptoms, such as anxiety, behavioural disorders, physical illnesses, and even chronic delinquency (Bowlby, Miller, & Winnicott, 1939). As Winnicott became more experienced in his work with evacuated children, he began to discover the awful truth of his clinical predictions, encountering such troubling symptoms as enuresis, skin irritations, head-banging, and a whole host of other severe manifestations (Winnicott, 1945e; Winnicott & Britton, 1947).

Some of the evacuated children in Winnicott's hostels, most of whom had experienced considerable emotional disruptions before the war had even begun, displayed extreme delinquency, as well as overtly psychotic reactions. Work with them, therefore, represented a new clinical departure for Winnicott, who had previously had very limited exposure to childhood delinquency (Clare Winnicott, 1984). The symptomatology of the youngsters included, among others, bed-wetting, faecal incontinence, stealing in gangs, the burning of hay-ricks, truancy from school, truancy from the hostel, train wrecking, and fraternizing with local soldiers (Winnicott & Britton, 1947). One nine-year-old boy from London exhibited such distress that he could not be contained well enough in the hostel, and even the tolerant Winnicott described him as "stark staring mad" (Winnicott, 1949b, p. 72)—an unusually unenlightened phrase for him to have used in discussing a patient. Winnicott attempted to help the boy by inviting him into his home for a period of three months, in the hope that he and his wife Alice might serve as surrogate parents. Winnicott (1949b, p. 72) remembered this period as "three months of hell", and that caring for the boy "was really a whole-time job for the two of us together, and when I was out the worst episodes took place" (Winnicott, 1949b, p. 72). In principle, this meant that Alice, a tormented woman in her own right, had to provide much of the care for this aggressive boy while Winnicott tended to the other children in the hostels and provided supervision and teaching for the hostel staff (cf. Clare

Winnicott, 1984). Not only did Alice lack any training in nursing or in psychotherapy, but, as we have already indicated, she herself suffered from psychiatric problems; therefore the imposition of this boy must have exacerbated the strain in the Winnicott household quite considerably.

Several colleagues of Winnicott have told me that this child was not the only patient to have lived residentially with Donald and Alice in their home at Sydney House in Hampstead (e.g. Barbara Dockar-Drysdale, personal communication, 13 July 1991; Michael Fordham, personal communication, 13 February 1994), and thus the amount of psychological disturbance in their house must have created gargantuan problems. Michael Fordham described the atmosphere at Pilgrim's Lane as unbearably "chaotic". During this period, Winnicott worked with many people diagnosed as "schizophrenic", and his reminiscences of the World War II era reveal much about the degree to which his psychotherapeutic endeavours claimed his time and energy: "I hardly noticed the blitz, being all the time engaged in analysis of patients who are notoriously and maddeningly oblivious of bombs, earthquakes and floods" (Winnicott, 1945b, p. 137). Might we not conjecture that in view of Winnicott's almost total absorption in his psychoanalytic practice, Alice felt abandoned by her husband and overwhelmed by her unofficial "caseload"? Winnicott himself had already begun to have dreams of his wife appearing in the guise of a castrating bear (Strachey, 1925); and so the wartime experiences only exaggerated the strains of an already troubled marriage.

One also wonders why Winnicott permitted psychotic patients to live in his home—a most unusual form of management or treatment by anybody's standards, but most especially for a classical Freudian psychoanalyst. It may be that Winnicott had hoped that these patients might provide Alice with some companionship; conversely, I suspect that in part Winnicott invited highly disturbed patients into his home as an unconscious means of angering and burdening his wife, in a desperate effort to facilitate the end of their crumbling marital relationship. Not surprisingly, the partnership collapsed, at Donald's particular request, and the Winnicotts separated in 1949, the year of their silver wedding anniversary. Dr Katharine Rees (personal communication, 23 September 1991, in Goldman, 1993), a former psychiatric social worker from the Psychology Department at the Paddington Green Children's Hospital, who knew Winnicott relatively well, has suggested that Donald stayed with Alice until she became strong enough to tolerate being without him. No doubt her psychoanalytic treatment with Dr Clifford Scott helped to fortify her. After the end of the marriage, Winnicott continued to communicate with his wife on an intermittent basis. A small number of letters, written by Alice to her former husband after the dissolution of their marriage, have survived, and they can only be described as heartbreaking in the extreme.

After the end of the marriage, Alice moved to Meadow Cottage, on Loddon Drive West, in Wargrave, Berkshire. She seems to have spent her time in lonely pursuits—the roster of members of her undergraduate college at the University of Cambridge lists her occupation as "Potter and Artist" (*Newnham College Roll: Letter, January, 1950*, p. 183)—though we do not know how extensively she maintained these pursuits after she left London. On 9 November 1958, she wrote to her beloved ex-husband about her work at the local Women's Institute, and of her interest in gardening, painting, and writing. She also acknowledged the letter that Donald had sent to her for her birthday, and she informed him that her former sisters-in-law, Violet and Kathleen, had sent her a scarf for her birthday (Alice Winnicott, 1958a). Donald often posted her books; he even presented her with a copy of his newly published *Collected Papers: Through Paediatrics to Psycho-Analysis* (Winnicott, 1958a; cf. Alice Winnicott, 1958b). This volume contained the revised version of Winnicott's paper on "Hate in the Countertransference" (Winnicott, 1958b), which provided a painful glimpse of moments from the last phase of the marriage, devoted to the residential care of a psychotic boy.

Winnicott certainly supported his one-time spouse financially, and he had the means to do this. On 19 November 1958, Alice wrote: "*As far as finance is concerned I am quite well off thanks to you + seem to save a bit every year. I have some in deposit at the bank + they pay me interest (5% I think) so it is quite a good investment*" (Alice Winnicott, 1958b). As the years progressed, the letters became increasingly plaintive, and Alice began to lament that Donald did not communicate more often, though his sisters do seem to have remained in contact with her. Alice's (1959a) letter of 12 November 1959 contains the following sad note: *"Thank you too for writing on my birthday. I was totally alone, as I am now. V. and K. wrote. I wish I saw them sometimes."* After Winnicott sent Alice a book called *Arabian Sands*, she responded, *"This will help to while away the long winter evenings"* (Alice Winnicott, 1959b).

It seems unlikely that Winnicott visited Alice personally, in view of his absorption in his second marriage, and his increasingly international career. By 1960, Alice wrote sadly: *"I have had only swans for company this year—a father, mother + baby"* (Alice Winnicott, 1960). She then provided Donald with a description of all the many different birds that she had seen, concluding: *"Do write to me. I wish I could see you"* (Alice Winnicott, 1960).

By 1961, Alice had moved to a farm in Cardiganshire, in Wales, where she would spend the rest of her life unhappily and in a rather bereaved state, reminiscing about the earlier, happier days of her marriage and the pleasant times that she had spent at the Winnicott family home in Plymouth. Winnicott kept sending Alice reading material, including his own books as well as a pamphlet about the ruins at Stonehenge. Alice sent him a pair of gloves and also a special diary from the Royal Horticultural Society, which contained tips about planting and about pests (Alice Winnicott, 1961a). On 1 September 1961, she wrote: *"Do you ever go to Rockville now to stay there? It seems such a little while ago somehow since I was there, busy cutting up oranges for the Mater to make marmalade, feeding the goldfish in the pond, or crossing to Oreston with you in the ferry."* Later in the same letter, she continued in an even more heart-wrenching manner: *"I wish so much you could have been happy with us. My old mare has a baby foal + they are grand together, living just behind us"* (Alice Winnicott, 1961b). No doubt Alice found herself lamenting the children that she and Donald never had together. Tragically, she suffered through her declining years in relative obscurity with virtually only her elder sister Mary, a palsy sufferer, for company. Alice Winnicott died on 19 November 1969, in the Bronglais Hospital in Aberystwyth, from bronchopneumonia, hypothermia, and renal failure, completely forlorn, and practically unremembered.

The 1940s provided Winnicott with an enormous amount of domestic chaos and upheaval, including the death of his father Sir Frederick Winnicott, on 31 December 1948, at the age of ninety-three. Quite soon thereafter, Winnicott also sustained the first in a long series of coronaries, which would plague him until his death. This first attack coincided not only with his father's death, but also with the final breakdown of his marriage. In order to convalesce, Winnicott rested from his work at the Paddington Green Children's Hospital for approximately three months (Irmi Elkan, personal communication, 6 October 1994). Winnicott suffered great emotional strain at this time, and on many evenings he could not bear to return to his house at Pilgrim's Lane. Instead, he spent many nights sleeping in his consulting room on Queen Anne Street—undoubtedly an uncomfortable arrangement in every respect (Irmi Elkan, personal communication, 6 October 1994). He also had to contend with a large amount of highly taxing yet always interesting clinical work during this time. One of his patients, a severely anorexic girl, only twelve years of age, caused Winnicott much anxiety, and he arranged to have her admitted to one of the general paediatric wards at Paddington Green. Sadly, she found the ingestion of real food far too difficult, and she became very ill. Winnicott visited her regularly in her hospital room, and this facilitated an improvement in the child's condition; but after his heart attack he could no longer visit, and the young girl deteriorated, refused all food, and eventually died (Irmi Elkan, personal communication, 6 October 1994).

As a point of interest, it is not quite true for Winnicott to have written that he hardly noticed the Blitz because of his absorption in his work with psychotic men and women. In fact, on 3 March 1943, during one particular meeting of The British Psycho-Analytical Society at its headquarters at 96, Gloucester Place, an air-raid siren began to wail, and bombs exploded at intervals. As the members of the audience sat engrossed listening to a paper on the war neuroses (Rosenberg, 1943), Winnicott stood up and stated, "I should like to point out that there is an air-raid going on" (quoted in Little, 1985, p. 19). Apparently, few people took much notice of what Winnicott had said, and the speaker, Dr Elizabeth Rosenberg (who would later be better remembered by her married name as Elizabeth Zetzel) continued to read her paper (cf. Zetzel, 1969). Characteristically, Winnicott remained vigilant not only of the internal world of the psychoanalytic society, but of the external reality of the bombs as well.

In 1951, two years after the end of his marriage, Donald Winnicott married for the second time. As described earlier, he had met his new bride, Clare Britton, when they were both working with evacuated children. Miss Britton had qualified as a social worker in 1939, and she had already acquired a certain amount of practical field-work experience. Together, Britton and Winnicott worked hard to oversee the psychiatric hostels, and they became such recognized experts on both the management and the treatment of disturbed evacuated youngsters that the Curtis Committee invited both of them to submit oral and written evidence about their experiences; and this partly formed the basis of The Children Act of 1948 (Clare Winnicott, 1984). Without doubt, Winnicott and Britton began a romantic liaison long before his divorce from Alice had become finalized. Dr Josephine Lomax-Simpson (1990) has recorded that, during their period of service for the Government Evacuation Scheme, Donald Winnicott and Clare Britton shared a flat, in Oxford, above a building known as the MacFisheries. Lomax-Simpson often visited this building because her father, the architect of Unilever House and other buildings, had designed it.

In any case, the relationship between Donald Winnicott and Clare Britton began on a collegial basis. Winnicott supervised Britton's clinical work, and she would later recall her sessions with her future husband as "the highlight of the week" and "invaluable learning experiences" (Clare Winnicott, 1984, p. 3). The two of them even collaborated on a paper for publication concerning "The Problem of Homeless Children" (Winnicott & Britton, 1944), followed soon thereafter by another joint article on "Residential Management as Treatment for Difficult Children" (Winnicott & Britton, 1947). Winnicott rarely collaborated on writing projects. To the best of my knowledge, he did so on only two other occasions; at the start of his career he co-authored his first medical paper with a paediatric colleague (Winnicott & Gibbs, 1926), and he also wrote a book review in conjunction with his analytic patient and colleague, Masud Khan (Winnicott

& Khan, 1953). And, of course, he signed his name to a joint letter with John Bowlby and Emanuel Miller (Bowlby, Miller, & Winnicott, 1939). Thus, Winnicott must have felt a special attraction for Clare Britton, an appeal enhanced not only by her evident professional gifts but also by her beauty. One of her former social work trainees described her to me as "a bit of a blonde bombshell", and Dr Michael Fordham (personal communication, 13 February 1994) described her, rather technically, as an "anima woman"—a Jungian term for a *femme fatale*. Before long, the professional relationship became transformed into a love relationship, and it seems likely that Winnicott initiated divorce proceedings with Alice Winnicott so that he would be able to marry Clare Britton.

By 1952, Winnicott had purchased the lease to a large and beautiful house for his new bride, located at 87, Chester Square, in the exclusive Belgravia district. Winnicott rented the house from the Grosvenor Estate, owned by the Duke of Westminster (Colin J. Mackenzie-Grieve, personal communication, 10 October 1994). Eventually, he moved his private practice into Chester Square, and he ceased to use his consulting room in Queen Anne Street. After Clare Winnicott qualified as a psychoanalyst, she, too, treated her patients there.

Donald and Clare enjoyed a more compatible relationship, and Clare shared not only her husband's professional interest in children and in psychotherapy but also his passion for dancing (Clare Winnicott, 1978). The French psychoanalyst Serge Lebovici recalled, "At a conference in Rome I was particularly struck by how much he seemed to be in love with his wife; what she told me did not seem in any way exaggerated, when she spoke of the way he danced with her at conference receptions" (quoted in Clancier, 1984b, p. 134). The new marriage seemed based as much on friendship and on shared professional interests as on any sensual grounds. Under Winnicott's guidance, his new wife undertook further training, and she eventually qualified as a psychoanalyst in 1961, having undergone a period of psychoanalytic treatment first with Dr Clifford Scott (who had also treated Alice Winnicott), and then with the tempestuous Melanie Klein. (After Winnicott's death, Clare underwent further treatment with Lois Munro and then with Dr Peter Lomas: Charles Rycroft, personal communication, 27 January 1996.)

Clare Winnicott found her analysis with Dr Scott somewhat unsatisfactory, and she told her husband that she wished to undergo a re-analysis with Melanie Klein, explaining, "I think she's tough enough for me" (interview, 18 September 1981, cited in Grosskurth, 1986, p. 451). Winnicott had no objections to Clare pursuing a psychoanalytic treatment with the latter, even though his allegiance to Mrs Klein had become increasingly strained. Donald Winnicott approached Klein on his wife's behalf to arrange for the treatment, reminding Klein that she owed him a favour in exchange for his having treated her young son Erich many years previously. Klein consented, and she began to work with Clare, who appreciated Klein's terrific memory and her sense of solidity and strength. Nevertheless, Clare shared her husband's objection that Klein neglected the external world, pontificating to her patient, "It's no good your talking about your mother", because "We can't do anything about it now" (ibid., p. 451). Shortly before Klein's death, Clare Winnicott brought a dream to her session, and Klein spent a full twenty-five minutes offering an interpretation, which Clare timed by her own watch! Mrs Winnicott became enraged and spluttered, "How dare you take my dream and serve it up to me?" (ibid., p. 452), and she stormed out of the consulting room.

Winnicott seems to have interceded on his wife's behalf, but Klein replied that his wife could not be analysed, because "She's too aggressive" (ibid., p. 452). Winnicott urged his wife to return to the sessions, otherwise her training at The Institute of Psycho-Analysis would have become jeopardized. One week later, Clare Winnicott returned, seething, "I have come back on your terms, Mrs. Klein, not on mine" (ibid., p. 452). The treatment continued apace, and shortly before her death on 22 September 1960, Melanie Klein informed her colleagues that Clare Winnicott should be graduated as a fully accredited psychoanalyst.

During her professional lifetime, Clare Winnicott wrote a small number of interesting papers on social work and psychoanalysis (e.g. Britton, 1955; Clare Winnicott, 1963, 1980), as well as a small collection of essays (Clare Winnicott, 1964); she also worked as a tutor in child care on the Child Care course at the London School of Economics and Political Science. She received her appointment as lecturer in charge of the new social work training course there in 1947; subsequently she became lecturer on the Applied Social Studies course from 1957 until 1964. In that year she became the Director of Child Care Studies in the Children's Department for the Home Office, a post in which she remained until her enforced retirement in 1971 (cf. Clare Winnicott, undated). During this time, she worked out of the Central Training Council in Child Care at the Home Office building in Horseferry House, Dean Ryle Street, Westminster, not far from her home in Chester Square. Eventually, she received an O.B.E. (Officer of the Order of the British Empire) for this important work. Clare Winnicott also became a founder member of the Robertson Centre—an organization designed to promote the work of James and Joyce Robertson (1989), pioneering investigators in child care whose famous films helped to document the devastating effects of separation between children and parents during hospital treatment.

Without doubt, Clare Winnicott stimulated her husband, and she encouraged his creativity. Not surprisingly, Winnicott produced his most original and his most important books and papers during the time of his second marriage. He even dedicated one of his books, *The Family and Individual Development* (Winnicott, 1965b, n.p.), very simply, "To Clare". Shortly after the couple met, Winnicott wrote to Clare, "Your effect on me is to make me keen and productive and this is all the more awful—because when I am cut off from you I feel paralysed for all action and originality" (quoted in Clare Winnicott, 1978, p. 32). Those who saw the couple together could tell how much they really loved one another (e.g. Clancier, 1984b). Winnicott even told his colleague Peter Tizard (1971) that he probably would have died twenty years earlier if he had not met Clare. It may well have saddened Winnicott not to have had sons or daughters of his own, especially as he loved other people's progeny, and he did mention his despair to at least one of his students (Silvia Oclander-Gordon, personal communication, 14 December 1991). Winnicott's inability to become a biological father may explain, in part, why he so readily invited some of his fragile and needy patients to live in his home.

Winnicott's marriage to Clare Britton not only enhanced his physical well-being, but it seems evident that his capacity for work improved dramatically as well, and his productivity escalated to new heights. During his marriage to Alice Taylor, Winnicott published only one book—a textbook on paediatrics (Winnicott, 1931a). In the course of his marriage to Clare Britton, on the other hand, he produced six more books before his death (Winnicott, 1957a, 1957b, 1958a, 1964a, 1965a, 1965b), and he wrote enough papers, lectures, and correspondence to fill another twelve volumes published after his death (Winnicott, 1971a, 1971b, 1978, 1984a, 1986a, 1986b, 1987a, 1987b, 1988, 1989, 1993, 1996). Clare Winnicott also had a great ability to nurture her husband. In her presence, he could even enjoy the luxury of abrogating his own extensive caretaking responsibilities. On one occasion, she damaged her foot and developed bruises. Winnicott left the house to purchase some crêpe bandage. He returned after two hours with a gold bracelet for his wife, but he had forgotten to buy her the bandage (Clare Winnicott, 1978).

During the 1950s and 1960s, Winnicott enjoyed a rich and busy life, filled with countless public lectures and many hours of clinical work, not to mention teaching, supervision, and writing, as well as a considerable amount of administration for various professional organizations. He particularly cherished the numerous opportunities granted to him to discuss his ideas in public. Winnicott always talked well, and whenever he lectured, the hall would be filled to capacity (Gillespie, 1971b). Shortly after the conclusion of the Second World War, he spoke to the monthly Friday night staff seminar at the famous Cassel Hospital. One psychiatric nurse recollected that the team would not let him leave, and that he continued talking until well after midnight. On another occasion, in 1965, Winnicott spoke to a group of colleagues, and Miss Doris Wills, a child psychotherapist who worked with Anna Freud and Dorothy Burlingham, wrote to him, thanking him for his participation. Winnicott had obviously once again attracted a large crowd, and Miss Wills (1965) felt prompted to write that: *"Your presence as you may know always draws considerable numbers, someone murmured to me, 'Dr. Winnicott's presence is as good as the Beatles'!"* Winnicott always spoke the King's English (Khan, 1975), in slow, measured tones; and though high-pitched, his voice could be very reassuring and soothing. From 1936 on, he taught a regular course on human growth and development to teachers at the

Institute of Education in London, at the personal invitation of his friend and colleague, Dr Susan Isaacs (Winnicott, 1953f, 1967c; Clare Winnicott, 1988); and from 1947 on he lectured to students of social work at the London School of Economics and Political Science (Clare Winnicott, 1988), including a series of talks on "A Clinical Approach to Family Problems", thus extending his influence throughout the various branches of the mental health profession.

Winnicott always took great pains in the preparation of his talks. As he wrote to his colleague Michael Balint rather immodestly: *"Even a Winnicott paper has to be thought out a little bit beforehand"* (Winnicott, 1952d). He also noted that his papers required a period of unconscious gestation: "For instance, when I write a paper for this Society on any subject I nearly always find myself dreaming dreams which belong to that subject" (Winnicott, 1949d, p. 177, fn. 2). As his widow, Clare Winnicott (1988, p. ix), commented: "His lectures could be free and seem unstructured only because they were based on a central core of integrated knowledge." In view of Winnicott's extraordinarily congested timetable, it nearly boggles the mind how he managed to prepare his endless talks and manuscripts at all.

Winnicott quickly developed a fine reputation as an engaging and spontaneous lecturer, and the British Broadcasting Corporation invited him to chat to parents on the radio. Between 1939 and 1962, he delivered some fifty broadcasts on a vast variety of topics, ranging from the contribution of fathers (Winnicott, 1944b), the only child (Winnicott, 1945d), the importance of visiting children in hospital (Winnicott, 1951b), and the dynamics of adoption (Winnicott, 1955d), to the psychology of step-parents (1955f), the role of jealousy (Winnicott, 1960f), and the vicissitudes of guilt (Winnicott, 1961f). In addition to his individual radio talks, Winnicott also prepared two full sets of memorable lectures for members of the public. Janet Quigley produced the first series in 1945, at the end of the Second World War; these talks subsequently appeared in pamphlet form under the title *Getting to Know Your Baby*, which contained the transcripts of six radio broadcasts (Winnicott, 1945a), and sold for one shilling. The cover of the little pamphlet bore a reproduction of a woodcut of a mother and baby, designed by Alice Winnicott. Interestingly, in order to arrive at the British Broadcasting Corporation recording studio in Langham Place in Central London, Winnicott recalled that he would have to drive his automobile "over the glass and rubble of the previous night's air-raid" (quoted in Bollas, Davis, & Shepherd, 1993, p. xiv).

Another producer, Miss Isa D. Benzie (also known as Mrs Royston Morley) of the Talks Department at the British Broadcasting Corporation, offered Winnicott the opportunity to prepare several more talks on the theme of "The Ordinary Devoted Mother". These aired in 1949–1950. Nine of the broadcasts from this series appeared in the pamphlet, *The Ordinary Devoted Mother and Her Baby: Nine Broadcast Talks (Autumn 1949)* (Winnicott, 1949a).

These broadcasts reached millions of people; and to this day, those who read the transcripts (Winnicott, 1957a, 1957b, 1964a, 1993) can still marvel at Dr Winnicott's polished and relaxed ability to communicate with parents and to offer them good advice and support without undermining what he regarded as their special capacity to understand their own children (Winnicott, 1949c). His reputation as a broadcaster on psychological topics became so great that at one point Eileen Molony (1958), producer of the BBC radio programme on "Parents and Children", pleaded with Winnicott to appear on her show: "Nobody will ever belief [sic] my programme is any good until you broadcast in it!!"

Winnicott not only lectured frequently, he also wrote in abundance. He received much assistance from his accomplished secretary, Mrs Joyce Coles, and from his dedicated amanuensis Prince Masud Khan. Mrs Coles typed and Mr Khan edited, and together they transformed Winnicott's manuscripts into several volumes of collected essays. Every Sunday morning Khan (1988) spent two or more hours at Winnicott's home at 87, Chester Square, Belgravia, applying himself to this task. At the present time, no fewer than twenty separate volumes bear the name of D. W. Winnicott as author, including one volume of selected letters (Winnicott, 1987b) and one further book of essays, entitled *Thinking About Children*, now in the final stages of preparation (Winnicott, 1996; cf. Davis, 1987; Farhi, 1991).

In addition to producing such a large number of books, chapters, articles, and reviews, as well as hospital memoranda (e.g. Winnicott, 1955h), Winnicott spent a great deal of time attending to his voluminous correspondence. This task became easier after his secretary, Joyce Coles, established a splendid filing system for him in 1957, retaining carbon copies of most of his professional letters. Yet although this undertaking stole much of his precious time, he even inflicted some additional letter-writing upon himself. For example, whenever a colleague delivered a paper to a Scientific Meeting of The British Psycho-Analytical Society, Winnicott would invariably send a congratulatory letter of some sort, expressing particular views that he had not necessarily always managed to verbalize during the discussion (cf. Winnicott, 1960g). Winnicott's letters became almost legendary, and upon receipt of one of them Dr Michael Balint (1960) replied, *"Of course I was waiting for your after-lecture letter which by now has become to all intents and purposes a psycho-analytic institution."* Winnicott (1960i) himself realized that his penchant for correspondence often exceeded normal bounds, and in a letter to the psychoanalyst Dr Ilse Hellman he confessed, *"I have got rather a name for writing letters, and I am trying to stop the habit."* After his death he left hundreds of fascinating unpublished letters, which his wife kept preserved in special ring binders (Rodman, 1987a).

As his reputation flowered and the ever high standard of his work became better known, Winnicott's colleagues rewarded him with numerous appointments, awards, and other distinctions. Within The British Psycho-Analytical Society, he served variously as a Training Analyst, as a member of the Board and Council, as Scientific Secretary, as Training Secretary, and as the chairman of a 1944 Symposium on the Psycho-Analytic Contribution to the Theory of Shock Therapy, not to mention the numerous seminars and lectures that he delivered to trainee psychoanalysts at The Institute of Psycho-Analysis. He also worked as the Physician-in-Charge of the Child Department of the London Clinic of Psycho-Analysis—a post that he held for some twenty-five years—arranging analytic treatment for children whose parents could not in most instances afford to pay for private psychotherapy. For a time, he also toiled arduously as Chairman of the Publications Committee of The Institute of Psycho-Analysis. Furthermore, Winnicott served as President of The British Psycho-Analytical Society on two separate occasions, first from 1956 until 1959 and, again, from 1965 until

1968. Dr John Bowlby served as the Vice-President during Winnicott's first term of office. After Winnicott's election to the presidency in 1956, The British Psycho-Analytical Society held a rather splendid and enjoyable dance in his honour (Lomax-Simpson, 1990).

Winnicott's younger colleagues, Dr John Padel (personal communication, 4 December 1991) and Dr Charles Rycroft (personal communication, 29 November 1993) recalled that Winnicott had no flair at all for committee work, and he did it rather badly, having no obsessional attention to detail. Instead, he specialized in bold and brave new ventures, including the launching of the Winter Lectures on psychoanalysis, which proved to be the first systematic attempt to disseminate psycho-analytic ideas to members of the general public. These talks, held in Porchester Hall on Porchester Road, London, formed the basis of the immensely popular public lecture series sponsored by The British Psycho-Analytical Society. Dr Thomas Hayley (1991), the psychoanalyst who co-ordinated the talks on behalf of Winnicott, noted that an average lecture attracted as many as four hundred guests, but when Winnicott himself spoke, the size of the gathering swelled to some six hundred individuals. Mrs Beta Copley (personal communication, 20 October 1994) recalled a time when Winnicott presented the case history of a rather ill medical doctor—presumably the man described at length in Winnicott's (1986a) book, *Holding and Interpretation: Fragment of an Analysis.* Copley reflected that Winnicott de-scribed his patient with such vividness that one could almost imagine the patient there in the room, sitting next to Winnicott.

His colleagues often invited him to become the head of his own faction within the psychoanalytic society, but he always refused to do so (Gillespie, 1971b; James, 1991), presumably for reasons of modesty. Interestingly, Winnicott completed two full terms as society President, just as his father had served as Lord Mayor of Plymouth for two terms of office. One would have thought that one stint as the President of The British Psycho-Analytical Society would have satisfied him, but perhaps a deep need to identify with and subsequently to vanquish his highly successful father might have stimulated his ambitiousness.

On the international psychoanalytic stage, Winnicott chaired the famous investigatory committee of The International Psycho-

Analytical Association, which delved into the dubious clinical practices of the French analyst Dr Jacques Lacan. In 1953, Winnicott and a number of colleagues (Dr Phyllis Greenacre, Mrs Hedwig Hoffer, and Dr Jeanne Lampl-de Groot) interviewed many of the members of Lacan's institution, the Société Française de Psychanalyse, as well as members of the classical Société Psychanalytique de Paris, amid allegations that Lacan conducted shortened psychoanalytic sessions. The committee justly expressed grave doubts about Lacan's work as a practitioner (cf. Hartmann, 1953, 1955; Clancier & Kalmanovitch, 1984; Roudinesco, 1993).

Winnicott also proved instrumental in helping to establish a psychoanalytic society in Finland with his British colleague, Miss Pearl King, through visiting and offering supervisory seminars on a number of occasions. Additionally, he undertook two large lecture tours to the United States of America, one in October, 1962, and another in October, 1963. We know from Winnicott's (1963c) own writings that at least one patient experienced some distress at his departure on these trips. He also returned to the United States of America on at least two further occasions, in October 1967 and then, finally, in November 1968, to address the New York Psychoanalytic Society (Winnicott, 1969b), and other institutions (Winnicott, 1968g; Robert Langs, personal communication, 21 April 1994).

Winnicott lectured in Scotland at various times. Continental appearances included lectures in Paris, Rome, Geneva, Copenhagen, Lisbon, Helsinki, and Amsterdam. Furthermore, he delivered at least one talk in Canada. He also gave numerous lectures in England to a vast variety of organizations. (See Appendix B.)

In the broader psychotherapeutic community, Winnicott worked tirelessly to promote worthy organizations. For example, he became one of the leading supporters in the development of the Association of Psychotherapists, the forerunner of the British Association of Psychotherapists (Scarlett, 1991). He also served on the Board of the Clinic for Nervous and Difficult Children, headed by Dr Margaret Lowenfeld, one of the truly independent pioneers of the discipline of Child Psychotherapy in Great Britain (Urwin, 1988; Davis, 1991), and he derived great satisfaction from helping his colleagues on a regular basis. He supplied numerous letters of recommendation for younger colleagues who applied to psychotherapy training programmes (e.g. Winnicott, 1964d); he wrote in support of the widow of a deceased psychoanalytic colleague, to help obtain money from the Royal Medical Benevolent Fund for the surviving family members (Winnicott, 1957i), he assisted scholars with their research (e.g. Roazen, 1975), and he also helped at least one colleague to arrange for a visa to live in Britain (Balkányi, 1957). He also received many requests for referrals from young practitioners who wanted patients for their private practices (e.g. Carr, 1963; Lomas, 1963), and Winnicott would frequently oblige.

Winnicott's honours included election in 1944 as a Fellow of the Royal College of Physicians (F.R.C.P.); he also received Fellowships of the Royal Society of Medicine and of the British Psychological Society. Moreover, he held the additional posts as Chairman of the Medical Section of the British Psychological Society, as President of the Paediatrics Section of the Royal Society of Medicine, and as President of the Association for Child Psychology and Psychiatry. By 1955, he had also become a lecturer in the Child Development Department at the Institute of Education of the University of London. Finally, in 1968 he also became an Honorary Member of the Royal Medico–Psychological Association, and winner of the coveted James Spence Medal for Paediatrics, an award named for one of Winnicott's personal heroes, Professor Sir James Spence, a distinguished children's doctor from Newcastle-upon-Tyne, who insisted that mothers and newborn babies should not be separated at birth—hitherto a very common procedure on maternity wards (Winnicott, 1948b). The Finnish Psychoanalytical Society also honoured Winnicott by inviting him to become an Honorary Member. These various elections and prizes indicate the respect that Winnicott engendered among his peers in psychoanalysis as well as in general medicine.

Undoubtedly, Winnicott must have had fantasies about receiving a Knighthood from Queen Elizabeth II; after all, his father, Frederick Winnicott, had earned a Knighthood, and Donald Winnicott must have regarded his own pioneering work on child welfare as rather more important than his father's civic activities. Towards the end of his life, Winnicott wrote a paper about the monarchy, and he mentioned that he lived quite near

Buckingham Palace. We do know that he had thoughts of meeting Queen Elizabeth II on his mind, and in his paper on "The Place of the Monarchy" (Winnicott, 1970c, p. 266), he even permitted himself to muse about the Monarch, noting that "she is a human being whom I might see in her car as I sit waiting in a taxi while she emerges from Buckingham Palace to perform some function which is part of her living out the role assigned to her by fate". Unfortunately, neither Winnicott, nor anyone else for that matter, has ever earned a Knighthood for services to psychoanalysis.

CHAPTER SEVEN

Private life

This sketch of Winnicott's biography has surveyed the basic contours of his life, but it may be of some additional value to learn more about Winnicott the *man*, thereby providing students with a greater appreciation of the psychobiographical antecedents of his developmental psychology and his contributions to the practice of psychoanalysis and psychotherapy. Physically, Winnicott had a fairly average body build, standing only 5'6" or 5'7" in height—most of my informants have estimated it at 5'7" (e.g. Barbara Dockar-Drysdale, personal communication, 1 October 1994). He had a slender waistline, and perhaps a somewhat largish head, so that he would resemble a garden "gnome" (Harry Karnac, personal communication, 3 August 1994; Malcolm Pines, personal communication, 3 October 1994), or an "impish elf" (Peter Giovacchini, personal communication, 10 July 1994). One of Lotte Meitner-Graf's famous photographs of Winnicott, conveniently reprinted in Anne Clancier and Jeannine Kalmanovitch's (1984) book about him, provides the best glimpse of his gnome-like bearing. He also had bright blue eyes, which could look rather "steely" and penetrating at times (Ruth Karnac, personal communication, 3 August 1994). His face bore the signs of a full and eventful life, furrowed with lines and craggy crevices (Malcolm Pines, personal communication, 3 October 1994). He seems to have worn his hair in a conservative style, though often on the longish side (Michael Fordham, personal communication, 13 February 1994), and he had a habit of stroking it from time to time (Irmi Elkan, personal communication, 6 October 1994). Sartorially, Winnicott dressed in fine suits. Upon receiving a new suit from his tailors, S. B. Rosenberg Limited in Southend-on-Sea, in Essex, he would write to his personal tailor, Cyril Rosenberg: *"The jacket and trousers arrived safely and I am glad to have them. They are very beautifully made, and I shall try to live up to their standard"* (Winnicott, 1966f). Nonetheless, in view of his frantically busy lifestyle, Winnicott often looked "crumpled" (Susanna Isaacs Elmhirst, personal communication, 30 May 1994; Harry Karnac, personal communication, 3 August 1994). He also tended to twist his limbs in various distracted and pretzel-like shapes, prompting his colleague Charles Rycroft to speak about Winnicott's odd "posturology" (Charles Rycroft, personal communication, 29 November 1993).

As we know, Winnicott worked very hard throughout his life, but he could also enjoy himself immensely, particularly during the course of his second marriage. In 1957, Dr Michael Balint, one of Winnicott's most valued and sympathetic colleagues, presented him with a copy of his newly published book *The Doctor, His Patient and the Illness* (Balint, 1957). Soon thereafter, Winnicott (1957k) wrote to Balint: *"I took your book to the south of France with me but somehow could not bring myself to remember that there was such a thing as psychology while I was away."* Winnicott's ability to forget about psychology from time to time stood him in good stead and permitted him to rest somewhat between long periods of challenging and demanding psychotherapeutic work and other professional commitments. Throughout his career, he took frequent holidays, not only to foreign countries, but often to Plymouth to visit his sisters and his childhood home, Rockville.

Of his many hobbies, Winnicott derived most pleasure from music, especially singing and playing the piano. Both of Winnicott's sisters exhibited great musical talent, and the Winnicott family home in Plymouth must have encouraged an appreciation of song (interview with Clare Winnicott: Neve, 1983). Winnicott himself played on a grand piano (Susanna Isaacs Elmhirst, personal communication, 30 May 1994). He owned stacks of music, and he particularly liked the compositions of Bach, Beethoven (especially the Late String Quartets), and even the Beatles (Clare Winnicott, 1978). He also adored the songs of the chanteuse Juliette Greco, and he would often purchase her records from the gramophone recordings section of Harry Karnac's bookshop in Gloucester Road (Harry Karnac, personal communication, 3 August 1994). Juliette Greco, a pouting and alienated French singer and songwriter, popular with the Beatnik movement, produced many albums featuring her well-known renditions of ballads such as "Déshabillez-moi", "Lola la rengaine", "Si tu t'imagines", and "L'Enfant secret" (which she had co-authored). This diversity of musical tastes offers us yet another indication of Winnicott's tremendous open-mindedness. Winnicott had few free hours in his hectic day for playing on the piano, so he had to steal brief moments whenever he could. Clare Winnicott recalled that "he would often dash up to the piano and play for a moment between patients, and invariably he celebrated the end of a day's work by a musical outburst fortissimo" (Clare Winnicott, 1978, pp. 30–31). Winnicott could play fairly well, sight-reading the sonatas of Brahms; and he especially enjoyed performing pieces by Bach, undoubtedly his favourite composer (interview with Clare Winnicott: Neve, 1983). His close friend, Mrs Barbara Dockar-Drysdale (personal communication, 13 July 1991), told me that Winnicott loved to sing to himself whenever he walked up or down the stairs, preferring the church hymns of his Wesleyan Methodist childhood. Another colleague, Mrs Marion Milner (personal communication, 24 October 1987), remembered that Winnicott had long harboured a secret ambition to write a musical comedy, a wish that clearly captures his playfulness and lightheartedness. In addition to playing piano, he also enjoyed the recorder—but he had to dispense with these pleasures when he developed arthritis in later years (Margaret I. Little, personal communication, 25 May 1985). His interest in music had begun at a very early age, and he always encouraged other people in the development of their own musical talents. Phyllis Fenn (personal communication, 18 September 1994), the daughter of Sir Frederick Winnicott's housekeeper, recalled that as a little girl she used to visit the Winnicott family home; Donald would, in typical fashion, patiently listen to her play the piano, and he urged her to continue with her music. He would even pepper his lectures with musical references. Irmi Elkan (personal communication, 6 October 1994) remembered that Winnicott once stunned an audience of social work trainees at the London School of Economics and Political Science by speaking about the ostensibly frivolous musical "The Boyfriend", by the composer and lyricist Sandy Wilson, as a perfect example of the difference between id relationships and ego-relatedness!

In the moments that remained, he read poetry (Clare Winnicott, 1978) and *The Times* newspaper, often expressing his views in letters to the Editor (e.g. Winnicott 1946, 1966e). He became very happy when Clare recited poems to him—in particular, the works of T. S. Eliot and Dylan Thomas, as well as Shakespeare's sonnets. Additionally, Winnicott felt a strong affinity for the moving work of William Wordsworth (cf. Turner, 1988; John Padel, personal communication, 4 December 1991). And he especially loved "The Owl and the Pussycat" by Edward Lear, eventually memorizing it himself (Clare Winnicott, 1978).

For drinking, he preferred Guinness (Winnicott, 1961g), and towards the end of his life he poured malt whisky into his tea, for medicinal purposes (Khan, 1988). During his first marriage, Winnicott maintained a fisherman's cottage on the West coast of Wales, which must have afforded him many periods of leisure; he would also loan the cottage to good friends from time to time—for example, to Dr Michael Fordham (personal communication, 13 February 1994). He also had a great fondness for smoking, sometimes twisting his arm all the way around the back of his neck and then puffing as if in an absent-minded haze (Charles Rycroft, personal communication, 29 November 1993; Harry Karnac, personal communication, 3 August 1994). Winnicott also took a certain amount of pride in his garden, which flourished on the roof of his house at Chester Square (Peter Giovacchini, personal communication, 10 July 1994).

When reading for pleasure, Winnicott preferred autobiographical and biographical writings, a perfectly consistent choice in view of his fascination with the life histories of his patients. He described himself as addicted to autobiographical works (Winnicott, 1967a), and he also enjoyed writing book reviews of works that he had read (e.g. Winnicott, 1941b, 1941c, 1951a, 1959a; Winnicott & Khan, 1953). From time to time, he might also write a preface to a book written by one of his colleagues (e.g. Winnicott, 1969d). Harry Karnac (1991, p. 27) recalled that, "at one stage, he was buying a lot of biographies and autobiographies of all sorts of people in different parts of the world and various periods in history. Since many of the subjects of these works struck me as rather undistinguished, I once let my curiosity get the better of me and asked him if there was some underlying reason for this choice of reading. 'Not really,' he replied. 'I only read them until they reach the age of four or five—after that they become far too boring'" (Harry Karnac, personal communication, 3 August 1994).

Winnicott first met Harry Karnac around 1958, after Karnac had begun recommending his books to customers. Winnicott came into the bookshop one day and thanked Mr Karnac for waving his banner—in other words, for promoting his publications. Winnicott enjoyed books so much that he often spent many hours on Saturday afternoons in the Gloucester Road offices of Harry Karnac, after having finished his morning clinic at the Paddington Green Children's Hospital. The two men became firm friends, and they would retreat to Karnac's private room in the bookshop and discuss general topics such as literature. Occasionally, Clare Winnicott would telephone to enquire what had kept her husband from coming back home (Harry Karnac, personal communication, 3 August 1994).

Winnicott's favourite television programmes included "Match of the Day", which broadcast highlights of sporting events, and "Come Dancing", which demonstrated ballroom techniques (Clare Winnicott, 1978). He also adored dressing up and dining out, and he very much delighted in his occasional forays into painting, regularly producing hundreds of Christmas cards each year by hand. As Christmas approached, Winnicott would often stay awake until 2.00 a.m., finishing his artwork. When Clare suggested that he had done enough for one night, Donald retorted, "Yes, I know, but I like painting" (quoted in Clare Winnicott, 1978, p. 30). Winnicott made many other journeys into the world of art. Dr Susanna Isaacs Elmhirst (personal communication, 30 May 1994), Winnicott's Clinical Assistant and later successor at the Paddington Green Children's Hospital, informed me that Winnicott obtained a picture of the acacia tree that stood in the hospital grounds, and he had this picture hung in a corridor of the building. Apparently, Winnicott loved trees, and he harboured a particular penchant for this acacia, even arranging for a preservation order to prevent the tree from being cut down.

He also enjoyed riding a bicycle at fast speeds (interview with Clare Winnicott: Neve, 1983)—a perpetual indulgence in child-like behaviour, though he would often drive his automobile quite slowly, being rather occupied by deep thoughts or engaging in conversations with his passenger (Gillespie, 1971b). He seems to have had very little time for any other athletic pursuits, however, and he may have regarded this as a loss, especially in view of his adolescent penchant for sporting activities; but he never mentioned any regrets about this, as far as I can ascertain.

Donald Winnicott (1957j) maintained an account with Midland Bank, at the branch on Wigmore Street. As for his health care and maintenance, he attended the surgery of Dr Norman Chisholm, a General Practitioner who worked at 1, Greenhill, on Hampstead High Street. Winnicott became a patient of Dr Chisholm's practice when he and Alice Winnicott lived in nearby Pilgrim's Lane. Although Winnicott moved to Belgravia thereafter, he still remained one of Dr Chisholm's patients, and eventually he registered his second wife, Clare, with this practice as well. Dr Chisholm had worked for a time with Dr Michael Balint (1957), the psychoanalyst who conducted pioneering work by introducing psychological concepts into the field of general medical practice. In view of Chisholm's psychological sophistication, Winnicott no doubt remained loyal to him. After Chisholm's retirement, Donald and Clare Winnicott sought medical treatment from Norman Chisholm's successor, a physician of Irish extraction called Dr James Finbarr Hoare.

As for his personality, most people who have reminisced about Winnicott have described him variously as a "loveable sort of man" (Lawrence Goldie, personal communication, 6 December 1990), "fair-minded" (James, 1991), possessed of an "extraordinary generosity" (Gillespie, 1971b, p. 228), "solitary, wilful and extremely modest" (Khan, 1971a, p. 225), "extraordinarily warm and friendly" (Robin Skynner, personal communication, 20 April 1994), "beguiling" (Michael Fordham, personal communication, 13 February 1994), and characterized by an "irrepressible ebullience of creative thought" (Khan, 1988, p. 2). One colleague described him, quite refreshingly, as "a *yeasty* person" (quoted in Little, 1981, p. 268). Professor Phyllis Grosskurth (1986, p. 399), a historian of psychoanalysis who interviewed many individuals who had known Winnicott personally, noted that "Almost everyone uses the word 'pixie' to describe him." Dr Josephine Lomax-Simpson (1990, p. 85), a psychoanalyst who knew Winnicott, called him an "elf-like ethereal man"— a sentiment echoed by Professor Paul Roazen (1994), another historian of psychoanalysis, who remembered Winnicott as a "wonderful pixie of a man", whose vibrancy has been ill served by the rather dour bust of Winnicott sculpted by the artist Oscar Nemon in his studio at St. James's Palace. This statue now stands on the stairway of Mansfield House, the home of The British Psycho-Analytical Society in New Cavendish Street, in the heart of Central London. Not surprisingly, it seems that Winnicott used to play with Nemon's plaster and make shapes out of it when he went to the sculptor's studio on Saturday mornings for posing sessions (Rodman, 1987c).

Apart from these glowing and revealing posthumous tributes, at least four other aspects of Winnicott's personality stand out quite sharply, and these all proved important in his work— namely, his modesty, his eccentricity, his sense of humour, and his capacity for sadism. As a modest man, Winnicott often began his public talks with remarks of this nature: "It might happen that nothing that I say will have any effect at all on what you do when you go back to your work" (Winnicott, 1968d, p. 2). He could accept that his insights might be irrelevant to somebody else, just as readily as he could admit to his patients that he did not understand something that they might have said. Once, in 1969, Winnicott had accepted an invitation to supervise a junior analyst, Dr Ishak Ramzy, at a conference, in front of an audience of psychoanalysts from around the world. However, at the last minute the seasoned seventy-three-year-old Dr Winnicott decided to enliven the proceedings by asking the younger analyst to supervise *him*, so that Winnicott could then present some new clinical material from an intriguing child-analytic case (Ramzy, 1978). Most aged clinicians would be horrified at the thought of abandoning their authority to a student or to a trainee, but

Winnicott could and did do so with considerable aplomb. Dr Michael Eigen, an American psychoanalyst, met Winnicott in the mid-1960s, whilst still a young post-graduate student; yet in spite of his youthful status, Eigen (1991, p. 85) noted that, "He treated me like an equal, like *someone*." And Harry Karnac also remembered Winnicott for his special modesty (personal communication, 3 August 1994). As the proprietor of Karnac Books for many years, Mr Karnac met many of the analysts whose books he sold in his shop. The authors would invariably pester Karnac to enquire as to how many copies of their works he had sold, but Winnicott never did this, and Harry Karnac found this rather "commendable" of him.

This modest analyst could also be eccentric and absent-minded, invariably crossing the street without looking (Clancier, 1984a). And when he found himself in the driver's seat, he often did not concentrate on the road. Dr William Gillespie (1971b, p. 228), a psychoanalytic colleague of long-standing wrote: "Especially I recall being given lifts in his veteran two-seater Rolls, which he would allow to drift along at 10 to 15 miles an hour while he talked and thought profoundly." It seems that Winnicott immersed himself so fully in deep and creative ideas that every now and then he had to sacrifice his awareness of some of the more mundane aspects of life.

And he could be very funny and very playful in his writing. At first glance, much of Winnicott's prose—especially his technical papers—appears somewhat dry and bloodless, but he certainly becomes funnier, and his wry sense of humour more apparent, with each subsequent re-reading. In his essay on the female birth-control pill, he begins by remarking, "Actually, you know, I've never had the Pill" (Winnicott, 1969e, p. 195)—rather an obvious statement, but very amusing when read in the right mood. We might also consider his advice to colleagues in his book *Playing and Reality*: "When the analyst knows that the patient carries a revolver, then, it seems to me, this work cannot be done" (Winnicott, 1971a, p. 92, fn. 1). Once again, Winnicott resorted to the self-evident to captivate and to amuse his interlocutors, as well as to impart a message of absolutely vital importance to psychotherapists.

Of course, nobody could be more nurturant and facilitative than Donald Winnicott; as we have noted, he enjoyed helping other people, and he did so unflinchingly during his whole career. He not only furnished untold letters of recommendation with unflagging cheerfulness and taught innumerable seminars with zest, but he enjoyed watching others develop. Professor E. James Anthony (personal communication, 18 May 1994) has furnished us with a splendidly relevant description: "He was the chairman of the examining board of the British Psychoanalytic Institute that assembled to assess my competence to become a member of the Institute. My membership paper was accepted and my answers to questions apparently passed muster, but what I recall very distinctly was his encouraging smile and his repeated efforts to set me (a nervous 'me') at ease. I also remember clinging to a piece of paper containing what I thought to be crucial concepts until it was soaked with sweat and I imagined wondering whether he perceived me with his remarkably observant eyes as clinging for dear life to my transitional object!" Another striking example of Winnicott's passion for being helpful might be his willingness to pay for the psychoanalytic treatment of a woman known as "Susan"—a very regressed patient who underwent a lengthy analysis with Mrs Marion Milner (letter to Judith Hughes, 8 April 1986, in Hughes, 1989; cf. Milner, 1969).

It would be sheer folly to assume that Winnicott had no unflattering qualities. In particular, he could be grandiose from time to time. Dr Charles Rycroft knew him well and worked closely with him as Acting Training Secretary in The Institute of Psycho-Analysis in 1949, during one of Winnicott's many bouts of cardiac illness. The two men also sustained an extensive correspondence, some of which survives to this day (e.g. Winnicott. 1953g, 1954c, 1955g, 1956g). Rycroft actually went so far as to describe Winnicott as "a crypto-prima donna" (interview, 22 December 1981, cited in Grosskurth, 1986, p. 399). Dr Rycroft (personal communication, 29 November 1993) remembered that when he attended Winnicott's private seminars at Chester Square and spoke his mind, Winnicott did not renew the invitation to return.

Furthermore, Winnicott could be rather frank and firm when the occasion demanded. He once wrote to Charles Rycroft about a paper delivered by a mutual colleague at The British Psycho-Analytical Society: *"Actually you missed a terrible evening—one of the worst I have experienced for a long time"* (Winnicott, 1956g). As another instance, it seems that at some point during the Second World War, Melanie Klein approached Winnicott and asked him to write a physician's letter that would exempt her son Eric Clyne from military service. (Erich Klein had changed his name to Eric Clyne in 1937, on the advice of Nathan Isaacs, husband of the psychoanalyst Susan Isaacs [Grosskurth, 1986]). Winnicott replied resolutely that he would write no such missive, and he added further that it would do Eric a power of good to serve his King and his country—or, if one reads between the lines, he seemed to imply that Eric Clyne would benefit from a period of separation from his overpowering mother (Charles Rycroft, personal communication, 29 November 1993). And Winnicott could be quite verbally brutal at times. He told one of his patients that he really hated her abusive mother (Little, 1985); and his paediatric colleague, Professor John Davis, reported that Winnicott once described a psychologically abusive parent in the following manner: "If that man were my patient, I would feel sorry for him but as he is my patient's father, I simply regard him as evil" (quoted in Davis, 1993b, p. 98). Furthermore, Anna Freud (1973, p. 285) reported that Winnicott "wrote such a hostile and denigrating review of one of my books for an official journal here that it was refused. And afterwards he said that he was sorry, he did not know why he had done it, he really liked the book. So that is how it is."

Overall, Winnicott's inner strengths permitted him to be "chirpy" (Davis, 1993a, p. 96), "puzzling, even irritating" (Johns, 1991), a "truthful person" (Little, 1985, p. 23), and "the diametrical opposite of a bore" (Tizard, 1971, p. 227). Mrs Beta Copley (personal communication, 20 October 1994), a child psychotherapist, found him a fount of generosity who helped his students at every turn. Furthermore, his unique range of qualities and resources shed illumination and insight among all those who knew him. He also had the capacity to live life to the very fullest, soaking up each new experience and then integrating new ideas and insights into his character structure in a very particular way.

Illness and death

Towards the late 1960s, Winnicott certainly began to slow down. By this time he had already suffered several heart attacks, and he started to look very old and craggy. In 1963, after forty years of service, he had to retire from his post at the Paddington Green Children's Hospital. This caused Winnicott considerable disappointment, and he wrote to his colleague, Dr John Rawlings Rees, that "I have been retired from Paddington Green because of my great age!" (Winnicott, 1963j). In compensation, he received the title of Honorary Consulting Physician, which he used from time to time. On one occasion, he returned to "The Green" (as he called it) to pay a visit to Dr Susanna Isaacs (now Dr Susanna Isaacs Elmhirst), the physician who had succeeded him. Winnicott entered the building without an appointment, and apparently the new secretary at the hospital did not recognize him, and she announced to Dr Isaacs, "There's a Doctor Winnicott to see you." Susanna Isaacs Elmhirst (personal communication, 30 May 1994) realized that Winnicott may have felt hurt at not having been properly acknowledged at the institution where he had worked so diligently for four decades, and so she apologized on behalf of her secretary when she saw him.

Nevertheless, in spite of his retirement from the National Health Service, Winnicott continued to work with extreme vigour on various clinical cases, writing projects, and administrative tasks. In particular, he seems to have derived very great pleasure from hosting in his home a weekly seminar for professional colleagues and for trainees, at which case material would be presented and discussed. The audience included a large number of young students from the Child Psychotherapy course at the Tavistock Clinic and from the Child Analysis course at the Hampstead Child-Therapy Clinic. Senior psychoanalysts, such as Dr Paula Heimann, found a real haven at Winnicott's seminars, and she attended regularly after the breakdown of her relationship with Melanie Klein (Grosskurth, 1986). Even Dr Ronald D. Laing (1958) joined in the proceedings during the early part of his short-lived career in psychoanalysis. On most occasions, Winnicott would present a case history of a child patient, and sometimes other members of the seminar would share clinical material as well. Winnicott rarely prepared a formal agenda for the seminars; instead, he would respond to the current preoccupations of the group members and provide relevant case histories (Simon Meyerson, personal communication, 26 October 1994). One regular participant at the seminars, Miss Rosalie Kerbekian (personal communication, 8 May 1993), then a trainee Educational Psychologist at the Tavistock Clinic, recalled that Winnicott used to serve cherries to the students. He also delighted Miss Kerbekian by commenting upon an especially pretty dress that she wore to one of the seminars. Another trainee, Miss Silvia Oclander, remembered that Winnicott would speak personally to the students at times, expressing sad feelings about never having had any children of his own (Silvia Oclander-Gordon, personal communication, 14 December 1991).

Mr Donald Campbell (personal communication, 2 May 1994), a Training Analyst at The Institute of Psycho-Analysis and a senior Member of The British Psycho-Analytical Society, recalled with great clarity his visits to Dr Winnicott's seminars in 1969 and 1970. Apparently, one did not need an invitation to attend; students and practitioners heard about the seminars by word of mouth, and one could pop in to the meetings on a very informal basis. The front door to 87, Chester Square would be left open to allow entry to latecomers. Winnicott would hold court in his well-appointed living room, seated in a stuffed chair, with students settled on the floor or standing at the back. The meetings would always be filled to capacity. According to Campbell (personal communication, 2 May 1994), Winnicott looked like a "little elf", and he held his body in a very childlike manner, often folding his legs underneath him or lounging in his chair with his limbs slung over the armrests—most unusual postures for a senior psychoanalyst. In spite of his elfin demeanour, the seventy-three-year-old Winnicott looked extremely "wizened" and well into his eighties, according to Campbell. He would generally show slides of children's squiggle drawings, and he would ramble on without abiding by any formal timekeeping constraints. Campbell also reported that at one of the meetings an intrepid student asked the aged Dr Winnicott why he continued to work so hard. Winnicott replied directly to the question and told his students that his entire generation of friends had died in the First World War, and that he continued to work so arduously because of survivor guilt.

These seminars proved immensely popular with trainees from various courses and with colleagues from a variety of mental health disciplines. Mr Simon Meyerson (personal communication, 26 October 1994), a clinical psychologist, noted that Winnicott opened both his mind and his heart to the students in a very human and responsive fashion. Everybody who attended these special meetings has recalled how clearly he has remained in their thoughts. No doubt the seminar sessions brought Winnicott much pleasure as well, and they permitted the childless psychoanalyst an opportunity to pass on the kernels of his wisdom to the next generation of colleagues.

On the administrative front, Winnicott devoted much of the 1960s to an important project—namely, raising money so that Oscar Nemon's plaster cast of Sigmund Freud could be bronzed and displayed in a prominent public venue. Efforts to arrange for a suitable statue of Sigmund Freud had begun as early as 1906, when Freud's colleague, Dr Paul Federn, one of the pioneers of Viennese psychoanalysis, had hoped to persuade Freud to pose. Sigmund Freud refused to do so, only relenting some twenty-five years later, when he finally sat for the eminent sculptor, Oscar Nemon. The plaster cast languished in Nemon's possession for many years, and, in 1964, Mrs Penelope Balogh, a psychotherapist from Hampstead, undertook the task of forming a committee to raise money so that the statue could at last be cast in bronze. Mrs Balogh, a great admirer of Donald Winnicott's works, approached him, and eventually Winnicott offered his staunch assistance to this crucial project (Gillespie, 1972). Winnicott agreed to serve as the Chairman of the committee, and Penelope Balogh became Treasurer. Mrs Coles functioned as Secretary, collecting the donations as they trickled in, and a friend, Mr Philip Soper, an accountant, acted as Auditor to the committee. The members of the committee also received assistance from a Mr McBride from the Camden County Council, and from the wife of Kenneth Robinson, the Minister of Health. It soon became clear that the committee would need to raise the princely sum of £10,000 to pay for the cost of bronzing and displaying Nemon's masterwork, and it was decided that the statue should be placed within a half-mile radius of Freud's final home at 20, Maresfield Gardens, London. For the next six years Winnicott would work tirelessly on this project (Gillespie, 1972).

The final years brought other treats as well, including a special black-tie gala dinner held in honour of Winnicott's seventieth birthday in 1966, at Mansfield House, the headquarters of The British Psycho-Analytical Society. Many senior analysts attended, and Winnicott invited his friend Harry Karnac and his wife Ruth as his special guests (Harry Karnac, personal communication, 3 August 1994). The elderly James Strachey delivered a speech at this dinner, recalling the rather impudent young man who had appeared in his consulting room for treatment more than forty years before.

By 1968, Penguin Books had sold some 50,000 copies of Winnicott's paperback collection, *The Child, the Family, and the Outside World* (Winnicott, 1964a), and a party was held for him at this time (Bollas, Davis, & Shepherd, 1993). Winnicott also participated in a formal banquet in 1966, during the course of his second term as President of The British Psycho-Analytical Society, to mark the completion of James Strachey's monumental editing and translation of Freud's (1953–1974) collected writings in English, a magisterial project undertaken in collaboration with Anna Freud, Alix Strachey, and Alan Tyson. As President, Winnicott sat next to Anna Freud at the banquet table. It would not be unreasonable to suppose that Winnicott derived great pleasure from this occasion, particularly in view of the fact that his former analyst, James Strachey, had undertaken the bulk of the translating work.

In April of 1968, shortly before the completion of his second term as President of The British Psycho-Analytical Society, Donald Winnicott renewed his efforts to raise money for the Freud statue. With the assistance of Miss Helen Boxall, an administrator at The Institute of Psycho-Analysis in London, and with aid from her secretarial colleagues, Winnicott wrote to all of the members of The International Psycho-Analytical Association, requesting contributions. By October of 1968, shortly before his lecture tour to New York City, 256 analysts from all over the world had donated some £3,000 to the fund, with another £1,500 promised. The British Psycho-Analytical Society, Winnicott's home institution for more than four decades, pledged a further £1,000 to the cause. Winnicott continued to pester the various psychoanalytic societies around the world for more money for the enterprise (Gillespie, 1972).

Eventually, however, all of Winnicott's hard work and his continuous care-taking of others began to exact its toll. And he did not always look after himself as well as he might have done. When Dr Peter Giovacchini (personal communication, 10 July 1994), a brilliant American psychoanalyst, came to visit Winnicott in London in May of 1968, Winnicott kept Dr and Mrs Giovacchini awake, talking, drinking, and gossiping until the dawn appeared—rather vigorous behaviour for a man seventy-two years of age. Dr Lawrence Goldie (personal communication, 6 December 1990), a classmate of Clare Winnicott's at The Institute of Psycho-Analysis, recalled seeing Donald Winnicott asleep at the wheel of his parked car, with his head hanging heavily, while waiting for Clare to emerge from her evening seminar. Goldie thought that Winnicott might be dead because he looked so unwell at that point. Professor E. James Anthony (personal communication, 18 May 1994), the distinguished child analyst, remembered that when he and Winnicott both went to address a psychoanalytic audience in Rome, Winnicott moved at a very slow pace through the streets of the old Eternal City. And the relative of one of Winnicott's child patients told me that he would often sleep during clinical sessions, presumably from exhaustion and ill health (cf. Little, 1985).

In the last two decades, he had increasingly great problems with his heart, and he suffered a very painful coronary, which nearly killed him, after he had delivered a memorable paper at the New York Psychoanalytic Society (Winnicott, 1969b). Winnicott journeyed to America in 1968 for what proved to be the last time, to speak at various institutions, including the William Alanson White Institute in Manhattan on 8 November (Winnicott, 1968g), the Kings County Hospital in Brooklyn (Robert Langs, personal communication, 21 April 1994), and the venerable New York Psychoanalytic Society towards the end of his visit, on 12 November. This visit caused him terrific agony, on both the personal and the professional front. The New York Psychoanalytic Society, the oldest psychoanalytic organization in the United States, is the equivalent of The British Psycho-Analytical Society in terms of its adherence to the classical values of psychoanalysis. Winnicott had already experienced some anxieties about the sort of reaction that he would encounter from his American counterparts (Eigen, 1991), and he chose to present a paper entitled "The Use of an Object". Apparently, he received a very frosty response from the venerable American analysts who struggled to comprehend Winnicott's prototypically British psychoanalytic vocabulary (Rudnytsky, 1989, 1991; cf. Goldman, 1993); and it seems that he did not in any way defend himself against their fiery criticisms. After the verbal critiques by Dr Bernard Fine, Dr Edith Jacobson, and Dr Samuel Ritvo, three very distinguished American psychoanalysts, Winnicott muttered that he now understood why the Americans had become embroiled in the fighting in Vietnam (Steven J. Ellman, personal communication, 15 May 1992, quoted in Goldman, 1993). After the talk concluded, he returned to his hotel room and had a massive coronary, which kept him stranded in New York City for a time (Eigen, 1991). He developed pulmonary oedema, compounded by an attack of Asian influenza, which he had contracted in Manhattan (Rodman, 1987d), and he had to undergo treatment in the cardiac care unit at the Lenox Hill Hospital on New York City's East Side, nearly dying in the process. He received fine medical attention from his physician in New York, Dr Michael Rosenblüth, a specialist in internal medicine.

Pulmonary oedema can be described as a clinical condition whereby the lungs become filled up with fluid from the bloodstream, resulting either from failure in the left side of the heart or from a fulminating viral or bacterial pneumonia, among other causes. Pulmonary oedema can also be a complication in patients with valvular heart disease. Symptoms can include strain on the heart, fatigue, shortness of breath, difficulty in breathing, sweatiness, strained speech, increased heartbeat, agitation, as well as discomfort while lying down. The patient also turns bluish in colour. The Asian influenza would also have worsened the oedema. No doubt Winnicott's passion for cigarettes had also exacerbated his cardiac condition, not to mention the stress of the visit overseas. He needed two nurses to accompany him on the flight from New York back to London (Kenneth Fenn, personal communication, 18 September 1994), which gives us some indication of the extent of his weakness at that time. Upon his return, Winnicott remarked to a younger colleague that "They will kill me one day", referring to the hostile American analysts (Ved Varma, personal communication, 13 March 1994).

Shortly after he resumed work in London, Winnicott (1969i, p. 181) wrote to the American psychoanalyst, Dr Robert Rodman about the question of the use of an object, noting, *"I have just read a paper on this to the New York Psychoanalytic Society but my ideas are not well formulated in this paper."* This strikes me as a typically masochistic response, and as a rather untrue one as well, because Winnicott stated his ideas with fervent clarity; yet he seems to have taken all the blame upon himself. Anna Freud very kindly wrote to him to enquire about his health at this time, and Winnicott (1969j, p. 185) responded rather tentatively: *"I am grateful to you for your letter which you wrote concerning my illness. Now I am convalescent at home all seems well, but I cannot yet plan for my future professionally."* He then began to discuss the events in New York with Miss Freud, noting:

> *If you were to ask me what about my paper, The Use of an*
> *Object, I would say that the answer is complex. I read the*
> *paper and got considerable personal benefit from the reaction*
> *of the three discussants, so that I am now in process of*
> *rewriting it in a quite different language. The unfortunate*
> *thing was that the three said discussants occupied the whole*
> *of the time so that there could be no response from the very*
> *large audience which collected for some reason unspecified.*
> *There was an internal TV arranged so that the overflow in*
> *the library could watch me, which I thought rather amusing.*
> *Actually I was already ill but I think this was not noticed.*
> [Winnicott, 1969j, p. 185]

To add insult to injury, soon after his return to London someone stole Winnicott's automobile (Winnicott, 1969k).

Dr Robert Langs, the noted American psychoanalyst, heard Winnicott speak to members of his psychoanalytic institute at the Kings County Hospital in Brooklyn at this time, and he told me that he could well understand why Winnicott's paper on "The Use of an Object" had provoked so much hostility from the New York community. In his training in the United States, Langs had learned that patients project their neurotic material onto the figure of the analyst. The analyst, in turn, does little more than interpret this material. Winnicott introduced a much more inter-actional model of treatment, in which the patient would *use* the analyst and would even attempt to *destroy* the analyst in order to maintain some sense of psychic equilibrium. The American prac-titioners of this generation objected to being "used" by their patients in the generous way in which Winnicott had permitted himself to be used; therefore, they attacked him (Robert Langs, personal communication, 21 April 1994). The paper on "The Use of an Object" (Winnicott, 1969b) proved so contentious that Winnicott felt a personal need to work this through in his own writings following the talk, and he did so in a number of manu-scripts (e.g. Winnicott, 1968e, 1968f, 1969f, 1970c, 1971a).

Once Winnicott had settled back into his London routine, he could attend to neglected tasks, such as arranging for the trans-fer of £50 to Dr Michael Rosenblüth, the American specialist who had supervised his treatment in New York. Apparently, Dr Rosenblüth had sent Winnicott no bill for his professional serv-ices, and so Winnicott (1969o) wrote to his bank to wire an honorarium overseas nonetheless. He also began to settle the estate of his first wife, Alice, who had died on 19 November 1969. Winnicott (1969n) contacted his bank manager to inform him: "*Sadly I have to report the death of Alice my first wife. I am letting you know of this because of the matter of alimony which has been paid automatically by yourselves monthly.*"

Winnicott (1969e) felt sad that he could not attend the International Psycho-Analytical Congress of The International Psycho-Analytical Association in Rome, and he reported that he had dreamed about having attended a large conference—no doubt a typical wish-fulfilment. After all, Winnicott had in fact participated in most of the bi-annual international psychoanalytic gatherings over the last two decades, and he probably missed his many colleagues and friends from overseas. The trip to America and its sequelae still continued to torment Winnicott throughout the year of 1969. The American astronauts had landed on the moon on 20 July 1969, and some months later Winnicott found himself staring at the moon and then suddenly realized, to his increasingly xenophobic dismay, "Oh damn, there's an American flag on it!" (Winnicott, 1969e, p. 207). In a poem on the "Moon Landing", Winnicott (1969e, p. 208) referred to the astronauts as "Clever devils", and then he vowed that "My moon has no flag" (Winnicott, 1969e, p. 209).

As the end approached, Winnicott laboured with some urgency to put his remaining typescripts in order so that they might soon be prepared for publication (Khan, 1988). Winnicott's amanuensis, Masud Khan, made many trips to Chester Square to help his mentor with the editing process; in particular, the two men devoted a good deal of time to the preparation of Winnicott's (1971a) book, *Playing and Reality*. And Mrs Coles, his secretary, typed and re-typed endless drafts of his papers. Khan (1988, p. 26) remembered that Winnicott became very tired during their working meetings: "Quite often he would drift into a somnolent quiet, almost snoozing." He also used the last months to work on his autobiography, *Not Less Than Everything*, which he never completed (Clare Winnicott, 1978). In his zeal to finish his writings, Winnicott often took on too many commitments, and he experienced difficulties honouring his various obligations. Professor E. James Anthony (personal communication, 18 May 1994), the eminent child psychiatrist and psychoanalyst, had to coax him a great deal to obtain Winnicott's (1970a) manuscript on "The Mother–Infant Experience of Mutuality" for the book that he was editing with Dr Therese Benedek, *Parenthood: Its Psychology and Psychopathology* (Anthony & Benedek, 1970).

In spite of many difficulties and much pain, Winnicott preserved his intelligence and his clinical acumen until the very end. Roughly six months before his death, he facilitated a seminar with a group of young Anglican priests, who asked the aged psychoanalyst to help them better understand how they might differentiate between people who could benefit from pastoral care and those who required more extensive psychiatric intervention. Winnicott paused before replying to this request, and then he told the priests: "If a person comes and talks to you and, listening to him, you feel he is *boring* you, then he is sick, and needs psychiatric treatment. But if he sustains your interest, no matter how grave his distress or conflict, then you can help him alright" (quoted in Khan, 1986, p. 1). Masud Khan (1986, p. 1), Winnicott's trusted editor and a psychoanalytic practitioner in his own right, observed: "I was deeply impressed by the wisdom of Winnicott's reply, and since then, whenever I see a person in consultation, this statement of his is never out of my mind."

As the weeks wore on, Winnicott's hair continued to fall out; his teeth started to rot as well, and he ultimately resorted to dentures. He also suffered from fretful, interrupted sleep, and he treated himself by gazing at the moon, which he enjoyed (Winnicott, 1969e). Furthermore, the aged psychoanalyst drank malt whisky, diluted with water, believing that the alcohol would take effect more quickly in this way, and he also put shots of malt whisky in his tea, to help to soothe the frequent angina pains (Khan, 1988), which would incapacitate him for days at a time. In his characteristically self-effacing manner, he spoke of himself as feeling merely "indisposed" (quoted in Khan, 1988, p. 33). These cardiac difficulties had plagued Winnicott for many years, and he turned to an American psychoanalyst, Dr Alfred Flarsheim, a former specialist in internal medicine, for help with his medical management (Peter Giovacchini, personal communication, 10 July 1994). Of greatest importance, Donald and Clare began to embark on the difficult but necessary psychological preparation for his impending death. He wrote a poem called

"Sleep", which dates from this period, and it demonstrates his ability to think expansively about mortality:

Let down your tap root
to the centre of your soul
Suck up the sap
from the infinite source
of your unconscious
And
Be evergreen.

[quoted in Clare Winnicott, 1978, p. 32]

By September of 1970, he became increasingly concerned about the fate of the Freud statue. It may be that Winnicott sensed his own impending death, and he strove to ensure the erection of Nemon's statue, as a symbol of immortality for Freud and, through the process of identification, for himself as well. During his convalescence in New York, the Board and Council of The British Psycho-Analytical Society and The Institute of Psycho-Analysis had agreed to take over the responsibility for the statue if Winnicott should ultimately prove unable to complete the final arrangements, but Winnicott insisted upon finishing this project to his own satisfaction. He sent out one final appeal to all the members of The International Psycho-Analytical Association for funds, and in the autumn of 1970, the statue could at last be launched. On 2 October 1970, Winnicott presided over the special unveiling ceremony, which took place on the green lawn by the Swiss Cottage Centre, not far from Maresfield Gardens. Numerous dignitaries attended, as well as psychoanalysts from all over the planet. Many members of the Freud family also participated in this special event, including several of Freud's great-grandchildren, who actually removed the wrappings from the statue. Other guests included the Mayor of the London Borough of Camden, who accepted the statue as a gift to the residents of that region of London; and Mrs Peter Glauber, an old friend of the late Paul Federn, the analyst who had originally encouraged Freud to sit for a sculpture portrait (Gillespie, 1972).

The French psychoanalyst, Dr Anne Clancier (1984b, p. 137), attended the festivities, and she remembered Winnicott's appearance at that time: "I, too, met him shortly before his death. It was at the inauguration of the statue of Freud. He was standing next to me while the speeches were being made: it was very cold and his cheeks and lips were blue. I knew he had a bad heart and I was afraid throughout the ceremony that he might die at any moment. He survived it however." Shortly thereafter, Winnicott even seemed to improve slightly, and he spoke in fine fettle at the funeral of his psychoanalytic colleague, Dr Walter G. Joffe, himself a former President of The British Psycho-Analytical Society.

The winter of 1970–1971 must have been painful for Winnicott. He had begun to say goodbye to his friends and colleagues. Yet in spite of his increasingly evident decline, he refused to stop work or to slow down, and he delivered his last public lectures, including a talk on "Cure" to a group of doctors and nurses at St. Luke's Church in Hatfield on 18 October 1970 (Winnicott, 1970b) and another on "Residential Care as Therapy", The David Wills Lecture, for the Association of Workers for Maladjusted Children, on 23 October 1970 (Winnicott, 1984b). He also received two exciting and prestigious lecture invitations in the final days of his life—notably, the opportunity to deliver the fifteenth annual Frieda Fromm-Reichmann Memorial Lecture, sponsored by The Washington School of Psychiatry in the United States of America (Weigert, 1970), as well as the chance to serve as the keynote speaker at The Association for the Psychiatric Study of Adolescents to be held in Guildford, Surrey (Meyerson, 1970). But Winnicott died before he could deliver these talks. Charles Rycroft (personal communication, 29 November 1993) has postulated that Winnicott suffered from an identification with the martyred Jesus Christ, masochistically torturing himself with more and more tasks. Winnicott himself knew that he had only a short time to live, and when he addressed a group of nurses in Cambridge, he prefaced his talk with an announcement that if he should drop dead in the middle of his speech, the nurses ought not to feel guilty about it (David Holbrook, personal communication, 8 February 1994). Winnicott spoke about his impending death with his students as well. Rosalie Kerbekian (personal communication, 8 May 1993) mentioned that Winnicott used to urge his students to telephone first before arriving for the seminars in the forthcoming term, in case he should have died. He told his younger colleagues that they would be very distressed if they should arrive and see his body being removed in a hearse.

Winnicott continued to use the final months of his life to prepare for death. His writing from the latter part of 1970 offers every indication that he knew that he would soon be dead. Indeed, he began his lecture on "Residential Care as Therapy", on 23 October 1970, with the following sentences: "A great deal of growing is growing downwards. If I live long enough I hope I may dwindle and become small enough to get through the little hole called dying" (Winnicott, 1984b, p. 220). But, mixed with the honest ability to stare death in the face, he often resorted to understandable defensive postures as well. On 7 January 1971, Winnicott (1971d) wrote a letter to Madame Jeannine Kalmanovitch, his French translator. As one looks at the letter, scribbled in Winnicott's own sprawling hand eighteen days before his decease, one can see quite clearly that Winnicott committed a death-orientated parapraxis. He wrote the date of composition at the top of the stationery, but he erred and put down 7.2.71 (in other words, 7 February 1971), instead of 7.1.71. Winnicott then took his heavy ink pen and changed the number 2 into the number 1, thus correcting his own mistake. I do have a strong hunch that the ailing Winnicott knew that he would not live as long as 7 February 1971, and his slip of the pen represented a wish to move the clock forward, perhaps as an expression of a desire to be alive and to cheat death for at least one month more, or possibly even as a yen to die and be done with it already. Years earlier, Winnicott had told his colleague, Mrs Barbara Dockar-Drysdale (1974), that he would rather be dead than live in a state of great illness. No doubt the tension between a life with a weakened heart and death preoccupied him considerably.

In his unfinished autobiography, *Not Less Than Everything*, Winnicott wrote extensively about death. After an epigraph from T. S. Eliot's *Four Quartets*, he continued by jotting down a line of his own composition: "Oh God! May I be alive when I die" (quoted in Clare Winnicott, 1978, p. 19). Once again, Winnicott's desire to be alive at the time of his death may represent his need to triumph over the reality of decay and disintegration. He next began to write in prose:

I died.

It was not very nice, and it took quite a long time as it seemed (but it was only a moment in eternity).

[quoted in Clare Winnicott, 1978, p. 19]

It seems that this whimsical depiction of his own death encapsulated Winnicott's urge to master the experience of dying, which, he sensed, would be quite imminent.

At some point in either November or December of 1970, Winnicott terminated his popular Thursday evening seminars for trainees and colleagues. Mrs Beta Copley (personal communication, 20 October 1994) recalled that Winnicott once spoke of himself as living on "borrowed time", and it seems that the burden had become really too much. On the night of the final seminar, Winnicott and the students discussed case material, and afterwards Clare Winnicott brought out two extremely big bowls, one filled with huge cherries and the other brimming with large strawberries. One of the seminar participants, Simon Meyerson (personal communication, 26 October 1994), a clinical psychologist at the Adolescent Unit of the Tavistock Clinic, commented on the piano in Winnicott's drawing room and asked Winnicott to play something. Dr Winnicott obliged readily, and he not only played the piano, but he burst into song for the students as well. Meyerson could not remember the exact title or the exact words of the ditty that Winnicott sang, but he summarized its essence for me as "My home is your home. Your home is my home." After Winnicott finished his rendition, and people felt quite overjoyed, the assembled gathering applauded the dying Dr Winnicott. Meyerson recalled Winnicott with great affection, very struck by "the infinity of his generosity".

One day, Winnicott went to visit Harry Karnac. Because of Winnicott's frailty, Karnac walked the old analyst to his car at the conclusion of their chat. Winnicott stopped Karnac in the street and produced a camera that one of the "bloody Americans" had given him, presumably during his trip to New York, and said that he really ought to try to use it. He took Karnac's photograph and then pasted it on the Christmas card that he sent him in December of 1970. Harry Karnac never saw Donald Winnicott again (personal communication, 3 August 1994). On

24 December 1970, Winnicott's dear chum from school days, John Alcock, died (Howard & Houghton, 1991)—Winnicott had known Alcock for more than sixty years. A few days later, on 31 December 1970, Winnicott's good friend Dr Michael Balint passed away suddenly, probably from acute ventricular fibrillation. Balint had also struggled with a history of cardiac problems, and his death must have shocked and saddened Winnicott quite considerably. Balint, born in the same year as Winnicott—1896—though several months later, represented in this respect an almost identical chronological sibling. In fact, Balint died on the twenty-second anniversary of the death of Sir Frederick Winnicott. Death seemed to hover all around.

The final days of Winnicott's life brought a series of further disappointments. He had written an outstanding professional paper on the important topic of stress in infancy for an edited volume on *Stresses in Childhood* (Varma, 1973). Outrageously, the commissioning editor at the University of London Press refused to publish Winnicott's article, because she resented his overtly psychoanalytic bias. The editor of the book, Dr Ved Varma, an educational psychologist, tried to assuage Winnicott's wounded pride, especially as he had invited Winnicott to write the article in the first place. Varma had already begun to plan a commemorative festschrift in honour of Winnicott, but this project could not be brought to fruition, for a variety of reasons. On 7 January 1971, Winnicott (1971e) wrote to Dr Varma:

> *Dear Mr Varma,*
>
> *Thank you for your letter + for the m/s returned*
> *I am truly most grateful to you for your generous gesture + am sorry that it could not come to realisation. What you tried to do will always be remembered by me, with pleasure.*
> *May your own affairs prosper—also good wishes for 1971*
> *Yours ever*
>
> *Donald W Winnicott*

This hitherto unpublished letter certainly indicates Winnicott's deep reservoir of tolerance and generosity, especially in view of the fact that Dr Varma had disappointed Winnicott on two separate projects. On the same day, Winnicott (1971d) also wrote to his French translator, Jeannine Kalmanovitch, discussing some of the practicalities of preparing his works for a French reader-ship. This undertaking, too, had various hiccups along the way.

Only a matter of days before his death, Winnicott received a welcome letter of appreciation from Frances Tustin, one of the child psychotherapists who had trained at the Tavistock Clinic. Her mentor, Esther Bick, regarded the liberal views of Winnicott with considerable contempt, and Mrs Bick discouraged her pupils from reading his works (though she did invite him to do some teaching for her students during the late 1950s, as we have already indicated). But after years of scepticism, Frances Tustin found that she really needed Winnicott's work to help her to understand the autistic children she tried to treat, and in par-ticular she profited from Winnicott's (1963a) very useful article on "The Mentally Ill in Your Caseload". Finally, Tustin (personal communication, 22 February 1994) wrote to Winnicott: *"Now that I am more experienced, I very much appreciate your work."* This expression of gratitude from a colleague steeped in the Kleinian tradition must have brought great pleasure to him.

The last hours of Winnicott's own life are rather poignant, and they deserve to be told. On Sunday evening, 24 January, 1971, his stalwart student, editor, and former analysand, Masud Khan, returned to London after a trip abroad. As he sorted through his post, he came upon the page proofs of Winnicott's as yet unpub-lished book, *Playing and Reality* (Winnicott, 1971a), which Khan had helped to prepare. The staff at Tavistock Publications had sent the typeset manuscript to Khan as Winnicott's appointed editor; therefore, Winnicott had not yet seen it. Khan knew that Winnicott would be pleased to hear about the book, and he considered telephoning him but refrained from doing so owing to the lateness of the hour—11.00 p.m. Sadly, Winnicott never received the good news about the impending publication of his new book. Only five hours later, he experienced heart failure, and he died quickly, at 4.00 a.m., on Monday, 25 January (Khan, 1971b; Judy Cooper, personal communication, 14 June 1988). Winnicott spent his last evening alive with his beloved wife, Clare, watching a comic film on television about old cars, entitled *Good Old Summertime*. The *Radio Times* (1971, p. 23) described this brief colour film as "A short diversion, filmed on a summer's day, with two veteran cars, three motorists and five girls". The programme aired on BBC 2 from 9.45 p.m. until 10.00 p.m. When the film ended, Winnicott murmured to Clare, "What a happy-making film!" (interview with Clare Winnicott: Neve, 1983, quoted in Rudnytsky, 1991, p. 193). In all likelihood, these were the last words that Winnicott spoke to his wife. Clare then fell asleep, and when she awoke she found her husband dead, seated on the floor, with his head snuggled on his armchair (Judy Cooper, personal communication, 14 June 1988). He passed away only months before his seventy-fifth birthday, and he was mourned by his widow and by thousands of devoted colleagues and students throughout the world.

The news of Winnicott's death took some time to reach his many international admirers, and prestigious lecture invitations continued to arrive at Chester Square, such as the opportunity to be a distinguished speaker at the forthcoming London meeting of the American College of Neuropsychiatrists (Cox, 1971). Joyce Coles (1971a, 1971b) remained in the employment of the widowed Mrs Winnicott in order to deal with the flurry of correspondence.

Four days after his death, on Friday, 29 January, friends and fellow psychoanalysts congregated at 3.00 p.m. to attend a memorial service, following the cremation at the Golders Green Crematorium in North-West London (Judy Cooper, personal communication, 14 June 1988)—the very venue where Winnicott had delivered a funeral oration for his mentor, the late Dr Ernest Jones (Winnicott, 1958e). The West Chapel at Golders Green was filled with devoted mourners who had come to pay their last respects. Ms Irmi Elkan (personal communication, 6 October 1994), one of the social workers who had worked with Winnicott at the Paddington Green Children's Hospital, recollected recognizing a young boy of twelve or thirteen, seated in the pew in front of her, as a former patient from Winnicott's practice. The child sobbed throughout the whole of the ceremony.

Dr William Gillespie and Professor Peter Tizard, two long-standing colleagues, delivered the funeral addresses, praising Winnicott for his outstanding and unparalleled contributions to psychoanalysis and to paediatrics. Peter Tizard, known to his friends as "Jack", spoke first. He had worked as a junior paediatrician for Winnicott at the Paddington Green Children's Hospital, and hence he had known him rather well over the previous twenty-two years. After introducing himself, Professor Tizard (1971, p. 226) quoted Ben Jonson's appraisal of William Shakespeare:

"I loved the man, and do honour his memory, on this side idolatry, as much as any."

Tizard then admitted that he approached his work for Winnicott with a certain amount of hesitation, having had "a poor opinion of the general usefulness of child psychiatry". But after a time he had realized what great gifts Winnicott possessed, and he reminded his audience that

Donald Winnicott had the most astonishing powers with children. To say that he understood children would to me sound false and vaguely patronizing; it was rather that children understood him and that he was at one with them. [p. 226]

The eulogist then paid tribute to Winnicott's professional work and to his stellar personal qualities, including his capacity for conversation, which Tizard regarded as rather important. He also remembered Winnicott as

a brilliant lecturer and a masterly exponent of what one might call the banana skin theory of laughter—the briefly anticipated disaster which does not take place—and in evoking this kind of laughter he had a comedian's sense of timing. [p. 227]

Tizard found a truly apt means of concluding his remarks, by expressing the view that

A true and vivid remembrance of Donald Winnicott will only last the lifetimes of those who knew him, but I like to think that those who remember us for a brief period of time will do so more kindly because of Donald Winnicott's influence on us. [p. 227]

Dr Gillespie (1971b), a sometime President of both The British Psycho-Analytical Society and of The International Psycho-Analytical Association, who had known Winnicott since 1932, spoke quite movingly:

Many of us here today, who have all too often made the journey to this spot to say a last farewell to one of our friends and colleagues, will feel a very special anguish at having to part in the end with Donald Winnicott, for he held a unique place in the hearts of all who knew him. I say "in the end" because the threat of this loss has been with us for many years. We knew that he would never spare himself in the face of the endless demands made upon him, and that he would probably have succumbed much earlier had it not been for the protective and loving care of his devoted wife, Clare. [p. 227]

Gillespie then proceeded to praise Winnicott for his work as President of The British Psycho-Analytical Society, and for having devoted so many of his "failing energies" (p. 227) to the campaign to erect Oscar Nemon's statue of Sigmund Freud. He concluded his tribute with a summary and an assessment of Winnicott's fine personal qualities and his work as a clinical psychoanalyst, noting that

Although Donald Winnicott was unquestionably pre-eminent as a child expert, he was supreme also as an analyst of adults and could fairly be described as an analyst's analyst, an analyst *of* analysts. [p. 228]

Finally, Gillespie concluded his funerary tribute with a very touching summation:

He had great things to give to psychoanalysis and he gave them unstintingly and with true altruism and unselfishness. We may truly say that he gave his life for his friends and patients. Our farewell to Donald Winnicott should be a heartfelt "Thank you". [p. 228]

Quite fittingly, the corpses of both Sigmund Freud and Melanie Klein had been cremated at this very same establishment years earlier. Thus, Donald Winnicott joined Professor Freud and Mrs Klein in the pantheon of psychoanalytic pioneers, having bequeathed a lifetime of crucial discoveries about the mental life of the child that remain very much in use today among contemporary clinicians.

Once the funeral service had concluded, a group of particularly close friends and colleagues, such as Barbara and Stephen

Dockar-Drysdale, Masud Khan, and others, returned to Chester Square to pay their further respects to the widow. Soon thereafter, an international campaign began to memorialize Winnicott, as he had affected so many people all around the world. Numerous obituaries appeared in a goodly selection of journals, including tributes by Dr William Gillespie (1971a) and by Dr Barbara Woodhead (1971) in the *British Medical Journal.* Masud Khan (1971a) wrote an obituary for *The International Journal of Psycho-Analysis*, published alongside the texts of the funeral tributes by Peter Tizard (1971) and William Gillespie (1971b). Khan's (1971a, p. 226) obituary stressed that, "With his death, psychoanalysis has lost one of its truly creative, courageous and self-critical thinkers." The National Association for Mental Health sponsored a memorial meeting for Winnicott at the Royal College of Physicians, chaired by the psychoanalyst Dr Martin James (Gillespie, 1972). Other organizations also commemorated the great pioneer of child psychiatry and psychoanalysis.

On 19 January 1972, The British Psycho-Analytical Society held a special Memorial Meeting in honour of Winnicott. Several days before the Memorial Meeting, the talented sculptor, Oscar Nemon, arrived at the headquarters of The British Psycho-Analytical Society at Mansfield House on New Cavendish Street to supervise the installation of the bust of Winnicott, which he had completed as a gift to the latter's psychoanalytic colleagues. Nemon arranged for the bust to be placed in the John Rickman Room at Mansfield House, named for one of Winnicott's deceased elder colleagues; and Mr Nemon directed both the placing and the lighting of Winnicott's head to his satisfaction (Klauber, 1972a). Today, Nemon's bust of Winnicott resides on the grand staircase at 63, New Cavendish Street, and one can also admire a reproduction of the sculpture on display in the foyer at the Royal College of Psychiatrists, in Belgrave Square, quite close to Winnicott's old home in Chester Square. The Winnicott Trust had donated this latter bust as a gift.

Many of Winnicott's friends, colleagues, and associates provided tributes at this special Memorial Meeting. Dr William Gillespie (1972), Mrs Marion Milner (1972), Mr Masud Khan (1972), and Dr Barbara Woodhead (1972), all senior analysts, delivered the principal speeches, and a number of other psychoanalysts, notably, Miss Charlotte Balkányi (1972), Miss Pearl

King (1972), Dr John Klauber (1972b), Dr Margaret Little (1972), and Mrs Edna Oakeshott (1972) made shorter contributions. A handful of distinguished guests also shared their reminiscences of Dr Winnicott, and these included Dr Mildred Creak (1972), the eminent child psychiatrist renowned for her work on the childhood psychoses, Dr Michael Fordham (1972), the pre-eminent Jungian analyst; Mrs Mary Waddington (1972), a teacher, and Mr Oscar Nemon (1972), the artist with whom Winnicott had worked so closely on the erection of the famous statue of Sigmund Freud. Dr John Klauber arranged for the publication of these tributes in a special edition of the *Scientific Bulletin* of The British Psycho-Analytical Society and The Institute of Psycho-Analysis, which included a beautiful obituary written by Winnicott's former Senior Registrar, Dr Susanna Isaacs (1972), and originally intended for the *St. Mary's Hospital Gazette.*

Dr William Gillespie, who had known Winnicott since the 1930s, provided a clear insight into the pioneering nature of Winnicott's work. Gillespie (1972) noted that

> it has been remarked, even if light-heartedly, that there is a certain resemblance between paediatrics and veterinary medicine, in that in neither case can one get much help from the patient's complaints or symptoms; in both cases one has to rely on physical signs and external information. [p. 1]

Gillespie, of course, commented that Winnicott believed that one could in fact receive a great deal of cooperation from one's child patients, reminding his audience that Winnicott

> must, I think, have identified strongly with them, or perhaps rather, in the case of infants, with the mother–child unity which he was to stress so strongly. [p. 1]

He remembered Winnicott as "an eternal child" (p. 2) and then proceeded to praise him for his tremendous talents and for his formidable intelligence, informing the audience that Winnicott often used to state that one must be clever in order to be a good psychoanalyst. Gillespie concluded his tribute by recounting Winnicott's sustained efforts to raise funds so that Nemon's statue of Sigmund Freud could at last be bronzed and displayed in public. The other tributes provided further opportunities for the British psychoanalysts to remember the wonderful talents of Donald Winnicott.

After the death of her husband, Clare Winnicott had to endure a second trauma. In the middle of 1971, the Home Office forced her to retire from the post that she herself had established as Director of Child Care Studies in the Children's Department, promoting the welfare of young people. Needless to say, having lost both her husband and her primary occupation, she experienced a great deal of psychological anguish. She therefore underwent a third course of psychoanalytic treatment with Dr Lois Munro, a sober and respected psychoanalyst who had served at one time as the Director of The London Clinic of Psycho-Analysis. The treatment began in September of 1971 and continued for some time, terminating before Dr Munro's death in 1973. Mrs Winnicott (1974, p. 1) respected Dr Munro greatly and spoke of her "courageous lack of fear at the human predicament". Clare Winnicott (1974, p. 2) also noted that, "The analytic work with Dr Munro was of necessity speciffically [sic] concerned with the whole process of mourning." Fortunately, Dr Munro proved a complete contrast to Mrs Klein, and in her memorial portrait the grateful Clare Winnicott (1974, p. 2) took particular pains to mention that "Dr Munro spoke infrequently in sessions", in contradistinction to the highly loquacious Melanie Klein. Clare must have found Dr Munro's unobtrusive style of practice a great relief.

After her husband's death, Mrs Winnicott also toiled tirelessly as Donald Winnicott's literary executor, editing his unpublished works for posthumous publication. She even spoke to the psychoanalytic bookseller and publisher Harry Karnac (personal communication, 3 August 1994) about the possibility of producing a standard edition of Winnicott's collected works. Sadly, this project did not materialize. She did, however, have the opportunity to launch a number of projects to commemorate the work of her late husband, most notably The Winnicott Memorial Fund Day at Bedford College, London, on 12 December 1975, at which time Dr Catriona Hood (1975), a psychoanalyst, delivered a paper on "What Does a Child Under Three Need?"— thus continuing Winnicott's own work on the treatment of very young children. She also helped to establish The Winnicott Trust, which dispensed the royalties from Winnicott's writings to worthy research projects in the field of infant mental health (cf. Murray, 1989, 1992). Additionally, Clare received an invitation to lay the foundation for the Donald Winnicott Centre, a treatment unit for physically and mentally handicapped children based at the Queen Elizabeth Hospital for Children in London (formerly the Queen's Hospital for Children), where Winnicott had worked for many years during the 1920s and 1930s (Hayward, 1976). Mrs Winnicott participated in the stone-laying on Wednesday, 25 May, 1977, and the following year, she attended the opening ceremonies of the Donald Winnicott Centre on Coate Street at 11.30 a.m., on Thursday, 26 October, 1978, in the presence of Alfred Morris, Esq., a Member of Parliament and the Minister for the Disabled. These events must have brought her considerable pleasure and pride.

After a few years, Clare Winnicott began to divest herself of some of Winnicott's personal possessions. Mr Peter Woolland (personal communication, 26 November 1994), the son of Winnicott's first cousin Marie, received a watch that Winnicott had treasured; and Dr Martin James (1991), a psychoanalyst who admired Winnicott immensely and who later became quite involved in the work of The Winnicott Trust, overseeing the dissemination of Winnicott's ideas, inherited a carrying case for papers. Tragically, Clare Winnicott suffered quite considerably from illness during her final years, and she had to endure extensive treatment at St. Thomas's Hospital in London for a slow and lingering melanoma of the foot (Susanna Isaacs Elmhirst, personal communication, 30 May 1994). The disease interfered with her professional work, and her patients became highly distressed. During this time, she sought further psychotherapeutic treatment from Dr Peter Lomas. Mrs Winnicott died eventually on 17 April 1984.

Winnicott's spinster sisters Violet and Kathleen spent their final years in decline at the family home of Rockville, and both ladies died in their dotage after having suffered from a variety of illnesses. With the deaths of Donald, Alice, Clare, Violet, and Kathleen Winnicott, all childless, the line of Sir Frederick Winnicott became completely extinguished. But though Donald Winnicott had no biological children, his extensive outpouring of books, articles, lectures, seminars, letters, and radio broadcasts serves as a remarkable legacy that will last longer than any human being ever could.

APPENDICES

APPENDICES

Winnicott's schoolmates

Winnicott's contemporaries
at The Leys School, Cambridge

Frank Dalziel ADAM died amid active fighting during the First World War on 16 July 1918.

Eric Cecil AIRTH emigrated to South Africa, and he worked as a mining engineer. He died in August 1971, only months after the passing of his old school colleague, Donald Winnicott.

Syed Mafid ALAM enrolled at Downing College at the University of Cambridge after he departed from The Leys School; his subsequent whereabouts have not been traced.

Leslie Gordon ATKINS died in action during the First World War on 24 May 1918.

William Norman CLELAND died on 27 April 1945. No other information could be obtained about this classmate.

Eric Edgar DAVIES became the manager of an export concern, and he emigrated to Santiago, Chile. Mr Davies also received the O.B.E. He passed away on 22 April 1988, probably the oldest of Winnicott's surviving classmates.

Edward Barcroft GEORGE died while fighting in the First World War in September 1916.

Wilfrid Arnold GRACE attended Queen's College at the University of Oxford, where he read Modern History. He subsequently

---

Sources: Stirland, 1963; Howard & Houghton, 1991.

became a headmaster at the Wakefield Grammar School in Yorkshire. He died on 25 July 1964.

Francis Stanley HELM died in 1946. I have not succeeded in obtaining any further information about this gentleman.

Eric Henry HICKMAN died in 1955. I have not located any additional information about Mr Hickman.

William Arthur HINCHCLIFFE became a solicitor and an Honorary Colonel in the Duke of Wellington's Regiment in the Territorial Army. He lived in Huddersfield, Yorkshire, and he died on 24 February 1968.

Richard Boyce HOLMAN died in 1955. His father, Francis Arthur Holman, had attended The Leys School in 1875 and 1876 as one of its first pupils.

Cecil Wilfrid HOUGH became an agriculturalist, and he lived at Romford, Essex. He died on 13 February 1979.

Charles William Heaton JOHNSON left The Leys School after one year, in 1911. He passed away on 30 October 1964.

Herbert LUMSDEN became a distinguished soldier, attaining the rank of Lieutenant-General in the British army. He won both the Distinguished Service Order and the Military Cross, and he died while fighting during the Second World War, in January 1945.

William Strang MACLAY died while fighting on 28 June 1915, the first casualty of the Class of 1914.

Andrew Montgomery REES died during the First World War, in 1918.

William Henry ROBINSON became a Major in the British Army, and he then worked as a merchant in Stoke-on-Trent, in Staffordshire. He died on 3 March 1966.

William Strang SCOTT served as a Lieutenant in the Cameronians during the First World War. He then settled in Bowling, in Glasgow, Scotland. He passed away on 3 December 1983.

Clifford Huddart WALKER left The Leys School in 1915. He fought in the First World War, and he settled in Bispham, in Blackpool, Lancashire.

Joseph Shenton WILLIAMS died in 1924. No further information could be obtained about him.

Winnicott's lectures

United States

October 1962

San Francisco Psychoanalytic Institute (Winnicott, 1962c)

Los Angeles Psychoanalytic Society (Winnicott, 1962e)

October 1963

San Francisco Psychoanalytic Society (Winnicott, 1963f)

Topeka Psychoanalytic Society (Winnicott, 1963b)

Boston Psychoanalytic Society (Winnicott, 1963c)

Atlanta Psychiatric Clinic (Winnicott, 1963d)

Philadelphia Psychiatric Society (Winnicott, 1963g)

McLean Hospital, Belmont, Massachusetts (Winnicott, 1963h)

October 1967

McLean Hospital, Belmont, Massachusetts (Winnicott, 1968b)

November 1968

William Alanson White Institute (Winnicott, 1968g)

New York Psychoanalytic Society (Winnicott, 1969b)

Canada

1960: McGill University, Montreal (Winnicott, 1961b)

France

1954: Seventeenth Conférence des Psychanalystes de Langues Romanes, Paris (Winnicott, 1955c)

1957: Twentieth International Psycho-Analytic Congress of The International Psycho-Analytical Association, Paris (Winnicott, 1958g)

Italy

1963: Eleventh European Congress of Child Psychiatry, Rome (Winnicott, 1963f)

1964: Symposium on "The Physiological, Neurological and Psychological Problems of the Neonate", Rome (Winnicott, 1964b)

Other European talks

1955: Nineteenth International Congress of The International Psycho-Analytical Association, in Geneva, Switzerland (Winnicott, 1956a)

1956: Eighth International Congress of Paediatrics in Copenhagen, Denmark (Winnicott, 1956d)

1958: The Fourteenth International Congress of Child Psychiatry in Lisbon, Portugal (Winnicott, 1958h)

1961: The Scandinavian Orthopsychiatric Congress in Helsinki, Finland (Winnicott, 1961e)

1965: The Twenty-Fourth International Psycho-Analytic Congress of The International Psycho-Analytical Association in Amsterdam, Holland, in 1965 (Winnicott, 1966b)

Scotland

1959: Association for Child Psychology and Psychiatry in Glasgow (Winnicott, 1959d)

1961: The Twenty-Second International Psycho-Analytic Congress of The International Psycho-Analytical Association in Edinburgh (Winnicott, 1962a)

England

The British Psycho-Analytical Society (e.g. Winnicott, 1935, 1941a, 1942, 1944c, 1944d, 1945b, 1948c, 1949b, 1949d, 1952a, 1953a, 1955a, 1956c, 1959b, 1962d, 1963e, 1965c, 1969h)

The Medical Section of the British Psychological Society (e.g. Winnicott, 1936, 1948a, 1948b, 1954a, 1970d)

St. Paul's School (Winnicott, 1945c)

The Nursery School Association (Winnicott, 1950c)

The London School of Economics and Political Science (e.g. Winnicott, 1951c)

The Section on Psychiatry of the Royal Society of Medicine (Winnicott, 1953b)

The Section on Paediatrics of the Royal Society of Medicine (Winnicott, 1953c)

The Association of Workers for Maladjusted Children (1955e, 1960d, 1984b)

The Association of Supervisors of Midwives (Winnicott, 1957d, 1957e)

The Royal College of Midwives (Winnicott, 1957f)

The Society for Psychosomatic Research (e.g. Winnicott, 1957g)

The Friends' House (Winnicott, 1958c)

The Family Service Units Caseworkers' Study Weekend (Winnicott, 1958i)

The Association of London County Council Child Welfare Officers (Winnicott, 1959c)

The Association of Psychiatric Social Workers (Winnicott, 1961a)

Goldsmiths' College, University of London (Winnicott, 1961b)

The Association of Social Workers (Winnicott, 1963a)

The Devon Centre for Further Education (Winnicott, 1965e)

The London Branch of the Nursery School Association of Great Britain and Northern Ireland (Winnicott, 1966c)

The 1952 Club of The British Psycho-Analytical Society (Winnicott, 1967c)

The Winter Lectures of The British Psycho-Analytical Society (Winnicott, 1968a)

The National Childbirth Trust (Winnicott, 1969c)

St. Luke's Church, Hatfield (Winnicott, 1970b)

Miscellaneous lectures (cf. Winnicott, 1944a, 1950a, 1950b, 1953c, 1954b, 1955b, 1956b, 1958d, 1958f, 1960a, 1960b, 1960c, 1960e, 1961c, 1961d, 1962b, 1964c, 1965d, 1966a, 1967b, 1968c, 1969g, 1974)

Winnicott's
Last Will and Testament

Donald Woods Winnicott spent the last evening of his life in the presence of his second wife, Elsie Clare Nimmo Britton Winnicott. Together, they watched television, and they both fell asleep on the floor. By the time Mrs Winnicott had awakened from her slumber, she discovered that her husband of nearly twenty years had died. Dr David Tizard, the physician who cared for the ageing and ailing Winnicott, determined that the great psychoanalyst had died from heart disease—in particular, left ventricular failure and myocardial infarction.

Winnicott had, of course, suffered from numerous coronary crises since the late 1940s, and so, as an intelligent man, he had prepared his Last Will and Testament in the event of his unexpected death. During the course of my research for the biography of Donald Winnicott, I have had the opportunity to consult Winnicott's final Will, drawn up on 18 May 1965, shortly after Winnicott's sixty-ninth birthday, as well as the Codicil to his will, witnessed on 31 January 1969, soon after the near-fatal coronary episode that occurred during his lecture trip to New York City. As the details of Winnicott's life and work have become of increasingly great interest during recent years, I thought it might be of value to scholars to have an opportunity to inspect these documents.

On reading the will, we should not be surprised to learn that Winnicott had bequeathed all his worldly possessions to his second wife, Clare Winnicott. As we know, Winnicott had said that Clare managed to extend his life by another twenty years (Gillespie,

1971b), and thus he remained eternally grateful to her. The legacy that she ultimately received included the deed to Winnicott's extremely large and valuable house in Belgravia, as well as the royalties from his extensive body of writings. Clare Winnicott used this money to establish The Winnicott Trust.

In 1969, Winnicott wrote a codicil to his will. He had only recently returned to London at this time, after having spent quite a few weeks in the Lenox Hill Hospital in New York City, recovering from pulmonary oedema and Asian influenza. He hovered on the brink of death for some time during the final months of 1968, but he managed to recover, and he returned to London in the early days of 1969. The codicil, dated 31 January 1969, provides additional monies to two particular legatees—Professor Anthony D. Bradshaw and Mrs Joyce Coles, both of whom occupied a special place in Winnicott's life.

Professor Bradshaw, a leading research botanist and nephew of Donald Winnicott, bore much of the burden of looking after Winnicott's first wife, Alice, who lived in retirement in Wales. From time to time, Winnicott sent money to Professor Bradshaw so that he could care for Alice more effectively. On 18 March 1969, Winnicott (1969m) wrote to Bradshaw:

> The thing I am writing to you about at the moment is that my illness made me think of what would happen if I were to die. It is extremely difficult to know what to do about this. What I have in fact done is to make a provision in my Will for £1000 which will be left to you in your name. It becomes your possession; nevertheless I think you will understand that I am hoping you would find that you could take some responsibility at any rate for a time for the special needs of Alice.

Mrs Joyce Coles, Winnicott's devoted private secretary from 1948 to 1971, took care of all aspects of Winnicott's work by typing his voluminous correspondence, arranging his appointments, maintaining notes on all his patients, and so forth. Winnicott simply could not have functioned as well as he did if Joyce Coles had not protected him from many of the practical demands of the outside world. Additionally, Mrs Coles also assisted in nursing Winnicott during his long period of convalescence.

The documents themselves may be described as rather straightforward, but I do hope that they will provide some pleasure to students of British psychoanalysis. I have reproduced the Will and the Codicil in their exact form, retaining any inelegancies of punctuation and phrasing that one will find on the original documents.

THE WILL

I DONALD WOODS WINNICOTT of 87, Chester Square, London S.W.1. in the County of London Fellow of the Royal College of Physicians hereby revoke all former Wills and testamentary dispositions made by me and declare this to be my last Will

1.   I APPOINT MIDLAND BANK EXECUTOR AND TRUSTEE COMPANY LIMITED (hereinafter called "the Company") and my Wife Clare Nimmo Winnicott (who together with the Company are hereinafter called "my Trustees") to be EXECUTORS and TRUSTEES of this my Will AND I DECLARE that the Company is so appointed upon its published Standard Conditions as now in force (as if the same were here set out) with remuneration as provided by those Conditions and the Company's Standard Scale of Fees in force at my death AND I DESIRE that the firm of Messrs. Lithgow Pepper & Eldridge of 84, Wimpole Street, London W.1. shall be employed as solicitors in connection with my estate unless the Company sees reason to the contrary.

2.   SUBJECT to the payment of all funeral and testamentary expenses death duties and debts I GIVE all my property both real and personal and whatsoever and wheresoever unto my said Wife Clare Nimmo Winnicott for her own absolute use and benefit.

A S   W I T N E S S my hand this Eighteenth day of May 1965.

SIGNED by the above named	)	
DONALD WOODS WINNICOTT as	)	
his last Will in the	)	
presence of us both pre-	)	
sent at the same time who	)	[signed: D.W. Winnicott.]
in his presence and in	)	
the presence of each other	)	
have hereunto subscribed	)	
our names as witnesses:-	)	

[signed:
M. R. Eldridge
84, Wimpole St, W.1
Solicitor

G Townsend
12 Links Road
London N.W.2
Solicitors Clerk.]

THE CODICIL

I DONALD WOODS WINNICOTT of 87 Chester Square London S.W.1. DECLARE this to be a Codicil to my Will which bears date the Eighteenth day of May One thousand nine hundred and sixty five

I GIVE the following pecuniary legacies free from all death duties whether payable in the United Kingdom or countries overseas

(a)   To PROFESSOR ANTHONY D. BRADSHAW of 60 Knowsley Road Liverpool 19 the sum of One thousands pounds

(b)   To my Secretary Mrs JOYCE COLES of 120 Corringway Ealing London W.5. the sum of One thousand pounds

In all other respects I confirm my said Will AS WITNESS my hand this Thirty first day of January One thousand nine hundred and sixty nine

SIGNED by the above named   )
DONALD WOODS WINNICOTT as)
a Codicil to his Last   )
Will in the presence of   )
us both present at the   )   [signed: D.W. Winnicott.]
same time who in his   )
presence and in the   )
presence of each other   )
have hereunto subscribed   )
our names as witnesses:-   )

[signed:
M.R Eldridge
84, Wimpole Street
London W.1
Solicitor

W H Thomson
Flat 3
48 Manchester Street
London W.1.
Clerk]

REFERENCES

In compiling the References to the voluminous works by Donald Winnicott, I have in all instances provided citations to the original published source for each work. Many of the articles and essays by Winnicott have appeared subsequently in their exact form, or in revised form, in various volumes of collected papers. For the sake of convenience, we have provided additional references to these editions.

Within any given publication year, Winnicott often published a great many articles, especially during the 1950s and 1960s. I have constructed my lettering system of Winnicott's texts in the following fashion: first, I have listed any books that appeared within a certain calendar year, followed by major and minor journal articles, in order of publication, beginning with *The International Journal of Psycho-Analysis*. Thereafter, I have listed shorter pieces such as reviews, followed by published letters, and thence followed by unpublished letters.

In the tradition of the historian of psychiatry, Henri Ellenberger, I have in all cases checked each source in its original published or unpublished format.

Alcock, Theodora (1948). Conclusions from Psychiatric Work with Evacuated Children: A Contribution to the Symposium on "Lessons for Child Psychiatry". Given at a Meeting of the Medical Section of the British Psychological Society, 27 February 1946. *British Journal of Medical Psychology*, 21: 181–184.

Alcock, Theodora (1963). *The Rorschach in Practice*. London: Tavistock Publications.

Anderson, James William (1982a). Notes on the Life of D.W. Winnicott. Unpublished typescript.

Anderson, James William (1982b). The Personal Roots of Winnicott's Originality. Unpublished typescript.

Anonymous (1961). Donald Winnicott. *St. Mary's Hospital Gazette*, 67: 137–138.

Anthony, E. James; & Benedek, Therese (Eds.) (1970). *Parenthood: Its Psychology and Psychopathology*. Boston, MA: Little, Brown and Company.

Baker, Derek (1975). *Partnership in Excellence. A Late-Victorian Educational Venture: The Leys School, Cambridge. 1875–1975*. Cambridge: The Governors of The Leys School.

Balint, Michael (1957). *The Doctor, His Patient and the Illness*. London: Pitman Medical Publishing Company.

Balint, Michael (1960). Letter to Donald W. Winnicott, 10 February. Box 2. File 8. Donald W. Winnicott Papers.

Balkányi, Charlotte (1957). Letter to Donald W. Winnicott, 30 November. Box 1. File 1. Donald W. Winnicott Papers.

Balkányi, Charlotte (1972). Contribution. *The British Psycho-Analytical Society and The Institute of Psycho-Analysis. Scientific Bulletin*, 57: 28.

Bick, Esther (1958a). Letter to Donald W. Winnicott, 22 September. Box 1. File 15. Donald W. Winnicott Papers.

Bick, Esther (1958b). Letter to Donald W. Winnicott, 10 October. Box 1. File 15. Donald W. Winnicott Papers.

Bollas, Christopher, Davis, Madeleine; & Shepherd, Ray (1993). Editors' Preface. In: Donald W. Winnicott, *Talking to Parents* (pp. xiii–xvi), 1993.

Bowlby, John (1958). Letter to Donald W. Winnicott, 21 July. Box 1. File 15. Donald W. Winnicott Papers.

Bowlby, John; Miller, Emanuel; & Winnicott, Donald W. (1939). Evacuation of Small Children. *British Medical Journal*. (16 December): 1202–1203.

Braddon, Russell (1962). *Joan Sutherland.* London: Collins.

Britton, Clare (1955). Casework Techniques in the Child Care Services. *Case Conference, 1* (No. 9): 3–15.

Brome, Vincent (1982). *Ernest Jones: Freud's Alter Ego.* London: Caliban Books.

Bryan, Douglas (1923). The British Psycho-Analytical Society: Quarterly Report. *International Journal of Psycho-Analysis, 4*: 245–246.

Carr, Helen (1963). Letter to Donald W. Winnicott, 14 September. Box 4. File 2. Donald W. Winnicott Papers.

Casement, Patrick J. (1991). Contribution to the Plenary Discussion. Conference on *Contributions of Donald Winnicott.* The British Psycho-Analytical Society. London, 2 March.

Clancier, Anne (1984a). A Yeast for Thought: Interview with Evelyne Kestemberg. In: Anne Clancier & Jeannine Kalmanovitch, *Winnicott and Paradox: From Birth to Creation,* transl. by Alan Sheridan (pp. 126–132). London: Tavistock Publications, 1987.

Clancier, Anne (1984b). An Inimitable Genius: Interview with Serge Lebovici. In: Anne Clancier & Jeannine Kalmanovitch, *Winnicott and Paradox: From Birth to Creation,* transl. by Alan Sheridan (pp. 133–138). London: Tavistock Publications, 1987.

Clancier, Anne; & Kalmanovitch, Jeannine (1984). *Winnicott and Paradox: From Birth to Creation,* transl. by Alan Sheridan. London: Tavistock Publications, 1987.

Cole, Estelle Maud (1921). A New Point in the Symbolism of Flute Playing. *International Journal of Psycho-Analysis, 2*: 202–203.

Cole, Estelle Maud (1922). A Few "Don'ts" for Beginners in the Technique of Psycho-Analysis. *International Journal of Psycho-Analysis, 3*: 43–44.

Coles, Joyce (1971a). Letter to Edith Weigert, 3 March. Box 8. File 14. Donald W. Winnicott Papers.

Coles, Joyce (1971b). Letter to John W. Cox, 19 April. Box 8. File 10. Donald W. Winnicott Papers.

Cooper, Judy (1989). Book Review of Adam Phillips, *Winnicott. Journal of the British Association of Psychotherapists, 20*: 112–113.

Cooper, Judy (1991). Book Review of Donald W. Winnicott, *The Maturational Processes and the Facilitating Environment: Studies in the Theory of Emotional Development. Journal of the British Association of Psychotherapists, 22*: 99–100.

Cooper, Judy (1993). *Speak of Me as I Am: The Life and Work of Masud Khan*. London: Karnac Books.

Cordess, Christopher (1992). Pioneers in Forensic Psychiatry. Edward Glover (1888–1972): Psychoanalysis and Crime—A Fragile Legacy. *Journal of Forensic Psychiatry*, 3: 509–530.

Cox, John W. (1971). Letter to Donald W. Winnicott, 9 April. Box 8. File 10. Donald W. Winnicott Papers.

Creak, Mildred (1972). Contribution to the Winnicott Memorial Meeting—19/1/72. *The British Psycho-Analytical Society and The Institute of Psycho-Analysis. Scientific Bulletin*, 57: 25.

Darwin, Charles (1859). *On the Origin of Species by Means of Natural Selection, or the Preservation of Favoured Races in the Struggle for Life*. London: John Murray.

Davis, John A. (1993a). Winnicott as Physician. *Winnicott Studies*, 7: 95–97.

Davis, John A. (1993b). Correspondence. *Winnicott Studies*, 7: 98.

Davis, Madeleine (1987). The Writing of D.W. Winnicott. *International Review of Psycho-Analysis*, 14: 491–502.

Davis, Madeleine (1991). Play and Symbolism in Lowenfeld and Winnicott. *Free Associations*, 2 (No. 23): 395–421.

Davis, Madeleine; & Wallbridge, David (1981). *Boundary and Space: An Introduction to the Work of D.W. Winnicott*. New York: Brunner/Mazel. [Revised edition London: Karnac Books, 1991.]

Dockar-Drysdale, Barbara (1974). My Debt to Winnicott. In: *The Provision of Primary Experience: Winnicottian Work with Children and Adolescents* (pp. 1–6). London: Free Association Books, 1990.

Donald W. Winnicott Papers (1949–71). Archives of Psychiatry. History of Psychiatry Section. Department of Psychiatry. The Oskar Diethelm Library of the History of Psychiatry. The New York Hospital. Cornell Medical Center. New York, NY.

Dyer, Raymond (1977). Interview with Eva Rosenfeld, 31 May. In: Anna Freud and Education: Studies in the History, Philosophy, Science and Application of Child Psychoanalysis. Doctoral Dissertation, Division of Education, University of Sheffield, 1980.

Eber, Milton; & Kunz, Lyle B. (1984). The Desire to Help Others. *Bulletin of the Menninger Clinic*, 48: 125–140.

Ede, Harold Stanley (1930). *A Life of Gaudier-Brzeska*. London: William Heinemann.

Ede, Harold Stanley (1931). *Savage Messiah*. London: William Heinemann.

Eigen, Michael (1991). Winnicott's Area of Freedom: The Uncompromisable. In: Nathan Schwartz-Salant & Murray Stein (Eds.), *Liminality and Transitional Phenomena* (pp. 67–88). Wilmette, IL: Chiron Publications.

Farhi, Nina (1991). Helping the Man Who Helped Children. *The Guardian*, 23 October, p. 39.

Fordham, Michael (1972). Tribute to D.W. Winnicott. *The British Psycho-Analytical Society and The Institute of Psycho-Analysis. Scientific Bulletin*, 57: 22–23.

Freud, Anna (1973). Letter to Heinz Kohut, 2 July. In: Heinz Kohut, *The Curve of Life: Correspondence of Heinz Kohut. 1923–1981*, ed. by Geoffrey Cocks (p. 285). Chicago, IL: University of Chicago Press, 1994.

Freud, Sigmund (1900). *Die Traumdeutung*. Vienna: Franz Deuticke. *The Interpretation of Dreams*. In: *The Standard Edition of the Complete Psychological Works of Sigmund Freud. Volumes IV and V*, ed. and transl. by James Strachey, Anna Freud, Alix Strachey, & Alan Tyson. London: Hogarth Press and The Institute of Psycho-Analysis, 1953.

Freud, Sigmund (1923). Letter to Joan Riviere, 2 July. In: Athol Hughes (Ed.), Letters from Sigmund Freud to Joan Riviere (1921–1939), transl. by Michael Molnar (p. 274). *International Journal of Psycho-Analysis*, 19 (1992): 265–284.

Freud, Sigmund (1924a). *Collected Papers: Volume I*, transl. by Joan Riviere. London: Hogarth Press and The Institute of Psycho-Analysis.

Freud, Sigmund (1924b). *Collected Papers: Volume II*, transl. by Joan Riviere. London: Hogarth Press and The Institute of Psycho-Analysis.

Freud, Sigmund (1925). *Collected Papers: Volume IV*, transl. by Joan Riviere. London: Hogarth Press and The Institute of Psycho-Analysis.

Freud, Sigmund (1953–1974). *The Standard Edition of the Complete Psychological Works of Sigmund Freud*, ed. and transl. by James Strachey, Anna Freud, Alix Strachey, & Alan Tyson. London: Hogarth Press and The Institute of Psycho-Analysis.

Fuller, Peter (1987). Mother and Child in Henry Moore and Winnicott. *Winnicott Studies*, 2: 72–86.

Gay, Peter (1988). *Freud: A Life for Our Time*. New York: W.W. Norton and Company.

Gillespie, William H. (1971a). D.W. Winnicott M.A., F.R.C.P. *British Medical Journal* (6 February): 351.

Gillespie, William H. (1971b). Donald W. Winnicott. *International Journal of Psycho-Analysis*, 52: 227–228.

Gillespie, William H. (1972). Commemorative Meeting for Dr. Donald Winnicott, 19 January 1972. *The British Psycho-Analytical Society and The Institute of Psycho-Analysis. Scientific Bulletin*, 57: 1–4.

Glover, Edward (1960). *Selected Papers on Psycho-Analysis. Volume II. The Roots of Crime*. London: Imago Publishing Company.

Glover, Edward (1969). In Praise of Ourselves. *International Journal of Psycho-Analysis*, 50: 499–502.

Goldman, Dodi (1993). *In Search of the Real: The Origins and Originality of D.W. Winnicott*. Northvale, NJ: Jason Aronson.

Grolnick, Simon A. (1990). *The Work and Play of Winnicott*. Northvale, NJ: Jason Aronson.

Grosskurth, Phyllis (1986). *Melanie Klein: Her World and Her Work*. New York: Alfred A. Knopf [reprinted London: Karnac Books, 1987].

Guthrie, Leonard G. (1907). *Functional Nervous Disorders in Childhood*. London: Henry Frowde and Hodder & Stoughton.

Hartman, Frank R. (1976). Biographical Sketches. In: Martin S. Bergmann & Frank R. Hartman (Eds.), *The Evolution of Psychoanalytic Technique* (pp. 42–79). New York: Basic Books.

Hartmann, Heinz (1953). Extrait du rapport du président, le Dr Heinz Hartmann, suivi de la discussion. 26 July. In: *La Scission de 1953: La Communauté psychanalytique en France. I*, ed. by Jacques-Alain Miller (pp. 138–142). *Ornicar?*, 7 (Supplement).

Hartmann, Heinz (1955). Extrait du rapport du président, le Dr Heinz Hartmann. 26 July. In: *La Scission de 1953: La Communauté psychanalytique en France. I*, ed. by Jacques-Alain Miller (p. 160). *Ornicar?*, 7 (Supplement).

Hayley, Thomas T. S. (1991). Thomas Forrest Main (1911–1990). *International Journal of Psycho-Analysis*, 72: 719–722.

Hayward, Edward A. (1976). Letter to Clare Winnicott, 7 June. Box 2. File 23. Clare Winnicott Collection. Contemporary Medical Archives Centre. The Wellcome Institute for the History of Medicine. London.

Hood, Catriona (1975). What Does a Child Under Three Need? Unpublished typescript. Box 2. File 26. Clare Winnicott Collection.

Contemporary Medical Archives Centre. The Wellcome Institute for the History of Medicine. London.

Horder, Mervyn (1966). *The Little Genius: A Memoir of the First Lord Horder.* London: Gerald Duckworth and Company.

Horder, Thomas J. (1915). *Cerebro-Spinal Fever.* London: Henry Frowde and Hodder & Stoughton.

Horder, Thomas (1953). *Fifty Years of Medicine.* London: Gerald Duckworth and Company.

Howard, Maurice F.; & Houghton, Geoffrey C. (Eds.) (1991). *The Handbook and Directory of The Leys School* (Twentieth Edition). Sawston, Cambridge: Crampton and Sons.

Hughes, Athol (1991). Joan Riviere: Her Life and Work. In: Athol Hughes (Ed.), *The Inner World and Joan Riviere. Collected Papers: 1920–1958* (pp. 1–43). London: Karnac Books.

Hughes, Judith M. (1989). *Reshaping the Psychoanalytic Domain: The Work of Melanie Klein, W.R.D. Fairbairn, and D.W. Winnicott.* Berkeley, CA: University of California Press.

Isaacs, Susan (1930). *Intellectual Growth in Young Children.* London: Routledge and Kegan Paul.

Isaacs, Susan (1933). *Social Development in Young Children: A Study of Beginnings.* London: George Routledge and Sons.

Isaacs, Susan; Brown, Sybil Clement; & Thouless, Robert H. (Eds.) (1941). *The Cambridge Evacuation Survey: A Wartime Study in Social Welfare and Education.* London: Methuen and Company.

Isaacs, Susanna (1972). Donald Woods Winnicott: 1896–1971. *The British Psycho-Analytical Society and The Institute of Psycho-Analysis. Scientific Bulletin, 57*: 29–32.

Jacobs, Michael (1995). *D.W. Winnicott.* London: Sage Publications.

James, Martin (1991). Has Winnicott Become a Winnicottian?: The Importance of Psychiatry. Lecture at the Squiggle Foundation, London, 16 February.

Johns, Jennifer (1991). A Search for Winnicott. Conference on *Contributions of Donald Winnicott.* The British Psycho-Analytical Society, London, 2 March.

Jones, David (1943a). Postcard to Harold Stanley Ede, 10 March. Kettle's Yard Archive. Kettle's Yard. University of Cambridge, Cambridge.

Jones, David (1943b). Letter to Harold Stanley Ede, 27 March. Kettle's Yard Archive. Kettle's Yard. University of Cambridge, Cambridge.

Jones, David (1943c). Letter to Harold Stanley Ede, 17 May. Kettle's Yard Archive. Kettle's Yard. University of Cambridge, Cambridge.

Jones, David (1944). Letter to Harold Stanley Ede, 13 March. Kettle's Yard Archive. Kettle's Yard. University of Cambridge, Cambridge.

Jones, Ernest (1937). Letter to Sigmund Freud, 23 February. In: Sigmund Freud & Ernest Jones, *The Complete Correspondence of Sigmund Freud and Ernest Jones: 1908–1939*, ed. by R. Andrew Paskauskas (pp. 755–756). Cambridge, MA: Belknap Press of Harvard University Press, 1993.

Jones, Ernest (1957). Letter to Donald W. Winnicott, 15 September. Box 1. File 3. Donald W. Winnicott Papers.

Jones, Mervyn; & Ferris, Paul (1959). Dr. Ernest Jones: Portrait Assembled from Reminiscences of People Who Knew Him. British Broadcasting Corporation, Home Service, 15 March.

Kahr, Brett (in preparation a). *Donald Winnicott: The Life and Work of a Pioneer Psycho-Analyst*. London: Karnac Books.

Kahr, Brett (Ed.) (in preparation b). *The Winnicott Centenary Papers*. London: Karnac Books.

Karnac, Harry (1991). On Psychoanalytic Bookselling 1950–1989. *The British Psycho-Analytical Society Bulletin*, 27 (No. 8): 21–27.

Khan, M. Masud R. (1971a). Donald W. Winnicott: Bridging Paediatrics and Psychoanalysis. *International Journal of Psycho-Analysis*, 52: 225–226.

Khan, M. Masud R. (1971b). Letter to Alfred Flarsheim, 2 February. Box 8. File 11. Donald W. Winnicott Papers.

Khan, M. Masud R. (1972). Text for the Winnicott Memorial Meeting, 19 January 1972. *The British Psycho-Analytical Society and The Institute of Psycho-Analysis. Scientific Bulletin*, 57: 11–14.

Khan, M. Masud R. (1975). Introduction. In: Donald W. Winnicott, *Through Paediatrics to Psycho-Analysis* (pp. xi–l). London: Hogarth Press and The Institute of Psycho-Analysis, 1975 [reprinted London: Karnac Books, 1992].

Khan, M. Masud R. (1986). Introduction. In: Donald W. Winnicott, *Holding and Interpretation*, 1986a (pp. 1–18).

Khan, M. Masud R. (1987). Foreword. In: Anne Clancier & Jeannine Kalmanovitch, *Winnicott and Paradox: From Birth to Creation* transl. by Alan Sheridan (pp. xvi–xvii). London: Tavistock Publications.

Khan, M. Masud R. (1988). *When Spring Comes: Awakenings in Clinical Psychoanalysis*. London: Chatto and Windus.

King, Pearl (1972). Tribute to Donald Winnicott. *The British Psycho-Analytical Society and The Institute of Psycho-Analysis. Scientific Bulletin*, 57: 26–28.

King, Pearl (1988). Early Divergences Between the Psycho-Analytical Societies in London and Vienna. In: Edward Timms & Naomi Segal (Eds.), *Freud in Exile: Psychoanalysis and Its Vicissitudes* (pp. 124–133). New Haven, CT: Yale University Press.

King, Pearl (1991a). Biographical Notes on the Main Participants in the Freud–Klein Controversies in the British Psycho-Analytical Society, 1941–45. In: Pearl King & Riccardo Steiner (Eds.), *The Freud–Klein Controversies: 1941–45* (pp. ix–xxv). London: Tavistock/Routledge.

King, Pearl (1991b). Background and Development of the Freud–Klein Controversies in the British Psycho-Analytical Society. In: Pearl King & Riccardo Steiner (Eds.), *The Freud–Klein Controversies: 1941–45* (pp. 9–36). London: Tavistock/Routledge.

King, Pearl; & Steiner, Riccardo (Eds.) (1991). *The Freud–Klein Controversies: 1941–45*. London: Tavistock/Routledge.

Klauber, John (1972a). Editorial. *The British Psycho-Analytical Society and The Institute of Psycho-Analysis. Scientific Bulletin*, 57: i.

Klauber, John (1972b). Contribution by Dr. John Klauber. *The British Psycho-Analytical Society and The Institute of Psycho-Analysis. Scientific Bulletin*, 57: 24.

Klein, Melanie (1932). *Die Psychoanalyse des Kindes*. Vienna: Internationaler Psychoanalytischer Verlag. *The Psycho-Analysis of Children*, transl. by Alix Strachey. London: Hogarth Press and The Institute of Psycho-Analysis. [Also in: *Writings, Volume 2*, 1975.]

Klein, Melanie (1946). Notes on Some Schizoid Mechanisms. *International Journal of Psycho-Analysis*, 27: 99–110. [Also in: *Writings, Volume 3*, 1975 (pp. 1–24).]

Klein, Melanie (1950). On the Criteria for the Termination of a Psycho-Analysis. *International Journal of Psycho-Analysis*, 31: 78–80. [Also in: *Writings, Volume 3*, 1975 (pp. 43–47).]

Klein, Melanie (1957). *Envy and Gratitude: A Study of Unconscious Sources*. London: Tavistock Publications. [Also in: *Writings, Volume 3*, 1975 (pp. 176–235).]

Klein, Melanie (1959). Our Adult World and Its Roots in Infancy.

Human Relations, 12: 291–303. [Also in: *Writings, Volume 3*, 1975 (pp. 257–263).]

Klein, Melanie (1961). *Narrative of a Child Analysis: The Conduct of the Psycho-Analysis of Children as Seen in the Treatment of a Ten-Year-Old Boy.* London: Hogarth Press and The Institute of Psycho-Analysis. [Also in: *Writings, Volume 4*, 1975c.]

Klein, Melanie (1975a). *The Writings of Melanie Klein, Volume 2: The Psycho-Analysis of Children*, ed. by Roger Money-Kyrle, Betty Joseph, Edna O'Shaughnessy, & Hanna Segal. London: Hogarth Press, 1975.

Klein, Melanie (1975b). *The Writings of Melanie Klein, Volume 3: Envy and Gratitude and Other Works*, ed. by Roger Money-Kyrle, Betty Joseph, Edna O'Shaughnessy, & Hanna Segal. London: Hogarth Press, 1975 [reprinted London: Karnac Books, 1991].

Klein, Melanie (1975c). *The Writings of Melanie Klein, Volume 4: Narrative of a Child Analysis*, ed. by Roger Money-Kyrle, Betty Joseph, Edna O'Shaughnessy, & Hanna Segal. London: Hogarth Press, 1975.

Kubie, Lawrence S. (1957). Letter to Donald W. Winnicott, 20 August. Box 1. File 3. Donald W. Winnicott Papers.

Laing, Ronald D. (1958). Letter to Donald W. Winnicott, 21 April. Box 1. File 11. Donald W. Winnicott Papers.

Little, Margaret I. (1972). Contribution by Dr. Margaret Little. *The British Psycho-Analytical Society and The Institute of Psycho-Analysis. Scientific Bulletin, 57*: 20–21.

Little, Margaret I. (1981). Donald Winnicott: A Note. In: *Transference Neurosis and Transference Psychosis: Toward Basic Unity* (pp. 265–268). New York: Jason Aronson.

Little, Margaret I. (1985). Winnicott Working in Areas Where Psychotic Anxieties Predominate: A Personal Record. *Free Associations, 1* (No. 3): 9–42.

Little, Margaret I.; & Langs, Robert J. (1981). Dialogue: Margaret Little/Robert Langs. In: Margaret I. Little, *Transference Neurosis and Transference Psychosis: Toward Basic Unity* (pp. 269–306). New York: Jason Aronson.

Lomas, Peter (1963). Letter to Donald W. Winnicott, 25 February. Box 4. File 2. Donald W. Winnicott Papers.

Lomax-Simpson, Josephine (1990). Book Review of Adam Phillips, *Winnicott. Group Analysis, 23*: 85–86.

Meisel, Perry; & Kendrick, Walter (1985). Introduction. In: James

Strachey & Alix Strachey, *Bloomsbury/Freud: The Letters of James and Alix Strachey. 1924–1925*, ed. by Perry Meisel & Walter Kendrick (pp. 3–49). New York: Basic Books.

Meyerson, Simon (1970). Letter to Donald W. Winnicott, 30 November. Box 8. File 11. Donald W. Winnicott Papers.

Miller, Alice (1979). The Drama of the Gifted Child and the Psycho-Analyst's Narcissistic Disturbance. *International Journal of Psycho-Analysis, 60*: 47–58.

Milner, Marion (1972). For Dr. Winnicott Memorial Meeting 19 January 1972. *The British Psycho-Analytical Society and The Institute of Psycho-Analysis. Scientific Bulletin, 57*: 5–10.

Milner, Marion (1978). D.W. Winnicott and the Two-Way Journey. In: Simon A. Grolnick, Leonard Barkin, & Werner Muensterberger (Eds.), *Between Reality and Fantasy: Transitional Objects and Phenomena* (pp. 37–42). New York: Jason Aronson.

Milner, Marion (1969). *The Hands of the Living God: An Account of a Psycho-Analytic Treatment*. London: Hogarth Press and The Institute of Psycho-Analysis.

Molnar, Michael (Ed.) (1992). *The Diary of Sigmund Freud: 1929–1939. A Record of the Final Decade*, transl. by Michael Molnar. London: Hogarth Press.

Molony, Eileen (1958). Letter to Donald W. Winnicott, 24 October. Box 1. File 8. Donald W. Winnicott Papers.

Murray, Lynne (1989). Winnicott and the Developmental Psychology of Infancy. *British Journal of Psychotherapy, 5*: 333–348.

Murray, Lynne (1992). The Impact of Postnatal Depression on Infant Development. *Journal of Child Psychology and Psychiatry and Allied Disciplines, 33*: 543–561.

Nemon, Oscar (1972). Contribution. *The British Psycho-Analytical Society and The Institute of Psycho-Analysis. Scientific Bulletin, 57*: 24–25.

Neve, Michael (1983). Interview with Clare Winnicott, June 1983. In: Peter L. Rudnytsky, *The Psychoanalytic Vocation: Rank, Winnicott, and the Legacy of Freud* (pp. 180–193). New Haven, CT: Yale University Press, 1991.

Newnham College Roll: Letter. January, 1950 (1950). Cambridge: W. Heffer and Sons.

Newman, Alexander (1995). *Non-Compliance in Winnicott's Words: A Companion to the Writings and Work of D.W. Winnicott*. London: Free Association Books.

Oakeshott, Edna (1972). Contribution by Mrs. E. Oakeshott. *The British Psycho-Analytical Society and The Institute of Psycho-Analysis. Scientific Bulletin*, 57: 21.

Padel, John (1991). The Psychoanalytic Theories of Melanie Klein and Donald Winnicott and Their Interaction in the British Society of Psychoanalysis. *Psychoanalytic Review*, 78: 325–345.

Partridge, Maurice (1950). *Pre-Frontal Leucotomy: A Survey of 300 Cases Personally Followed Over 1½–3 Years.* Oxford: Blackwell Scientific Publications.

Pfister, Oskar (1913). *Die Psychoanalytische Methode: Eine Erfahrungswissenschaft–Systematische Darstellung.* Berlin: Julius Klinkhardt. *The Psychoanalytic Method*, transl. by Charles Rockwell Payne. London: Kegan Paul, Trench, Trubner and Company, 1915.

Phillips, Adam (1988). *Winnicott.* London: Fontana Press.

Radio Times (1971). Entry for *Good Old Summertime* (23 January–29 January): 23.

Ramzy, Ishak (1978). Editor's Foreword. In: Donald W. Winnicott, *The Piggle: An Account of the Psychoanalytic Treatment of a Little Girl*, ed. by Ishak Ramzy (pp. xi–xvi). London: Hogarth Press and The Institute of Psycho-Analysis.

Rayner, Eric (1991). *The Independent Mind in British Psychoanalysis.* London: Free Association Books.

Riviere, Joan (1929). Womanliness as a Masquerade. *International Journal of Psycho-Analysis*, 10: 303–313. [Also in: Athol Hughes (Ed.), *The Inner World and Joan Riviere. Collected Papers: 1920–1958.* London: Karnac Books, 1991.]

Riviere, Joan (1932). Jealousy as a Mechanism of Defence. *International Journal of Psycho-Analysis*, 13: 414–424. [Also in: Athol Hughes (Ed.), *The Inner World and Joan Riviere. Collected Papers: 1920–1958.* London: Karnac Books, 1991.]

Riviere, Joan (1936a). A Contribution to the Analysis of the Negative Therapeutic Reaction. *International Journal of Psycho-Analysis*, 17: 304–320. [Also in: Athol Hughes (Ed.), *The Inner World and Joan Riviere. Collected Papers: 1920–1958.* London: Karnac Books, 1991.]

Riviere, Joan (1936b). On the Genesis of Psychical Conflict in Earliest Infancy. *International Journal of Psycho-Analysis*, 17: 395–422. [Also in: Melanie Klein, Paula Heimann, Susan Isaacs, & Joan Riviere (Eds.), *Developments in Psychoanalysis.* London:

Hogarth Press and The Institute of Psycho-Analysis, 1952; reprinted London: Karnac Books, 1989.]

Riviere, Joan (1958a). Letter to Donald W. Winnicott, 12 June. Box 1. File 13. Donald W. Winnicott Papers.

Riviere, Joan (1958b). Letter to Donald W. Winnicott, 7 December. Box 1. File 13. Donald W. Winnicott Papers.

Roazen, Paul (1975). *Freud and His Followers*. New York: Alfred A. Knopf.

Roazen, Paul (1994). Freud's Patients. Conference on *The Return of the Repressed: Psychoanalysis and Its Histories*. Psychoanalytic Forum. Institute of Contemporary Arts. London, 19 February.

Robertson, James; & Robertson, Joyce (1989). The Robertson Centre. In: *Separation and the Very Young* (pp. 197–232). London: Free Association Books.

Robinson, Chris (1991). *Victorian Plymouth*. Plymouth: Pen and Ink Publishing.

Rodman, F. Robert (1987a). Preface. In: Donald W. Winnicott, *The Spontaneous Gesture*, 1987b (pp. ix–x).

Rodman, F. Robert (1987b). Introduction. In: Donald W. Winnicott, *The Spontaneous Gesture*, 1987b (pp. xiii–xxxiii).

Rodman, F. Robert (1987c). Editorial Caption to Photograph. In the Buckingham Palace Studio of Oscar Nemon. In: Donald W. Winnicott, *The Spontaneous Gesture*, 1987b (photographic insert).

Rodman, F. Robert (1987d). Footnote. In: Donald W. Winnicott, Letter to Anna Freud, 20 January. In: Donald W. Winnicott, *The Spontaneous Gesture*, 1987b (p. 185).

Rosenberg, Elizabeth (1943). A Clinical Contribution to the Psychopathology of the War Neuroses. *International Journal of Psycho-Analysis*, 24: 32–41.

Roudinesco, Élisabeth (1993). *Jacques Lacan: Esquisse d'une vie, histoire d'un système de pensée*. Paris: Éditions Fayard.

Rudnytsky, Peter L. (1989). Winnicott and Freud. *Psychoanalytic Study of the Child*, 44: 331–350. New Haven, CT: Yale University Press.

Rudnytsky, Peter L. (1991). *The Psychoanalytic Vocation: Rank, Winnicott, and the Legacy of Freud*. New Haven, CT: Yale University Press.

Rycroft, Charles (1994). Psychoanalysis 1937–1993: Reminiscences of a Survivor. *Newsletter*. School of Psychotherapy and Counselling, Regent's College (Winter, Supplement): 1–4.

Scarlett, Jean (1991). Getting Established: Initiatives in Psychotherapy Training Since World War Two. *British Journal of Psychotherapy*, 7: 260–267.

Segal, Hanna (1991). Foreword. In: Athol Hughes (Ed.), *The Inner World and Joan Riviere. Collected Papers: 1920–1958* (pp. xi– xiv). London: Karnac Books.

Sherman, Murray H. (1983). Lytton and James Strachey: Biography and Psychoanalysis. In: Norman Kiell (Ed.), *Blood Brothers: Siblings as Writers* (pp. 329–364). New York: International Universities Press.

Sinason, Valerie (1992). *Mental Handicap and the Human Condition: New Approaches from the Tavistock.* London: Free Association Books.

Stirland, John (Ed.) (1963). *The Leys School: Handbook and Directory* (Sixteenth Edition). Sawston, Cambridge: Crampton and Sons.

Stirland, John (1975). Some "Shining Lights". *The Leys Fortnightly.* Centenary Edition: 47–54.

Strachey, Alix (1924). Letter to James Strachey, 29 December. In: James Strachey & Alix Strachey, *Bloomsbury/Freud: The Letters of James and Alix Strachey. 1924–1925*, ed. by Perry Meisel & Walter Kendrick (pp. 165–166). New York: Basic Books, 1985.

Strachey, Alix (1925). Letter to James Strachey, 12 May. In: James Strachey & Alix Strachey, *Bloomsbury/Freud: The Letters of James and Alix Strachey. 1924–1925*, ed. by Perry Meisel & Walter Kendrick (pp. 262–263). New York: Basic Books, 1985.

Strachey, James (1924a). Letter to Alix Strachey, 9 October. In: James Strachey & Alix Strachey, *Bloomsbury/Freud: The Letters of James and Alix Strachey. 1924–1925*, ed. by Perry Meisel & Walter Kendrick (pp. 83–84). New York: Basic Books, 1985.

Strachey, James (1924b). Letter to Alix Strachey, 18 November. In: James Strachey & Alix Strachey, *Bloomsbury/Freud: The Letters of James and Alix Strachey. 1924–1925*, ed. by Perry Meisel & Walter Kendrick (pp. 119–120). New York: Basic Books, 1985.

Strachey, James (1925). Letter to Alix Strachey, 11 February. In: James Strachey & Alix Strachey, *Bloomsbury/Freud: The Letters of James and Alix Strachey. 1924–1925*, ed. by Perry Meisel & Walter Kendrick (pp. 329–330). New York: Basic Books, 1985.

Strachey, James (1930). Some Unconscious Factors in Reading. *International Journal of Psycho-Analysis, 11*: 322–331.

Strachey, James (1931). The Function of the Precipitating Factor in the Aetiology of the Neuroses: A Historical Note. *International Journal of Psycho-Analysis, 12*: 326–330.

Strachey, James (1934). The Nature of the Therapeutic Action of Psycho-Analysis. *International Journal of Psycho-Analysis, 15*: 127–159.

Strachey, James (1939). Preliminary Notes Upon the Problem of Akhenaten. *International Journal of Psycho-Analysis, 20*: 33–42.

Strachey, James (1940). Letter to Edward Glover, 23 April. In: Eric Rayner (1991). *The Independent Mind in British Psychoanalysis* (pp. 17–18). London: Free Association Books.

Strachey, James (1960). Letter to Donald W. Winnicott, 8 January. Box 2. File 12. Donald W. Winnicott Papers.

Strachey, James (1963). Joan Riviere (1883–1962). *International Journal of Psycho-Analysis, 44*: 228–230.

Swerdloff, Bluma (1965a). Interview with Theodor Reik, 3 June. In: The Reminiscences of Theodor Reik. Psychoanalytic Project. Oral History Research Office. Butler Library. Columbia University. New York, NY.

Swerdloff, Bluma (1965b). Interview with Raymond de Saussure, 29 July. Psychoanalytic Project. Oral History Research Office. Butler Library. Columbia University. New York, NY.

Swerdloff, Bluma (1965c). Interview with Michael Balint, 7 August. In: The Reminiscences of Michael Balint. Psychoanalytic Project. Oral History Research Office. Butler Library. Columbia University. New York, NY.

Tizard, J. Peter M. (1971). Donald W. Winnicott. *International Journal of Psycho-Analysis, 52*: 226–227.

Turner, John (1988). Wordsworth and Winnicott in the Area of Play. *International Review of Psycho-Analysis, 15*: 481–497.

Urwin, Cathy (1988). Margaret Lowenfeld. In: Cathy Urwin & John Hood-Williams (Eds.), *Child Psychotherapy, War and the Normal Child: Selected Papers of Margaret Lowenfeld* (pp. 3–139). London: Free Association Books.

Varma, Ved P. (Ed.) (1973). *Stresses in Childhood*. London: University of London Press.

Waddington, Mary (1972). Contribution by Mrs. Mary Waddington. *The British Psycho-Analytical Society and The Institute of Psycho-Analysis. Scientific Bulletin, 57*: 21.

Weigert, Edith (1970). Letter to Donald W. Winnicott,. 31 December. Box 8. File 11. Donald W. Winnicott Papers.

Weyand, Alexander M. (1952). *The Olympic Pageant.* New York: Macmillan Company.

Wills, Doris (1965). Letter to Donald W. Winnicott, 27 June. Box 5. File 7. Donald W. Winnicott Papers.

Winnicott, Alice (1958a). Letter to Donald W. Winnicott, 9 November. Box 1. File 15. Donald W. Winnicott Papers.

Winnicott, Alice (1958b). Letter to Donald W. Winnicott, 19 November. Box 1. File 15. Donald W. Winnicott Papers.

Winnicott, Alice (1959a). Letter to Donald W. Winnicott, 12 November. Box 2. File 6. Donald W. Winnicott Papers.

Winnicott, Alice (1959b). Letter to Donald W. Winnicott, 25 November. Box 2. File 6. Donald W. Winnicott Papers.

Winnicott, Alice (1960). Letter to Donald W. Winnicott, undated. Box 2. File 14. Donald W. Winnicott Papers.

Winnicott, Alice (1961a). Letter to Donald W. Winnicott, 3 January. Box 3. File 7. Donald W. Winnicott Papers.

Winnicott, Alice (1961b). Letter to Donald W. Winnicott, 1 September. Box 3. File 7. Donald W. Winnicott Papers.

Winnicott, Clare (1963). Face to Face with Children. In: Joan F. S. King (Ed.), *New Thinking for Changing Needs* (pp. 28–50). London: Association of Social Workers.

Winnicott, Clare (1964). *Child Care and Social Work: A Collection of Papers Written Between 1954 and 1963.* Welwyn, Hertfordshire: Codicote Press.

Winnicott, Clare (1974). Dr. Lois Munro: A Personal Tribute. Unpublished typescript. Box 2. File 26. Clare Winnicott Collection. Contemporary Medical Archives Centre. The Wellcome Institute for the History of Medicine. London.

Winnicott, Clare (1977). Donald Winnicott Centre. Queen Elizabeth Hospital for Children. Stone-laying Ceremony, Wednesday, 25 May 1977. Unpublished typescript. Box 2. File 23. Clare Winnicott Collection. Contemporary Medical Archives Centre. The Wellcome Institute for the History of Medicine. London.

Winnicott, Clare (1978). D.W.W.: A Reflection. In: Simon A. Grolnick, Leonard Barkin, & Werner Muensterberger (Eds.), *Between Reality and Fantasy: Transitional Objects and Phenomena* (pp. 17–33). New York: Jason Aronson.

Winnicott, Clare (1980). Fear of Breakdown: A Clinical Example. *International Journal of Psycho-Analysis*, *61*: 351–357.

Winnicott, Clare (1984). Introduction. In: Donald W. Winnicott, *Deprivation and Delinquency*. 1984a (pp. 1–5).

Winnicott, Clare (1988). Preface. In: Donald W. Winnicott, *Human Nature*, 1988 (p. ix).

Winnicott, Clare (Undated). Committee of Enquiry into the Death of Maria Colwell. Unpublished typescript. Box 2. File 26. Clare Winnicott Collection. Contemporary Medical Archives Centre. The Wellcome Institute for the History of Medicine. London.

Winnicott, Donald W. (1919). Letter to Violet Winnicott, 15 November. In: *The Spontaneous Gesture*, 1987b (pp. 1–4).

Winnicott, Donald W. (1920a). A Shropshire Surgeon. *St. Bartholomew's Hospital Journal*, *27*: 103.

Winnicott, Donald W. (1920b). St. Bartholomew's Hospital Amateur Dramatic Club. *St. Bartholomew's Hospital Journal*, *27*: 152–154.

Winnicott, Donald W. (1921a). A Reminder to the Binder. *St. Bartholomew's Hospital Journal*, *28*: 107.

Winnicott, Donald W. (1921b). The Snag. *St. Bartholomew's Hospital Journal*, *28*: 188.

Winnicott, Donald W. (1930). Short Communication on Enuresis. *St. Bartholomew's Hospital Journal*, *37*: 125–127.

Winnicott, Donald W. (1931a). *Clinical Notes on Disorders of Childhood*. London: William Heinemann (Medical Books).

Winnicott, Donald W. (1931b). Haemoptysis: Case for Diagnosis. *Proceedings of the Royal Society of Medicine*, *24*: 855–856.

Winnicott, Donald W. (1931c). Pre-Systolic Murmur, Possibly Not Due to Mitral Stenosis. *Proceedings of the Royal Society of Medicine*, *24*: 1354.

Winnicott, Donald W. (1934). Papular Urticaria and the Dynamics of Skin Sensation. *British Journal of Children's Diseases*, *31*: 5–16.

Winnicott, Donald W. (1935). The Manic Defence. In: *Collected Papers*, 1958a (pp. 129–144).

Winnicott, Donald W. (1936). Appetite and Emotional Disorder. In: *Collected Papers*, 1958a (pp. 33–51).

Winnicott, Donald W. (1939). The Psychology of Juvenile Rheumatism. In: Ronald G. Gordon (Ed.), *A Survey of Child Psychiatry* (pp. 28–44). London: Humphrey Milford and Oxford University Press.

Winnicott, Donald W. (1941a). The Observation of Infants in a Set Situation. *International Journal of Psycho-Analysis*, *22*: 229–249. [Also in: *Collected Papers*, 1958a (pp. 52–69).]

Winnicott, Donald W. (1941b). Book Review of John C. Flügel, *The Moral Paradox of Peace and War*. *The New Era in Home and School*, *22*: 183.

Winnicott, Donald W. (1941c). Book Review of Susan Isaacs, Sybil Clement Brown, & Robert H. Thouless (Eds.), *The Cambridge Evacuation Survey: A Wartime Study in Social Welfare and Education*. *The New Era in Home and School*, *22*: 256–257.

Winnicott, Donald W. (1942). Child Department Consultations. *International Journal of Psycho-Analysis*, *23*: 139–146. [Also in: *Collected Papers*, 1958a (pp. 70–84).]

Winnicott, Donald W. (1943a). Delinquency Research. *The New Era in Home and School*: *24*: 65–67.

Winnicott, Donald W. (1943b). Treatment of Mental Disease by Induction of Fits. In: *Psycho-Analytic Explorations*, 1989 (pp. 516–521).

Winnicott, Donald W. (1944a). General Discussion. *Transactions of the Ophthalmological Society of the United Kingdom*, *64*: 46–52.

Winnicott, Donald W. (1944b). What About Father? In: *Getting to Know Your Baby*, 1945a (pp. 16–21).

Winnicott, Donald W. (1944c). Introduction to a Symposium on the Psycho-Analytic Contribution to the Theory of Shock Therapy. In: *Psycho-Analytic Explorations*, 1989 (pp. 525–528).

Winnicott, Donald W. (1944d). Kinds of Psychological Effect of Shock Therapy. In: *Psycho-Analytic Explorations*, 1989 (pp. 529–533).

Winnicott, Donald W. (1945a). *Getting to Know Your Baby*. London: William Heinemann (Medical Books). [Also in: *The Child and the Family*, 1957a (pp. 7–12).]

Winnicott, Donald W. (1945b). Primitive Emotional Development. *International Journal of Psycho-Analysis*, *26*: 137–143. [Also in: *Collected Papers*, 1958a (pp. 145–156).]

Winnicott, Donald W. (1945c). Talking About Psychology. . . . *The New Era in Home and School*, *26*: 179–182. [Also in: *The Child and the Outside World*, 1957b (pp. 125–133).]

Winnicott, Donald W. (1945d). The Only Child. In: *The Child and the Family*, 1957a (pp. 107–111).

Winnicott, Donald W. (1945e). The Evacuated Child. In: *The Child and the Outside World*, 1957b (pp. 83–87).

Winnicott, Donald W. (1946). Letter to the Editor of *The Times*, 6 November. In: *The Spontaneous Gesture*, 1987b (p. 9).

Winnicott, Donald W. (1948a). Children's Hostels in War and Peace: A Contribution to the Symposium on "Lessons for Child Psychiatry". Given at a Meeting of the Medical Section of the British Psychological Society, 27 February 1946. *British Journal of Medical Psychology*, *21*: 175–180.

Winnicott, Donald W. (1948b). Pediatrics and Psychiatry. *British Journal of Medical Psychology*, *21*: 229–240. [Also in: *Collected Papers*, 1958a (pp. 157–173).]

Winnicott, Donald W. (1948c). Reparation in Respect of Mother's Organized Defence Against Depression. In: *Collected Papers*, 1958a (pp. 91–96).

Winnicott, Donald W. (1949a). *The Ordinary Devoted Mother and Her Baby: Nine Broadcast Talks (Autumn 1949)*. London: C.A. Brock and Company.

Winnicott, Donald W. (1949b). Hate in the Counter-Transference. *International Journal of Psycho-Analysis*, *30*: 69–74. [Also in: *Collected Papers*, 1958a (pp. 194–203).]

Winnicott, Donald W. (1949c). A Man Looks at Motherhood. In: *The Child and the Family*, 1957a (pp. 3–6).

Winnicott, Donald W. (1949d). Birth Memories, Birth Trauma, and Anxiety. In: *Collected Papers*, 1958a (pp. 174–193).

Winnicott, Donald W. (1949e). Letter to Noel Harris, 19 November. Box 8. File 1. Donald W. Winnicott Papers.

Winnicott, Donald W. (1950a). Some Thoughts on the Meaning of the Word Democracy. *Human Relations*, *3*: 175–186. [Also in: *Home Is Where We Start From*, 1986b (pp. 239–259).]

Winnicott, Donald W. (1950b). Knowing and Learning. In: *The Child and the Family*, 1957a (pp. 69–73).

Winnicott, Donald W. (1950c). The Deprived Child and How He Can Be Compensated for Loss of Family Life. In: *The Family and Individual Development* (pp. 132–145). London: Tavistock Publications, 1965.

Winnicott, Donald W. (1950d). Letter to the Editor of *The Times*, undated. In: *The Spontaneous Gesture*, 1987b (p. 21).

Winnicott, Donald W. (1951a). Book Review of Joanna Field, *On Not Being Able to Paint*. *British Journal of Medical Psychology*, *24*: 75–76. [Also in: *Psycho-Analytic Explorations*, 1989 (pp. 390–392).]

Winnicott, Donald W. (1951b). Visiting Children in Hospital. In: *The Child and the Family*, 1957a (pp. 121–126).

Winnicott, Donald W. (1951c). Notes on the General Implications of Leucotomy. In: *Psycho-Analytic Explorations*, 1989 (pp. 548–552).

Winnicott, Donald W. (1951d). Letter to James Strachey, 1 May. In: *The Spontaneous Gesture*, 1987b (p. 24).

Winnicott, Donald W. (1952a). Anxiety Associated with Insecurity. In: *Collected Papers*, 1958a (pp. 97–100).

Winnicott, Donald W. (1952b). Letter to Ernest Jones, 22 July. In: *The Spontaneous Gesture*, 1987b (p. 33).

Winnicott, Donald W. (1952c). Letter to Melanie Klein, 17 November. In: *The Spontaneous Gesture*, 1987b (pp. 33–37).

Winnicott, Donald W. (1952d). Letter to Michael Balint, 3 March. Balint Archives. Département de Psychiatrie. Université de Genève. Geneva, Switzerland.

Winnicott, Donald W. (1953a). Transitional Objects and Transitional Phenomena: A Study of the First Not-Me Possession. *International Journal of Psycho-Analysis*, 34: 89–97. [Also in: *Playing and Reality*, 1971a (pp. 1–25).]

Winnicott, Donald W. (1953b). Psychoses and Child Care. *British Journal of Medical Psychology*, 26: 68–74. [Also in: *Collected Papers*, 1958a (pp. 219–228).]

Winnicott, Donald W. (1953c). Symptom Tolerance in Paediatrics. *Proceedings of the Royal Society of Medicine*, 46: 675–684. [Also in: *Collected Papers*, 1958a (pp. 101–117).]

Winnicott, Donald W. (1953d). Discussion of "Grief and Mourning in Infancy". In: *Psycho-Analytic Explorations*, 1989 (pp. 426–432).

Winnicott, Donald W. (1953e). Letter to Esther Bick, 11 June. In: *The Spontaneous Gesture*, 1987b (pp. 50–52).

Winnicott, Donald W. (1953f). Letter to Sylvia Payne, 7 October. In: *The Spontaneous Gesture*, 1987b (pp. 52–53).

Winnicott, Donald W. (1953g). Letter to Charles F. Rycroft, 25 June. Collection of Charles F. Rycroft, London.

Winnicott, Donald W. (1954a). Mind and Its Relation to the Psyche–Soma. *British Journal of Medical Psychology*, 27: 201–209. [Also in: *Collected Papers*, 1958a (pp. 243–254).]

Winnicott, Donald W. (1954b). Play in the Analytic Situation. In: *Psycho-Analytic Explorations*, 1989 (pp. 28–29).

Winnicott, Donald W. (1954c). Letter to Charles F. Rycroft, 5 February. Collection of Charles F. Rycroft, London.

Winnicott, Donald W. (1955a). Metapsychological and Clinical Aspects of Regression within the Psycho-Analytical Set-Up. *International Journal of Psycho-Analysis*, *36*: 16–26. [Also in: *Collected Papers*, 1958a (pp. 278–294).]

Winnicott, Donald W. (1955b). Childhood Psychosis: A Case Managed at Home. *Case Conference*, *2* (No. 7): 3–8. [Also in: *Collected Papers*, 1958a (pp. 118–126).]

Winnicott, Donald W. (1955c). Régression et repli, transl. by Anne Berman. *Revue Française de Psychanalyse*, *19*: 323–330.

Winnicott, Donald W. (1955d). On Adoption. In: *The Child and the Family*, 1957a (pp. 127–130).

Winnicott, Donald W. (1955e). Group Influences and the Maladjusted Child: The School Aspect. In: *The Family and Individual Development*, 1965b (pp. 146–154).

Winnicott, Donald W. (1955f). For Stepparents. In: *Talking to Parents*, 1993 (pp. 7–13).

Winnicott, Donald W. (1955g). Letter to Charles F. Rycroft, 21 April. In: *The Spontaneous Gesture*, 1987b (p. 87).

Winnicott, Donald W. (1955h). Memorandum from Paddington Green Children's Hospital, Psychology Department, on Homosexuality and the Law, to the Wolfenden Committee. Unpublished typescript. Collection of The Winnicott Trust, London.

Winnicott, Donald W. (1956a). On Transference. *International Journal of Psycho-Analysis*, *37*: 386–388.

Winnicott, Donald W. (1956b). Primary Maternal Preoccupation. In: *Collected Papers*, 1958a (pp. 300–305).

Winnicott, Donald W. (1956c). The Antisocial Tendency. In: *Collected Papers*, 1958a (pp. 306–315).

Winnicott, Donald W. (1956d). Paediatrics and Childhood Neurosis. In: *The Maturational Processes and the Facilitating Environment*, 1965a (pp. 316–321).

Winnicott, Donald W. (1956e). Letter to W. Clifford M. Scott, 26 December. Cited in: Phyllis Grosskurth, *Melanie Klein: Her World and Her Work*. New York: Alfred A. Knopf, 1986.

Winnicott, Donald W. (1956f). Letter to Joan Riviere, 3 February. In: *The Spontaneous Gesture*, 1987b (pp. 94–97).

Winnicott, Donald W. (1956g). Letter to Charles F. Rycroft, 8 November. Collection of Charles F. Rycroft. London.

Winnicott, Donald W. (1957a). *The Child and the Family: First Relationships*, ed. by Janet Hardenberg. London: Tavistock Publications.

Winnicott, Donald W. (1957b). *The Child and the Outside World: Studies in Developing Relationships*, ed. by Janet Hardenberg. London: Tavistock Publications.

Winnicott, Donald W. (1957c). The Mother's Contribution to Society. In: *The Child and the Family*, 1957a (pp. 141–144).

Winnicott, Donald W. (1957d). The Contribution of Psycho-Analysis to Midwifery. Part I. *Nursing Mirror and Midwives Journal* (17 May): xi–xii. [Also in: *Babies and Their Mothers*, 1987a (pp. 69–81).]

Winnicott, Donald W. (1957e). The Contribution of Psycho-Analysis to Midwifery. Part II. *Nursing Mirror and Midwives Journal* (24 May): 553–554. [Also in: *The Family and Individual Development*, 1965b (pp. 106–113).]

Winnicott, Donald W. (1957f). Advising Parents. In: *The Family and Individual Development*, 1965b (pp. 114–120).

Winnicott, Donald W. (1957g). Excitement in the Aetiology of Coronary Thrombosis. In: *Psycho-Analytic Explorations*, 1989 (pp. 34–38).

Winnicott, Donald W. (1957h). Introductory Remarks on the Occasion of the Eighth Ernest Jones Lecture, Dr. Margaret Mead on "Changing Patterns of Parent–Child Relations in an Urban World". Box 1. File 2. Donald W. Winnicott Papers.

Winnicott, Donald W. (1957i). Letter to John G. Hunt, 14 February. Box 1. File 11. Donald W. Winnicott Papers.

Winnicott, Donald W. (1957j). Letter to the Manager of the Wigmore Street Branch of Midland Bank, 6 March. Box 1. File 1. Donald W. Winnicott Papers.

Winnicott, Donald W. (1957k). Letter to Michael Balint, 3 October. Box 1. File 1. Donald W. Winnicott Papers.

Winnicott, Donald W. (1957l). Letter to Katherine Jones, 9 October. Box 1. File 3. Donald W. Winnicott Papers.

Winnicott, Donald W. (1958a). *Collected Papers: Through Paediatrics to Psycho-Analysis*. London: Tavistock Publications. [Reprinted as *Through Paediatrics to Psycho-Analysis*. London: Hogarth Press and the Institute of Psycho-Analysis; reprinted London: Karnac Books, 1992.]

Winnicott, Donald W. (1958b). Hate in the Countertransference. In: *Collected Papers*, 1958a (pp. 194–203).

Winnicott, Donald W. (1958c). Psycho-Analysis and the Sense of Guilt. In: John D. Sutherland (Ed.), *Psycho-Analysis and Contemporary Thought* (pp. 15–32). London: Hogarth Press and The Institute of Psycho-Analysis.

Winnicott, Donald W. (1958d). Ernest Jones. *International Journal of Psycho-Analysis*, *39*: 298–304. [Also in: *Psycho-Analytic Explorations*, 1989 (pp. 393–404).]

Winnicott, Donald W. (1958e). Ernest Jones: Funeral Addresses. Spoken at Golders Green Crematorium on Friday, 14 February, 1958. *International Journal of Psycho-Analysis*, *39*: 305–306. [Also in: *Psycho-Analytic Explorations*, 1989 (pp. 405–407).]

Winnicott, Donald W. (1958f). The Capacity to Be Alone. *International Journal of Psycho-Analysis*, *39*: 416–420. [Also in: *The Maturational Processes and the Facilitating Environment*, 1965a (pp. 29–36).]

Winnicott, Donald W. (1958g). Discussion sur la contribution de l'observation directe de l'enfant à la psychanalyse, transl. by J. Koenig. *Revue Française de Psychanalyse*, *22*: 205–211.

Winnicott, Donald W. (1958h). Child Analysis. *A Criança Portuguesa*, *17*: 219–229. [Also in: *The Maturational Processes and the Facilitating Environment*, 1965a (pp. 115–123).]

Winnicott, Donald W. (1958i). The Family Affected by Depressive Illness in One or Both Parents. In: *The Family and Individual Development*, 1965b (pp. 50–60).

Winnicott, Donald W. (1958j). Letter to Joan Riviere, 13 June. In: *The Spontaneous Gesture*, 1987b (pp. 118–119).

Winnicott, Donald W. (1959a). On Envy. *Case Conference*, *5*: 177–178.

Winnicott, Donald W. (1959b). Classification: Is There a Psycho-Analytic Contribution to Psychiatric Classification? In: *The Maturational Processes and the Facilitating Environment*, 1965a (pp. 124–139).

Winnicott, Donald W. (1959c). Casework with Mentally Ill Children. In: *The Family and Individual Development*, 1965b (pp. 121–131).

Winnicott, Donald W. (1959d). The Fate of the Transitional Object. In: *Psycho-Analytic Explorations*. 1989 (pp. 53–58).

Winnicott, Donald W. (1960a). String. *Journal of Child Psychology and Psychiatry and Allied Disciplines*, *1*: 49–52. [Also in: *The Maturational Processes and the Facilitating Environment*, 1965a (pp. 153–157).]

Winnicott, Donald W. (1960b). The Theory of the Parent–Infant Relationship. *International Journal of Psycho-Analysis*, *41*: 585–595. [Also in: *The Maturational Processes and the Facilitating Environment*, 1965a (pp. 37–55).]

Winnicott, Donald W. (1960c). Ego Distortion in Terms of True and False Self. In: *The Maturational Processes and the Facilitating Environment*, 1965a (pp. 140–152).

Winnicott, Donald W. (1960d). The Relationship of a Mother to Her Baby at the Beginning. In: *The Family and Individual Development*, 1965b (pp. 15–20).

Winnicott, Donald W. (1960e). Aggression, Guilt and Reparation. In: *Deprivation and Delinquency*, 1984a (pp. 136–144).

Winnicott, Donald W. (1960f). Jealousy. In: *Talking to Parents*, 1993 (p. 41–64).

Winnicott, Donald W. (1960g). Letter to Wilfred R. Bion, 17 November. In: *The Spontaneous Gesture*, 1987b (p. 131).

Winnicott, Donald W. (1960h). Letter to James Strachey, 11 January. Box 2. File 12. Donald W. Winnicott Papers.

Winnicott, Donald W. (1960i). Letter to Ilse Hellman, 21 July. Box 2. File 9. Donald W. Winnicott Papers.

Winnicott, Donald W. (1961a). The Effect of Psychotic Parents on the Emotional Development of the Child. *British Journal of Psychiatric Social Work*, *6*: 13–20. [Also in: *The Family and Individual Development*, 1965b (pp. 69–78).]

Winnicott, Donald W. (1961b). Integrating and Disruptive Factors in Family Life. *Canadian Medical Association Journal* (15 April): 814–818. [Also in: *The Family and Individual Development*, 1965b (pp. 40–49).]

Winnicott, Donald W. (1961c). Psychoanalysis and Science: Friends or Relations? In: *Home Is Where We Start From*, 1986b (pp. 13–18).

Winnicott, Donald W. (1961d). Varieties of Psychotherapy. In: *Deprivation and Delinquency*, 1984a (pp. 232–240).

Winnicott, Donald W. (1961e). Psycho-Neurosis in Childhood. In: *Psycho-Analytic Explorations*, 1989 (pp. 64–72).

Winnicott, Donald W. (1961f). Feeling Guilty. In: *Talking to Parents*, 1993 (pp. 95–103).

Winnicott, Donald W. (1961g). Letter to Messrs. Arthur Guinness Son and Company, 31 October. Box 3. File 3. Donald W. Winnicott Papers.

Winnicott, Donald W. (1962a). The Theory of the Parent–Infant Relationship: Further Remarks. *International Journal of Psycho-Analysis, 43*: 238–239. [Also in: *Psycho-Analytic Explorations*, 1989 (pp. 73–75).]

Winnicott, Donald W. (1962b). Ego Integration in Child Development. In: *The Maturational Processes and the Facilitating Environment*, 1965a (pp. 56–63).

Winnicott, Donald W. (1962c). Providing for the Child in Health and in Crisis. In: *The Maturational Processes and the Facilitating Environment*, 1965a (pp. 64–72).

Winnicott, Donald W. (1962d). The Aims of Psycho-Analytical Treatment. In: *The Maturational Processes and the Facilitating Environment*, 1965a (pp. 166–170).

Winnicott, Donald W. (1962e). A Personal View of the Kleinian Contribution. In: *The Maturational Processes and the Facilitating Environment*, 1965a (pp. 171–178).

Winnicott, Donald W. (1963a). The Mentally Ill in Your Caseload. In: Joan F. S. King (Ed.), *New Thinking for Changing Needs* (pp. 50–66). London: Association of Social Workers. [Also in: *The Maturational Processes and the Facilitating Environment*, 1965a (pp. 217–229).]

Winnicott, Donald W. (1963b). The Development of the Capacity for Concern. *Bulletin of the Menninger Clinic, 27*: 167–176. [Also in: *Deprivation and Delinquency*, 1984a (pp. 100–105).]

Winnicott, Donald W. (1963c). Dependence in Infant Care, in Child Care, and in the Psycho-Analytic Setting. *International Journal of Psycho-Analysis, 44*: 339–344. [Also in: *The Maturational Processes and the Facilitating Environment*, 1965a (pp. 249–259).]

Winnicott, Donald W. (1963d). From Dependence Towards Independence in the Development of the Individual. In: *The Maturational Processes and the Facilitating Environment*, 1965a (pp. 83–92).

Winnicott, Donald W. (1963e). Communicating and Not Communicating Leading to a Study of Certain Opposites. In: *The Maturational Processes and the Facilitating Environment*, 1965a (pp. 179–192).

Winnicott, Donald W. (1963f). Psychotherapy of Character Disorders. In: *The Maturational Processes and the Facilitating Environment*, 1965a (pp. 203–216).

Winnicott, Donald W. (1963g). Psychiatric Disorder in Terms of Infantile Maturational Processes. In: *The Maturational Processes and the Facilitating Environment*, 1965a (pp. 230–241).

Winnicott, Donald W. (1963h). Hospital Care Supplementing Intensive Psychotherapy in Adolescence. In: *The Maturational Processes and the Facilitating Environment*, 1965a (pp. 242–248).

Winnicott, Donald W. (1963i). Two Notes on the Use of Silence. In: *Psycho-Analytic Explorations*, 1989 (pp. 81–86).

Winnicott, Donald W. (1963j). Letter to John Rawlings Rees, 24 May. Box 4. File 3. Donald W. Winnicott Papers.

Winnicott, Donald W. (1963k). Letter to C. W. E. Cave, 24 June. Box 4. File 2. Donald W. Winnicott Papers.

Winnicott, Donald W. (1964a). *The Child, the Family, and the Outside World*. Harmondsworth, Middlesex: Penguin Books.

Winnicott, Donald W. (1964b). The Neonate and His Mother. *Acta Pediatrica Latina*, 17: 747–758. [Also in: *Babies and Their Mothers*, 1987a (pp. 35–49).]

Winnicott, Donald W. (1964c). The Value of Depression. *British Journal of Psychiatric Social Work*, 7: 123–127. [Also in: *Home Is Where We Start From*, 1986b (pp. 71–79).]

Winnicott, Donald W. (1964d). Letter to A. Patricia de Berker, 9 March. Box 4. File 9. Donald W. Winnicott Papers.

Winnicott, Donald W. (1964e). Letter to Hedwig Walder, 9 October. Box 4. File 13. Donald W. Winnicott Papers.

Winnicott, Donald W. (1965a). *The Maturational Processes and the Facilitating Environment: Studies in the Theory of Emotional Development*. London: Hogarth Press and The Institute of Psycho-Analysis [reprinted London: Karnac Books, 1990].

Winnicott, Donald W. (1965b). *The Family and Individual Development*. London: Tavistock Publications.

Winnicott, Donald W. (1965c). The Psychology of Madness: A Contribution from Psycho-Analysis. In: *Psycho-Analytic Explorations*, 1989 (pp. 119–129).

Winnicott, Donald W. (1965d). Notes on Withdrawal and Regression. In: *Psycho-Analytic Explorations*, 1989 (pp. 149–151).

Winnicott, Donald W. (1965e). New Light on Children's Thinking. In: *Psycho-Analytic Explorations*, 1989 (pp. 152–157).

Winnicott, Donald W. (1966a). Becoming Deprived as a Fact: A Psychotherapeutic Consultation. *Journal of Child Psychotherapy*, 4: 5–12. [Also in: *Therapeutic Consultations in Child Psychiatry*, 1971b (pp. 315–331).]

Winnicott, Donald W. (1966b). Comment on Obsessional Neurosis and "Frankie". *International Journal of Psycho-Analysis*, 47: 143–144. [Also in: *Psycho-Analytic Explorations*, 1989 (pp. 158–160).]

Winnicott, Donald W. (1966c). The Child in the Family Group. In: *Home Is Where We Start From*, 1986b (pp. 128–141).

Winnicott, Donald W. (1966d). The Ordinary Devoted Mother. In: *Babies and Their Mothers*, 1987a (pp. 3–14).

Winnicott, Donald W. (1966e). Letter to the Editor of *The Times*, 13 January. Box 5. File 15. Donald W. Winnicott Papers.

Winnicott, Donald W. (1966f). Letter to Cyril Rosenberg, 11 July. Box 5. File 14. Donald W. Winnicott Papers.

Winnicott, Donald W. (1967a). The Persecution that Wasn't. *New Society* (25 May): 772–773. [Also in: *Deprivation and Delinquency*, 1984a (pp. 200–201).]

Winnicott, Donald W. (1967b). Preliminary Notes for "Communication Between Infant and Mother, Mother and Infant, Compared and Contrasted". In: *Babies and Their Mothers*, 1987a (pp. 107–109).

Winnicott, Donald W. (1967c). D.W.W. on D.W.W. In: *Psycho-Analytic Explorations*, 1989 (pp. 569–582).

Winnicott, Donald W. (1968a). Communication Between Infant and Mother, Mother and Infant, Compared and Contrasted. In: Walter G. Joffe (Ed.), *What is Psychoanalysis?* (pp. 15–25). London: Baillière, Tindall and Cassell. [Also in: *Babies and Their Mothers*, 1987a (pp. 89–103).]

Winnicott, Donald W. (1968b). Clinical Regression Compared with Defence Organization. In: Stanley H. Eldred & Maurice Vanderpol (Eds.), *Psychotherapy in the Designed Therapeutic Milieu* (pp. 3–11). Boston, MA: Little, Brown and Company. [Also in: *Psycho-Analytic Explorations*, 1989 (pp. 193–199).]

Winnicott, Donald W. (1968c). Infant Feeding and Emotional Development. *Maternal and Child Care*, 4: 7–9.

Winnicott, Donald W. (1968d). Delinquency as a Sign of Hope. *Prison Service Journal*, 7: 2–9. [Also in: *Home Is Where We Start From*, 1986b (pp. 90–100).]

Winnicott, Donald W. (1968e). Clinical Illustration of "The Use of an Object". In: *Psycho-Analytic Explorations*, 1989 (pp. 235–238).

Winnicott, Donald W. (1968f). Comments on My Paper "The Use of an Object". In: *Psycho-Analytic Explorations*, 1989 (pp. 238–240).

Winnicott, Donald W. (1968g). Letter to L. Joseph Stone, 18 June. In: *The Spontaneous Gesture*, 1987b (pp. 177–178).

Winnicott, Donald W. (1969a). James Strachey: 1887–1967. *International Journal of Psycho-Analysis*, 50: 129–131. [Also in: *Psycho-Analytic Explorations*, 1989 (pp. 506–510).]

Winnicott, Donald W. (1969b). The Use of an Object. *International Journal of Psycho-Analysis*, 50: 711–716. [Also in: *Playing and Reality*, 1971a (pp. 86–94).]

Winnicott, Donald W. (1969c). Breastfeeding as a Communication. *Maternal and Child Care*, 5: 147–150. [Also in: *Babies and Their Mothers*, 1987a (pp. 23–33).]

Winnicott, Donald W. (1969d). Foreword. In: Marion Milner, *The Hands of the Living God: An Account of a Psycho-Analytic Treatment* (pp. ix–x). London: Hogarth Press and The Institute of Psycho-Analysis.

Winnicott, Donald W. (1969e). The Pill and the Moon. In: *Home Is Where We Start From*, 1986b (pp. 195–209).

Winnicott, Donald W. (1969f). The Use of an Object in the Context of *Moses and Monotheism*. In: *Psycho-Analytic Explorations*, 1989 (pp. 240–246).

Winnicott, Donald W. (1969g). Development of the Theme of the Mother's Unconscious as Discovered in Psycho-Analytic Practice. In: *Psycho-Analytic Explorations*, 1989 (pp. 247–250).

Winnicott, Donald W. (1969h). Contribution to a Symposium on Envy and Jealousy. In: *Psycho-Analytic Explorations*, 1989 (pp. 462–464).

Winnicott, Donald W. (1969i). Letter to F. Robert Rodman, 10 January. In: *The Spontaneous Gesture*, 1987b (pp. 180–182).

Winnicott, Donald W. (1969j). Letter to Anna Freud, 20 January. In: *The Spontaneous Gesture*, 1987b (p. 185).

Winnicott, Donald W. (1969k). Letter to Michael B. Conran, 8 May. In: *The Spontaneous Gesture*, 1987b (pp. 188–191).

Winnicott, Donald W. (1969l). Letter to Robert Tod, 6 November. In: *The Spontaneous Gesture*, 1987b (pp. 196–197).

Winnicott, Donald W. (1969m). Letter to Anthony D. Bradshaw, 18 March. Box 8. File 10. Donald W. Winnicott Papers.

Winnicott, Donald W. (1969n). Letter to the Manager of the Wigmore Street Branch of Midland Bank, 20 November. Box 8. File 1. Donald W. Winnicott Papers.

Winnicott, Donald W. (1969o). Letter to the Manager of the Wigmore Street Branch of Midland Bank, 27 November. Box 8. File 1. Donald W. Winnicott Papers.

Winnicott, Donald W. (1970a). The Mother–Infant Experience of Mutuality. In: E. James Anthony & Therese Benedek (Eds.), *Parenthood: Its Psychology and Psychopathology* (pp. 245–256). Boston, MA: Little, Brown and Company. [Also in: *Psycho-Analytic Explorations*, 1989 (pp. 251–260).]

Winnicott, Donald W. (1970b). Cure. In: *Home Is Where We Start From*, 1986b (pp. 112–120).

Winnicott, Donald W. (1970c). The Place of the Monarchy. In: *Home Is Where We Start From*, 1986b (pp. 260–268).

Winnicott, Donald W. (1970d). Individuation. In: *Psycho-Analytic Explorations*, 1989 (pp. 284–288).

Winnicott, Donald W. (1971a). *Playing and Reality*. London: Tavistock Publications.

Winnicott, Donald W. (1971b). *Therapeutic Consultations in Child Psychiatry*. London: Hogarth Press and The Institute of Psycho-Analysis.

Winnicott, Donald W. (1971c). The Concept of a Healthy Individual. In: John D. Sutherland (Ed.), *Towards Community Mental Health* (pp. 1–15). London: Tavistock Publications. [Also in: *Home Is Where We Start From*, 1986b (pp. 22–38).]

Winnicott, Donald W. (1971d). Letter to Jeannine Kalmanovitch, 7 January. In: Anne Clancier & Jeannine Kalmanovitch (1984), *Winnicott and Paradox: From Birth to Creation*, transl. by Alan Sheridan (photographic insert). London: Tavistock Publications, 1987.

Winnicott, Donald W. (1971e). Letter to Ved P. Varma, 7 January. Collection of Ved P. Varma. London.

Winnicott, Donald W. (1974). Fear of Breakdown. *International Review of Psycho-Analysis, 1*, 103–107. [Also in: *Psycho-Analytic Explorations*, 1989 (pp. 87–95).]

Winnicott, Donald W. (1978). *The Piggle: An Account of the Psychoanalytic Treatment of a Little Girl*, ed. by Ishak Ramzy. London: Hogarth Press and The Institute of Psycho-Analysis.

Winnicott, Donald W. (1984a). *Deprivation and Delinquency*, ed. by

Clare Winnicott, Ray Shepherd, & Madeleine Davis. London: Tavistock Publications.

Winnicott, Donald W. (1984b). Residential Care as Therapy. In: *Deprivation and Delinquency*, 1984a (pp. 220–228).

Winnicott, Donald W. (1984c). Freedom. In: *Home Is Where We Start From: Essays by a Psychoanalyst*, 1986b (pp. 228–238).

Winnicott, Donald W. (1986a). *Holding and Interpretation: Fragment of an Analysis*. London: Hogarth Press and The Institute of Psycho-Analysis [reprinted London: Karnac Books, 1989].

Winnicott, Donald W. (1986b). *Home Is Where We Start From: Essays by a Psychoanalyst*, ed. by Clare Winnicott, Ray Shepherd, & Madeleine Davis. Harmondsworth, Middlesex: Penguin Books.

Winnicott, Donald W. (1987a). *Babies and Their Mothers*, ed. by Clare Winnicott, Ray Shepherd, & Madeleine Davis. Reading, MA: Addison-Wesley Publishing Company.

Winnicott, Donald W. (1987b). *The Spontaneous Gesture: Selected Letters of D.W. Winnicott*, ed. by F. Robert Rodman. Cambridge, MA: Harvard University Press.

Winnicott, Donald W. (1988). *Human Nature*, ed. by Christopher Bollas, Madeleine Davis, & Ray Shepherd. London: Free Association Books.

Winnicott, Donald W. (1989). *Psycho-Analytic Explorations*, ed. by Clare Winnicott, Ray Shepherd, & Madeleine Davis. London: Karnac Books.

Winnicott, Donald W. (1993). *Talking to Parents*, ed. by Clare Winnicott, Christopher Bollas, Madeleine Davis, & Ray Shepherd. Reading, MA: Addison-Wesley Publishing Company.

Winnicott, Donald W. (1996). *Thinking About Children*, ed. by Jennifer Johns, Ray Shepherd, & Helen Taylor Robinson. London: Karnac Books. In press.

Winnicott, Donald W.; & Britton, Clare (1944). The Problem of Homeless Children. *The New Era in Home and School*, 25: 155–161.

Winnicott, Donald W.; & Britton, Clare (1947). Residential Management as Treatment for Difficult Children: The Evolution of a Wartime Hostels Scheme. *Human Relations*, 1: 87–97. [Also in: *Deprivation and Delinquency*, 1984a (pp. 54–72).]

Winnicott, Donald W.; & Gibbs, Nancy (1926). Varicella Encephalitis and Vaccinia Encephalitis. *British Journal of Children's Diseases*, 23: 107–127.

Winnicott, Donald W.; & Khan, M. Masud R. (1953). Book Review of

W. Ronald D. Fairbairn, *Psychoanalytic Studies of the Personality. International Journal of Psycho-Analysis, 34*: 329–333. [Also in: *Psycho-Analytic Explorations,* 1989 (pp. 413–422).]

Woodhead, Barbara (1971). D.W. Winnicott M.A., F.R.C.P. *British Medical Journal* (20 February): 464.

Woodhead, Barbara (1972). Contribution to Winnicott Memorial Meeting, 19 January 1972. *The British Psycho-Analytical Society and The Institute of Psycho-Analysis. Scientific Bulletin, 57*: 15–19.

Woolf, Virginia (1928). Letter to Vanessa Bell, 25 May. In: Nigel Nicolson & Joanne Trautmann Banks (Eds.), *A Change of Perspective: The Letters of Virginia Woolf. Volume III. 1923–1928* (pp. 499–502). London: Hogarth Press, 1977.

Yates, Sybille L. (1932). Book Review of Donald W. Winnicott, *Clinical Notes on Disorders of Childhood. International Journal of Psycho-Analysis, 13*: 242–243.

Zetzel, Elizabeth R. (1969). 96 Gloucester Place: Some Personal Recollections. *International Journal of Psycho-Analysis, 50*: 717–719.

INDEX